How to Try Your Own Case in Court—and Win!

THE FIRST NON-LAWYER'S COMPLETE GUIDE TO:

- Small Claims Court
  - Traffic Infraction
    - Negligence (Personal Injury)
      - Unlawful Detainer (Eviction)
        - Collection
          - Strategies for Winning Court Trials

How to Try Your Own Case in Court— and Win!

The Honorable Mel Red Recana

Presiding Judge, Los Angeles Municipal Court

with

Wanda Sue Parrott

Book One

Basic Instructions for the Non-Lawyer

1997
Galde Press, Inc.
Lakeville, Minnesota

First Edition
First Printing, 1997

Library of Congress Cataloging-in-Publication Data

Recana, Mel Red.
    How to try your own case in court—and win! / Mel Red Recana. —
1st ed.
        p.   cm.
    Includes index.
    ISBN 1–880090–31–7 (pbk.)
    1. Pro se representation—United States—Popular works.   2. Civil
procedure—United States—Popular works.   I. Title.
KF8841.R43   1996
347.73'5—dc20
[347.3075]   96–27216
                                                                                CIP

Galde Press, Inc.
PO Box 460
Lakeville, Minnesota 55044

Dedication

If you need legal representation for your court trial—
but think you cannot afford a lawyer—
this book is dedicated
to you.

"Many seek the favor of a ruler,
but from the Lord a man gets justice."
—Proverbs 29:26

Contents

*A chapter marked with an asterisk (*) denotes optional "bonus" material that the reader may select at his own discretion. Unmarked chapters indicate basic instructions every person serving as his own lawyer should read.

Acknowledgments

I would like to say a few words to everyone who contributed to the creation of this book: the good Lord, my Creator*; my wife, Rory, for encouraging me to write it; my sons, Julian, Eric, and Bill, who served as critics of the manuscript through several stages of evolvement; my friend, Taekwondo Master James Bae, for his suggestions about how non-lawyers and persons from foreign countries could best be helped to understand how the American courts operate; Mrs. Lou Ann Berardi, English teacher at Loyola High School in Los Angeles, for editing my first rough draft; Wanda Sue Parrott, who translated and articulated my thoughts into easy-to-understand English and organized the book in its final form; and to Wolcott's Business Forms, Los Angeles, California, for granting permission to reproduce the legal forms which appear in Chapter 25. I could not have done this without you. Thank you all!

—MEL RED RECANA

---

*"In all my ways I acknowledge Him and He directs my path."—Proverbs 3:6

Opening Remarks

Shortly after my appointment to the Bench in 1981, I realized that many litigants were appearing in court without attorneys. I gave each person the same well-intentioned advice: *Get a lawyer.* Maybe I should not have been as taken aback as I was when, again and again, such litigants responded by saying, *"Your Honor, I cannot afford a lawyer."*

These people were telling the truth. Many of them earned less than five dollars per hour, while the average lawyer in Los Angeles charged from $100 to $180 per hour for professional services. A litigant living on a limited income, naturally, believed he would have to work between three and five full days just to pay for one hour of an attorney's services!

After taxes were deducted from his paycheck, the same person believed he would have to put in one to two full weeks of work time just to pay for one hour of professional legal counsel. If two hours of legal services were required, a lawyer's fee could cost a litigant almost all of a month's income!

They Hoped and Lost
Without knowing the alternatives which might have helped them with their legal needs, such litigants were choosing to appear in court without legal representation—and hoping for the best outcome; instead, the worst frequently happened.

Thus, these litigants, who believed telling the truth to the judge was all that was required to win in court, lost more than just their cases; many also lost faith in the American system of justice, which seemed to favor only affluent persons who could afford to pay for lawyers' services.

The Swelling Ranks of Lawyerless Litigants
During my first six years on the Bench, the ranks of these *Pro Pers* (persons appearing as their own legal counsel) swelled, and the fact became apparent to me that a similar dilemma existed in courtrooms across the nation.

I can relate to litigants who could not afford lawyers because there was a time when I might not have been able to afford an attorney if I had needed one; therefore, my personal background and professional experience qualified me to write this book for non-lawyers facing trial without legal counsel.

A Humble Beginning

When I was a child in Guinobatan, Albay, in the Philippines, my family was very poor. My mother died when I was thirteen and my father raised us. He was a professional boxer who later became a policeman. He had a third grade education but he instilled in me the importance of a college diploma as the key to a good and happy life.

My father taught me not to let lack of money discourage me from setting goals and working to attain them. With such encouragement, I became a do-it-yourselfer at an early age. The fact that his philosophy worked was proven the day I served as valedictorian of my high school graduating class.

In order to afford law school, I had to work as a court reporter (I had learned short-hand in high school). I was so poor, for one semester at night I walked ten miles in order to get home from school; torrential rains were often blowing with hurricane force. This validated the old saying, "If there is a will, there is a way."

From Law School to Los Angeles

In 1964 I graduated from the University of the East in Manila, passed the Bar Examination, and spent three-and-a-half years practicing law in the Philippines. I then came to California, becoming the first Filipino lawyer to pass the California Bar Examinations without having to return to law school. While in general practice with another Filipino attorney in Southern California, G. Monty Manibog, I handled family law, civil cases (contracts, personal injury, unlawful detainers, and real estate), immigration cases, and criminal matters involving trials before juries.

Back in the Philippines, there had been no jury trials, so I found the American system of jurisprudence exciting.

Falling in Love—With Law

I fell so in love with the jury trial that I became the first Filipino deputy district attorney for the County of Los Angeles, and in that capacity I tried cases nearly every day. After three years as a prosecutor, I went back into private practice, handling both civil and criminal matters, but specializing in criminal defense and personal injury cases.

Then, in 1981 my role reversed. Instead of appearing before a judge, I became one!

Elevation to the Bench

Saturday, June 13, 1981, the date I took my oath, was a historical event and perhaps the biggest day of my life, also. It was the Philippine Independence Day celebration, and I was given the honor of becoming the first Filipino in the continental United States to wear a judge's robe. Who could have predicted that a poor child like me would one day be addressed as "Your Honor"? Only one person: my father. I am grateful to be so honored and thanked him for encouraging me to practice the never-give-up philosophy which forms the fundamental premise of this book.

Author's Qualifications

Why am I qualified to tackle writing one book which incorporates techniques laymen can use for trying every type of civil case in court? Because I have been on both sides of the Bench.

As a Judge of the Municipal Court, I have sat as a Superior Court judge *pro tem* and as a California Court of Appeal justice *pro tem*. In 1986 I started teaching Trial Technique and Procedure in a Southern California law school, and I also fell in love with teaching.

Therefore, this book is a culmination of my own life's experiences, coupled with my great regard for the law, which began when my father inspired me to rise above the adverse conditions of our humble circumstances and pursue my dreams until they become realities.

If a person like me can do it, so can you.

Glimpse of Future Litigation

Underneath my judge's robe, I am still the same person who once earned only twenty dollars per month. When a person tells me that he does not have a lawyer because he cannot afford legal counsel, I understand. Therefore, while I still recommend that a litigant's best chance of winning in trial is through professional legal representation, I also realize the trend in do-it-yourself litigation is not likely to reverse for many years, if ever.

As the twentieth century winds toward its conclusion, I see glimpses of America's future parading before me daily in court. Today there may be one hundred people representing themselves in court for every ten persons who did so in the past; after the turn of the century, their ranks may swell tenfold until there are one thousand lay persons serving as their own legal counsel for every one hundred who do so today.

Who are most of these litigants? Average men and women from all walks of life. People like us!

Help Is at Hand

Are you suing someone? Or being sued? If your answer is yes, you are already a litigant. If you cannot hire a lawyer, or are a do-it-yourselfer who welcomes the challenge of serving as your own attorney, this book will help you. It is written around the premise: *In America, a non-lawyer may serve as his own legal counsel, as long as he confines his lay lawyering to representation of no one but himself.*

This is a book whose time has come. It is your book.

May you use it to try your own case in court—and win!

How to Read This Book

The law is for everyone. So is this text, which is really two books in one:

- *Book One* consists of basic instructions every non-lawyer may follow from start to finish in the handling of his own lawsuit.

- *Book Two* comprises a non-lawyer's guide to the law, trial lawyers' techniques, and legalese (legal language), as well as a wealth of helpful personal tips which put the *Pro Per* at ease as his own legal counsel.

Everything you need to start immediately preparing to be your own civil trial lawyer is condensed into this volume. Before you start, however, there are three facts about which you should be aware.

First, complete instructions are given for trying four types of cases: small claims court cases, traffic infraction cases, negligence (personal injury) cases, and unlawful detainer (eviction) cases. If your specific type of case is not included, you may still benefit from this book. How? By creatively building your own trial presentation around the general principles of law and trial techniques explained in these pages.

Second, throughout the book the term referring to a person who is serving as his own attorney, *Pro Per*, is capitalized and italicized. Does this indicate the term is an official title or even a proper name? No. I took the liberty of capitalizing the term *Pro Per* to express my respect for the men and women who choose to exercise their constitutional right to legal representation by serving as do-it-yourselfers, and who put forth the time and energy required to learn how to do it properly.

Third, there are two ways you can learn to be your own lawyer by reading this book: the short, easy way or the longer, more complete way. Choose whichever method is best for you—or mix and match them to create your own *Pro Per*'s training program.

- *The Short, Easy Method*—Read only the chapters which are not subtitled as "bonus" chapters. These are the chapters recommended for every *Pro Per*, regardless of the type of case he will be trying in court. The non-bonus chapters cover all the basics you need to know about serving as your own trial lawyer.

- *The Longer, Complete Method*—Read both the non-bonus chapters and those subtitled "Bonus." The bonus material contains more comprehensive explanations of the law, trial techniques, and instructions about how to practice many of the same strategies lawyers use to win their cases in court. This material will help you try your own case against either another *Pro Per* or skilled trial lawyer.

Which method is recommended for your type of case? If yours is a small claims court case or traffic infraction matter, you need not study the bonus material—unless you are interested in so doing. However, in negligence (personal injury) and unlawful detainer (eviction) cases, the bonus material may provide you with the legal ammunition you need to win your case in court.

The most effective do-it-yourself approach is: Skim through the non-bonus chapters from start to finish by skipping over the bonus chapters; this will give you a basic understanding of what serving as your own attorney entails.

Then, read the book again, including any or all bonus material you feel will be beneficial to you.

This is Book One of two volumes; it contains basic instructions. The set of two books is organized into seven sections, beginning with easy-to-understand general information every *Pro Per* should know and progressing toward specific types of legal actions and suggestions about how to handle such matters in court. The last two sections consist of a layman's guide to trial techniques and terms known by all trial lawyers. While these advanced sections retain their legal flavor, they are explained in easy-to-understand everyday English that dispels the mystery surrounding trial strategies and their corresponding legal language, thus showing the *Pro Per* how he, too, may use them to win his case in court. The advanced instructions constitute Book Two.

A brief introduction to a section's contents appears at the start of each of the seven parts of the book, along with recommendations about which chapters you should read if you wish to prepare your case in the quickest, easiest manner.

How much legal know-how do you need to try your own matter in court—and win? In this aspect of your case, you must reach your own decision, which means: You be the judge!

PART I

HOW TO GET YOUR CASE IN COURT

PART I ANSWERS the most common questions asked by every person who may be involved in his first legal action. It is especially arranged to help the first-time *Pro Per* who feels he has the grounds for a lawsuit but does not know how to start legal proceedings.

This section, which includes an introduction to the American court system, contains everything you need to know about how to get your case into the proper court for your type of matter.

Recommendation: Read all seven chapters.

Chapter 1

Do You Really
Need a Lawyer?

SO, YOU ARE INVOLVED in a legal matter. If you are like the average person in such a situation, your reaction is: *I need a lawyer!* If you cannot afford to retain an attorney, you wonder: *How can I pay for costly legal services?* This leads to the biggest question: *What will happen to me if I do not get a lawyer?*

While such questions can be unnerving, there is no need to panic. Instead, read this book—which gives help to anyone who cannot afford to hire a lawyer but who needs to know the best way to proceed with his or her legal matters.

It is designed to help you try your own case in court—and win!!

Can You Really Try Your Own Case?

It may surprise you, but people can try certain types of cases in court *without the necessity of professional legal counsel.* It happens all the time, although most legal affairs—especially court trials—are best handled by professionals.

There are several types of lawsuits, however, in which *lawyers are not allowed to participate!* Yours may be one of them. Or, maybe you plan to retain professional legal counsel; however, if your budget is extremely limited, this book can help you save money *by sharing tips on how to do much of the preliminary casework yourself.*

Law for the Layman
The law was not written for lawyers only. It is everyone's law, and the unique American justice system allows non-lawyers an opportunity to participate in it equally. If you have never been involved in a court trial before, the next few pages will enlighten you on the trial as it applies to both professional attorneys and individuals who serve as their own legal counsel.

Introduction to the Trial
When both sides in a controversial issue have their case heard in court, the procedure is known as a *trial*. The opposing parties are *litigants*.

A *decision* resolving the controversial matter before the court is sought by the litigants who were unable to resolve the issue between themselves.

Such a decision is reached by the party or parties legally empowered to hear the case, usually a *trial judge* or a *jury*.

- The majority of the civil cases included in this book are heard by judges.

- Juries hear civil cases only when requested by the parties, who will have to pay the jury fees. In criminal cases, there are no jury fees.

The conclusion of a trial involves handing down the *Judgment* or the *Sentence*. In a civil case, the "judgment" dictates the terms to be performed by the party losing the case (such as payment for damages) while in a criminal matter the "sentence" specifies the punishment for a party who has been found guilty.

Introduction to Trial Counsel
In the average courtroom trial, one man or woman represents each of the litigants (opposing parties) by serving as his side's attorney-at-law (legal agent or representative).

Attorneys are also known as *lawyers* (practitioners of law) or *legal counselors* (givers of legal advice).

Professional licensed legal counselors are not the only individuals who try cases in court, however. Private persons acting as their own attorneys may also try their own cases in court. These non-lawyers who serve as their own counsel are functioning *in Propria Persona* (in their own behalf). In the legal community these lay lawyers are called *Pro Pers*. (Another term is *Pro Se*.)

Trial counsel include adult men and women of all ages, shapes, sizes and cultural backgrounds. There is no simple way to describe the typical trial counselor any more than a few words could tell you what the average party to a lawsuit is like; therefore, the pronoun "he" is used extensively throughout this book when referring to lawyers, *Pro Pers* and the parties they represent.

Introduction to the Non-lawyer

During trial, the counselors are the spokespersons for the parties they represent; therefore, if a comment needs to be made to a party in the action, it is addressed first to the counselor through the court. In other words, counsel do not talk to each other when court is in session. One counsel talks to the court, and opposing counsel responds by addressing the court.

If the party wishes to make a comment, it is delivered by his counselor.

There is an exception to this form of courtroom protocol, however: when an individual appears as a *Pro Per*, he is both his own legal counsel and the party in the action. *He speaks for himself at all times because there is no one else present to speak for him.* He is, literally, his own agent.

If you will be acting as a *Pro Per* in your case, there are a few things you should know at the outset:

1. The law allows anyone wishing to serve as his own attorney to do so. No special education or license is required to represent yourself in your own legal matter. In a criminal case, the court will discourage a non-lawyer from representing himself; it will even offer a free counselor if you are not financially able to pay for an attorney.

2. The law does not allow unlicensed individuals to practice law for anyone except themselves. Therefore, never attempt to serve as someone else's lawyer if you have not passed the Bar Examination and are not duly licensed by the state in which you would be practicing.

3. Never retain an unlicensed person to serve as your legal counselor either in court or out of it.

This book can help you learn to think like a lawyer, handle your case as thoroughly as an attorney would, and even try your lawsuit in court—to win. By following the instructions, you will be able to save untold dollars that might otherwise be spent on costly legal fees.

One thing the book cannot do, however, is make you into a lawyer. Therefore, even if you feel like a lawyer after practicing all the techniques contained in the following chapters, *never pass yourself off as an attorney to a judge or lawyer.* Be proud to be a *Pro Per* exercising the American right to serve as your own lawyer.

An attorney's service to his client ends when the trial has concluded or at the time they agree to terminate their attorney-client relationship. If a party has acted *in Propria Persona* he ceases to be his own lawyer when he is substituted out by a lawyer he retains.

Introduction to Your Case

What role do you play in your legal matter? Are you the injured party, or the party being accused of causing an injury, damage or other injustice?

In a civil matter, the party making the complaint is the *Plaintiff* (injured party).

In a criminal matter, the injured party is *The People* (of the State or United States), while the actual victim of the crime, who is loosely referred to as "the complainant," is technically just a witness in the case.

In both civil and criminal lawsuits, the party charged for his injurious conduct or an offense is known as the *Defendant.*

The following Case Analysis will help you assess the legal matter in which you are involved. You will be able to tell in an instant whether you have grounds for a lawsuit to be tried in court, and whether your best course of action lies in hiring an attorney or handling your own case as a *Pro Per.*

Case Analysis

1. Select one word which describes your role in your legal matter and write it on the line below: *Plaintiff, Defendant*

   I am the _____.

2. Why are you involved in the controversy leading to your lawsuit? How did you get into it? Write the cause of your involvement:

   I am involved because_____

   _____

   _____

   _____.

3. What do you want to get out of the lawsuit? If the case goes to trial, what do you expect to gain? Be specific.

   I wish to get _____

   _____

4. Can you prove you deserve what you hope to get out of the lawsuit? In the spaces below, list all the proof you can get to show you are deserving.

I have the following proof _____

_____

_____

_____

How to Judge Your Own Case

Your answers to the Case Analysis will let you to judge for yourself whether you actually have grounds for a lawsuit that can be tried in court. It will also help you decide whether you really need a lawyer or prefer to handle your own case as a *Pro Per.*

Easy Answers—If you had no trouble answering all of the questions, and you definitely can offer solid evidence as proof of your position, you probably have the makings of a case that stands a good chance of being won in court.

If yours is a civil (non-criminal) case that is uncomplicated, involving only one basic issue which your evidence proves to be true, and you are not seeking more than $5,000* in damages, serving as a *Pro Per* is not only possible, it is probable. In a civil case in which more than $5,000 is being sought you may wish to retain an attorney. If your case is criminal in nature, professional legal counsel is recommended.

Difficult Answers—If you had trouble answering any questions in the Case Analysis, you may lack valid grounds for a lawsuit. If you have neither physical proof nor witnesses who can testify on your behalf, you stand little or no chance of winning a lawsuit in or out of court. If the legal matter in which you are involved is a serious threat to your welfare, you may wish to get professional legal counseling about the best way to proceed. Or, delay making your decision about whether or not to hire a lawyer until after you have read this book.

Do You Really Need a Lawyer?

Many people who find themselves involved in legal matters jump to the conclusion they need lawyers — and end up spending money they could have saved by handling the situations themselves.

Others, thinking they can do it all themselves, end up by retaining professional legal counsel.

---

*California maximum for Small Claims Court as of January 1, 1991.

In either event, time and money are wasted.

Before deciding whether you really need a lawyer in your case, read the next chapter. It will help you make the right decision.

Chapter 2

What Kind of Case Do You Have?

MAKING THE RIGHT DECISION whether to retain an attorney or proceed as a *Pro Per* is vitally important. Until you are sure of the answer, you cannot really continue with preparations of the case.

What kind of case do you have? Would it be best-served by professional legal representation? Could you serve yourself just as well by appearing in court on your own behalf? Or, is yours the type of case that you must handle yourself?

This chapter will help you decide. The decision you make will be the right one.

Two Kinds of Lawsuits

Broadly speaking, there exist only two categories into which all lawsuits are divided: *criminal* and *civil.* Therefore, the legal action in which you are involved is either a criminal case or a civil case.

An easy way to understand the difference between the two is to think of them this way:

Criminal cases involve public wrongs. Those committing these "public wrongs" are considered society's "bad guys," threats to "the people" of a city, state or nation collectively rather than individually. Persons committing criminal acts are sometimes called "public enemies."

Civil cases involve private wrongs. Those committing these "private wrongs" are usually individuals whose acts or omissions cause damages to other persons.

While they may be adversaries in private, they pose no threat to the general welfare of the public-at-large.

What Kind of Case Do You Have?

Following are four lists containing breakdowns of the most commonly tried types of cases in the American courts system. Look through the terms which describe various issues upon which cases are tried in court. Circle the word that most closely describes the type of legal action in which you are involved.

GROUP A

Armed Robbery	Grand Theft
Arson	Kidnapping
Assault with a Deadly Weapon	Mayhem
Bribery	Molestation (child)
Burglary	Murder
Drug Sales	Perjury
Embezzlement	Rape
Extortion	Treason

GROUP B

Assault (simple)	Driving Under the Influence
Battery	Driving Without a License
Building Code Violation	Drunk in Public
Concealed Weapon	Operating Unlicensed Business
Disturbing the Peace	Petty Theft
Gambling	Trespassing

GROUP C
(Amount involved exceeds $25,000*)

Adoption**	Nuisance
Bills (collection/payment)	Personal Injury
Contract cases	Probate**
Divorce**	Product Liability
Eminent Domain**	Property Damage
Malpractice	Subrogation
Torts	

*In California as of January 1989 cases exceeding $25,000 are heard in Superior Court; this figure may vary in other areas.

**In California they are heard in Superior Court, regardless of the amount involved.

GROUP D
(More than $5,000 but less than $25,000 involved*)
A variety of lawsuits as in Group C.

GROUP E
(Less than $5,000** damages involved)

Bills (collection/payment)	Malpractice
Contracts	Personal Injury
Landlord-Tenant Disputes	Property Damage

What the Groups Mean

An explanation of each of the five groups appears below. The description for the group containing your word suggests both the case type and best approach to legal representation for a lawsuit in this category. If you cannot find a word that describes your case exactly, read the explanations of the groups to find the category in which your case belongs.

GROUP A—

These cases involve major crimes. Included are some of the most serious criminal matters. Known as "felonies," this class of crime is commonly associated with society's so-called "public enemies."

Persons convicted of felonies are called "felons." A small percentage of the population, felons pose the greatest threat to society's welfare.

If your lawsuit fits the Group A class of legal matters, your best course of action is to use the professional services of an attorney who specializes in criminal law. However, many defendants appear as *Pro Pers;* while they may benefit from the experience, few have ever won major lawsuits. If convicted, a felon may lose his reputation, his freedom and even his life.

If you are the defendant in a felony case, and you cannot afford to hire an attorney, the court will appoint a public defender to represent you at low cost, or even no cost, to you.

If you are the victim in a felony suit, you should report the crime to a law enforcement agency. You will be called as a witness by the prosecution.

---

*In California, $25,000 is the maximum amount allowed for civil cases tried in Municipal Court.

**The maximum amount allowed in the State of California for damages sought in Small Claims Court as of January 1991. This figure varies in different jurisdictions.)

You may also retain an attorney to file a suit for damages against the perpetrator of the crime.

You cannot prosecute a felony case as a *Pro Per.*

GROUP B—

Included on this list are several of the most common smaller crimes, which are legally known as "misdemeanors." This type of crime is punishable by fines, community service or incarceration. Sometimes punishment includes a combination of all three factors. The jail sentence for a misdemeanor is one year or less.

A much greater segment of the population is involved in misdemeanors than in the types of criminal activities described in Group A. However, while a misdemeanor on one's record may not carry as great a stigma or as severe a punishment as a felony conviction, every criminal action is serious and should not be treated lightly.

If you are the defendant (accused) in a misdemeanor case, you need a lawyer.

If you cannot afford one, the court will appoint a public defender to represent you.

If you are the complainant (accuser) in a misdemeanor case, you will be a witness for the People who are represented by a city or county prosecutor.

GROUP C—

Included in this list are a few of the matters most often tried in civil courts. Generally, every type of legal action not criminal in nature belongs to the "civil" category. Most civil suits involve unresolved disputes between private parties, either on an individual or group level.

The majority of all civil lawsuits seek some form of financial restitution or compensation for damages, injuries or other injustices. In California a major portion of all civil trials are for personal injuries in which defendants are covered by insurance companies.

Some *Pro Pers* try their own cases—and win. This is true of both plaintiffs (those who file the lawsuit) and defendants (those who defend themselves against claims brought against them).

Before making the decision to serve as your own legal counselor in your civil suit, consider the following factors: (1) This book can teach you everything you need to know about trying your own case in court, but you must make the winning effort; (2) between one and five years, or more, of your time might be involved between the date the lawsuit was filed and the day it finally comes to trial; (3) you might face a seasoned trial lawyer in court who knows how to win on technicalities, despite your being well-armed with overwhelming evidence to support your side's case.

If you enjoy a challenge, go for it. Be a *Pro Per.* If, however, patience is not your strongest virtue, let a lawyer handle your lawsuit.

GROUP D—
This group includes cases that would otherwise be in Group C, but the plaintiff is seeking damages from $5,000 to $25,000. You must choose whether to proceed as a *Pro Per* or retain a lawyer.

GROUP E—
Included in this list is a variety of cases with a unique feature-in-common:

They can be handled by individual *Pro Pers.* In fact, certain cases *must* be handled *in Propria Persona* because lawyers are not allowed to represent clients in the courts where such cases are heard.

Small Claims Court cases, for instance, require that a plaintiff file his own case, and appear on his own behalf in court; the defendant also appears as a *Pro Per.* Several small claims case types appear in Group E's list, including: matters relating to unpaid or uncollected bills; broken or unfulfilled contracts and agreements (known legally as Breach of Contract); and matters involving damage to property.

Small claims, as opposed to large claims, are those which are defined by law in the State of California as cases in which damages range between $1 and $5,000. Cases in which more than $5,000 is sought cannot be tried in Small Claims Court. (The maximum amount that can be sought in your area may be more or less than $5,000 for small claims cases. If you have a small claims case, never ask for more than is allowed by law in your area.)

Individuals may also serve as *Pro Pers* in matters involving minor traffic violations. Among these are tickets for parking, speeding, running red lights or stop signs, and a host of other infractions (non-misdemeanor traffic violations). Such matters are usually heard in traffic courts.

Private parties may also represent themselves in matters involving landlord-tenant disputes of various kinds. Cases involving eviction of tenants for non-payment of rent, or for other reasons, are the most common of these types of cases (known legally as Unlawful Detainer). These are generally Municipal Court cases, along with the last group of types appearing in the next paragraph.

Non-lawyers may or may not act as *Pro Pers* in various other types of relatively uncomplicated cases in which only one basic issue is being disputed and the amount being sought is fairly low. Insurance companies may or may not be involved in such cases, which include accidents of all types; malpractice suits in which a professional person or firm failed to deliver competent professional services; and, cases in which personal injuries were sustained.

---

*California maximum for Small Claims Court as of January 1, 1991.

If your lawsuit resembles one described in this paragraph, you must decide whether you wish to proceed on your own or retain legal counsel.

All the cases appearing in Group E are civil in nature. The vast majority of all lawsuits tried and disposed in court belong to this "small civil" category which is characterized by two main factors: *Little time and little money are involved.* Cases appearing in Group E are usually disposed in six months or less from initial date of filing.

If yours is a Group E lawsuit, you can try your own case in court—and win!

This book will tell you how.

Summarizing Your Case

Generally, the only difference between the major and minor civil cases is the amount involved.The legal issues in both major and minor lawsuits are the same except for divorce, eminent domain, probate and adoption cases, which should always be filed in Superior Court (or the equivalent court in your area), while bankruptcy and immigration matters are filed in Federal Court. These are complicated cases and, therefore, are not discussed in this book.

Check the box in the Case Summary below which best describes your case:

Case Summary

My Case Type	Group	Description	Recommended Form of Representation	
			Attorney	Pro Per
_____	A	Criminal-felony	X	
_____	B	Misdemeanor crime	X	
_____	C	Major civil	X	
_____	D	Civil*	—	—
_____	E	Minor civil		X

The law cannot prevent you from serving as your own attorney in any court of law except in very serious criminal cases in which the court will try to persuade you to accept court-appointed counsel or to retain your own lawyer. Whether to retain a lawyer or serve as your own attorney is a decision you must make for yourself. Decide wisely. Confucius said, "Wisdom is knowing when you do not know."

Taking the Next Step

If you decide to retain a lawyer, rather than handle your legal matter yourself, you may still benefit from this book in several ways: by knowing how to prepare pre-trial

---

*Make your own decision.

materials, you can save money that might otherwise go for legal fees; by understanding what a lawyer must do, you can help him do his best for you; and, knowing what the court expects from you will help you give the best of yourself in the team effort to win your case.

The next question is: *Does your case really belong in court?*

NOTES

Chapter 3

Do You Really Need to Go to Court?

ONTRARY TO A BELIEF popularized by numerous TV dramas centering around courtrooms, the trial is not always the best way to resolve a legal controversy. In fact, making a lawsuit out of a small issue can often be more harmful than helpful. To illustrate this point, I am including the highlights of a case that is typical of so many civil court cases.

The Trial Over a Tree

Two neighbors constantly argued over a peach tree growing in Mr. A's back yard. One branch which was heavily laden with fruit hung over the fence into Mrs. B's yard. Their controversy went like this:

MR. A: Good morning, Mrs. B. I saw you picking my peaches again.

MRS. B: They aren't yours. They're mine.

MR. A: They're on my tree. They belong to me.

MRS. B: Oh yeah? Well, they're in my yard, so they're mine.

MR. A: I'm warning you. Stop picking my peaches.

MRS. B: How can you stop me?

MR. A: I'll sue you.

Mrs. B: Oh yeah? Just try!

Mr. A: I will!

Mr. A leaped the fence, began picking peaches from Mrs. B's yard and tossing them into his yard. Angered, Mrs. B ran into the house and called the police, reporting that a theft of her property was in progress. The officers advised the neighbors to settle their own problem.

Mr. A reacted by sawing the branch from the tree. It fell into Mrs. B's yard. The unresolved controversy continued:

Mrs. B: When are you going to clean up the mess you made in my yard?

Mr. A: It's your branch. You wanted it. I gave it to you.

Mrs. B: The rotten peaches are drawing flies and gnats.

Mr. A: Spoiled fruit does that. You should have picked them when they were fresh.

Mrs. B: They were smashed by the fall.

Mr. A: That's not my fault. It's your responsibility.

Mrs. B: Oh yeah? We'll see about that!

Mrs. B paid a handyman fifty dollars to clear up the mess, and she filed a lawsuit against Mr. A for damages.

After hearing this civil case, the judge decided for Mrs. B; however, Mr. A was only ordered to pay one dollar in damages to Mrs. B, and both parties were ordered to split court costs.

Was anyone really the winner in this dispute? No. Both were losers because more than just valuable time and money were wasted by bringing this case to trial. A valuable relationship was sacrificed.

Small Issues, Big Consequences

The small issue about the peach tree led to major consequences in the lives of the two neighbors who became enemies—and are likely to remain each other's adversaries for life.

Is the case involving the peach tree unusual? No. Small cases of this nature are heard in civil courts around the nation every day of the work week. Such lawsuits are often based on petty controversies that have been blown out of proportion by the opposing parties. They involve "unresolved disputes" that usually could have been settled by the parties themselves *if both sides had been willing to negotiate.*

Negotiate First, Sue Later

If everyone in the country sued each other each time a dispute arose, the court calendars would be so overloaded that millions of cases never would be heard. Fortunately, the majority of minor disputes are settled in private; they never reach the status of lawsuit or come before a judge.

Most people resolve their own differences, either through acceptance of a situation they feel is not worth the time, effort, and money to change—or which can be negotiated.

If you are involved in a dispute that is not yet a lawsuit, you may wish to follow this rule of thumb: *Negotiate first, sue later.*

The word *negotiate* means "to discuss for the purpose of reaching a mutually satisfactory agreement."

Here is how negotiation might have worked between Mr. A and Mrs. B, not only to avoid a court trial, but to strengthen their relationship.

Example of Negotiation:

MR. A: Good morning, Mrs. B. I saw you picking peaches again.

MRS. B: I'm glad you brought it up. I couldn't resist. They are so good.

MR. A: They're delicious all right.

MRS. B: I was wondering if maybe I could buy your peaches.

MR. A: How many do you need?

MRS. B: I'd like to can several quart jars, seven or eight at the most.

MR. A: Sure. The tree's loaded. But I'll make you a deal.

MRS. B: What kind of deal.

MR. A: Pick only those hanging on your side of the fence. You can have them for…well…

MRS. B: How much, Mr. A?

MR. A: Oh, I think a couple of quarts of your canned peaches is fair.

MRS. B: You've got a deal. But let's make it four quarts.

Turn the Negative to Positive

Negotiation is the art of fair bargaining. In the above example, a potentially negative situation was turned into a positive one in which both parties benefitted.

In this example, both Mr. A and Mrs. B were considerate of how their actions affected the other party. Each was basically asking, "What can I do to help you, my friend?" While neither wanted to lose, each put the other's welfare on a par with his own; consequently, both got more than they bargained for. Why is this? Simply because we always get back more than we give!

A law of life seems to be: If we give of ourselves positively, good things are bound to return. If, however, we are negative and selfish, we will reap what we sow. This is true in all aspects of living, not only in the kind of situations discussed in this chapter, many of which never need to go to court if they can be successfully negotiated at the outset.

> *"Therefore, if your enemy hungers, feed him; if he thirsts, give him a drink; for in so doing you will heap coals of fire on his head.*
> *"Do not be overcome by evil, but overcome evil with good."*—Romans 12:20–21

How to Deal with Problem Negotiations

Some people are simply unwilling to negotiate. You cannot talk to them because they refuse to enter into a discussion. They will not listen to a reasonable offer, nor will they make any concessions.

There are several ways to handle the matter. Each will be discussed briefly below:

1. *Forget it*—If the legal matter in which you are involved has not been filed in court, it is not yet a lawsuit. It is simply an unresolved controversy. If you do not feel it is important enough to waste your time, energy, and money on trying to resolve, your best course of action may lie in following the ancient maxim: *Forgive and forget.*

2. *Forge ahead*—If the legal matter is important to you, whether it is or is not yet a lawsuit, you may wish to forge ahead to force it to conclusion. This implies taking your case just as far as you can in order to settle it once and for all—with the court trial being the culmination of all other efforts at reaching a settlement.

3. *Consult a lawyer*—He can tell you whether your case belongs in court or not.

If you make the decision to move ahead with court proceedings, the thought of going all the way to trial may not appeal to you. Alternative approaches to the courtroom trial are discussed in the next chapter.

Chapter 4

Do You Really Want to Go to Trial?

SUPPOSE YOU HAVE MADE the decision to take your case to court. You must now ask yourself: *do I really want to go to trial?*

Many lawsuits that are filed in court are settled without being tried. Before deciding which is the best way to proceed in your legal matter—to try or not to try your case—familiarize yourself with the good and bad news contained in this chapter.

The Bad News About Court

If you are like most people involved in a legal matter, you would like to get it over with as soon as possible. Right? Right. And the courts will help you try your case quickly? Right? Wrong!

The bad news about court—any court—is that you will probably have to wait a considerable length of time before your case goes to trial. In a few exceptional instances, you may have an even shorter wait, but there is an equal possibility it may be longer than you expect.

How long you must wait, from date of filing until the trial, depends on the type of legal matter slated to be heard. An overview of the court calendars across America is contained in this chart, which is divided into three basic sections: *Short Causes, Medium Causes, and Long Causes.*

How to Estimate Your "Time to Trial"

To gain a fairly good idea of how long you will have to wait for your case to be tried, after the initial papers have been filed in court, read through the following chart. It contains breakdowns of the three basic categories of cases pending trial. Your type of case should fit into one of these groups.

Estimated Time to Trial

Type of Cause	Description	Waiting Period
Short	Cases taking less than one hour to a day or less of court time. Most common types: small claims cases, minor traffic infractions, unlawful detainers.	6 weeks-6 months
Medium	Cases requiring more than half a day but less than three days of court time. Most common types: a wide range of civil actions, including personal injury, breach of contract, malpractice, property damage, product liability and other civil cases, often involving insurance companies.	9 months-5 years
Long	Criminal cases: felonies. Big crimes often require a year or more of a court's time for the trial. Criminal trials take precedence over civil cases.	1–3 years or less

(Note: In misdemeanor cases, unless the defendant agrees to a longer period, most courts will set the case for trial within forty-five days from the date defendant enters his plea of not guilty [thirty days if defendant is in custody]).

You can easily see that both Short Causes of the very briefest kind and Long Causes of the criminal kind stand the best chances of coming to trial quickly, but just about everything in between—shown here under the broad heading of Medium Causes—has to wait its good, long turn.

Why is this so? There are so many lawsuits lined up to be tried that they trail right off one year's court calendar onto the next.

Is anything being done to alleviate the backlogs on the courts' calendars? Indeed there is, and that is the good news we will discuss next.

The Good News About Court

The good news is: *you can take your case to court—and even win it—without a trial!*

Today's courts encourage "out-of-court settlement." An out-of-court settlement is an agreement reached by both parties without the participation of a judge.

Every case settled this way helps reduce the backlog of cases still waiting to be heard. There is also an advantage to you, the litigant: *you can save both time and money by settling your case out of court!*

Two-Party Compromise

An out-of-court settlement is achieved by meeting with the lawyer or *Pro Per* for the opposite side *for the specific purpose of negotiating an agreement.* Work out terms which are mutually satisfactory to both of you.

You may have to "give some and take some" in this process, known as *reaching a compromise.*

The law does not dictate where you must reach an out-of-court settlement. You may be riding in a car when the agreement is reached, sitting on a bicycle, talking by telephone, or walking down the street.

The law does require, however, that the parties report that a settlement has been reached, so the clerk of the court can duly note this fact on the court's records *and remove the matter from the calendar of pending trials.*

Dispute Settlement Service

Los Angeles County offers a "Dispute Settlement Service" (see illustration on the next page) as an alternative to the court trial. It works, through mediation, to resolve civil disputes between consumers and business, renters and property owners, businesses and vendors, and neighbors. It does not handle criminal, malpractice, and family law (including divorce) cases.

A similar service may be available in your area. Some of the names by which this type of program is known are *arbitration, mediation,* and *settlement conference.*

Taking the Next Step

If you cannot successfully reach an out-of-court settlement, your next step will be to try your case in court. Chapter 5 will tell you which is the right court for your kind of case.

A WAY TO SETTLE YOUR DISPUTE
WITHOUT GOING TO COURT

LOS ANGELES COUNTY DISPUTE SETTLEMENT SERVICE

IT'S EASY, FREE, FAST AND IT WORKS!
VISIT OUR OFFICE OR CALL
(213) 974-0825
8:30 A.M. TO 4:30 P.M. WEEKDAYS

You'll receive more information to help you decide if mediation will work for you. When you let us know you want our help, we'll schedule a mediation session at a convenient time for both parties.

IT WORKS . . .
Before you file to settle your claim in the court system, please consider mediation through the Los Angeles County Dispute Settlement Service. A mediator works with you to reach an agreeable solution so that both parties win. The mediator will not judge right or wrong but will assist both of you in reaching an agreement.

IT'S EASY . . .
Just come into our office or call and a trained counselor will answer your questions and provide you with information on how you can resolve your dispute quickly and easily.

IT'S FREE . . .
No court filing service fees, attorney's fees or any other cost for either party.

IT'S FAST . . .
You don't have to wait for a court date. Mediations are scheduled at the convenience of both parties, often within a few short weeks. And, you won't have to spend a full day in court waiting for your case to be heard.

THERE IS NO RISK . . .
On those rare occasions when a solution can't be reached, parties still have the opportunity to go to court.

Chapter 5

How to Take Your Case to Court

MANY CASES NEVER get to court for one reason: *the parties do not know to which court to turn.*

Before you can take your case to court, you must know which is the proper court to serve you. This chapter will acquaint you with the American court system so you need never wonder again where to turn for judicial help.

Big Courts, Small Courts—Which is Which?

When someone asks me to explain the difference between Municipal Court and Superior Court, I say, "It is easy to remember if you think of it this way: Municipal Court is inferior court."

This does not mean "muni court" is less important or less dignified than Superior Court, or, as it is called in some areas, "Circuit" Court. It is just that smaller cases, and frequently a greater number of cases, pass through municipal courts than in higher courts.

Municipal Court, where most *Pro Pers* stand the best chance of trying their own cases to win, functions along with the higher courts to balance justice by making it possible for everyone to be served. Think of the term "super" as it applies to higher courts: super means "big" or "great." The higher courts handle the bigger, or greater, cases.

In contrast, a municipal court is popularly called "the People's Court," because its purpose and function is to move as many cases through the system in as short a time as possible. Most are "smaller" cases.

Basic Facts Every *Pro Per* Should Know

If you are not fully aware of the different types of courts in your state, do not feel bad. You are not alone. Unless a person is involved in business which requires dealing with the courts—such as filing a lawsuit or being party to one—he may never have felt the need to learn the intricacies of the judicial system.

Because you plan to serve as your own legal counsel, you may wish to acquaint yourself with the basic structure and function of the court system in your area. This chapter provides a basic introduction to state courts.

Federal courts, which are separate from state courts and are not involved in the types of trials covered in this book, are not included in this summary. For further information about federal or state courts, contact your local law library.

How the Judicial System Is Structured

Visualize the four courts comprising the state judicial system as a pyramid or upright triangle. The judicial hierarchy begins at the broad-based bottom and culminates in the narrow apex or capstone.

Traditionally, the capstone of a pyramid represents supremacy, superiority, or ultimate dominion over everything beneath it; thus, a state's Supreme Court, represented by the peak of the pyramid, is the highest court in the state.

In descending levels, the court of appeal is above Superior Court, and Superior Court is higher than Municipal Court, which is depicted as the bottom of the pyramid in this diagram.

The type of case you will be trying as a *Pro Per* will be heard in one of the two courts appearing in the lower half of the pyramid: Municipal Court or Superior Court.

Introducing Municipal Court

A municipality is any area where groups of people live in concentration, such as a city, town, or township. Municipal Court serves the local population of such a city, town, or township; it is the court of the immediate community.

- *Municipal Court has jurisdiction over all misdemeanors.*
  A "misdemeanor" is a criminal case that is punishable by imprisonment not exceeding one year in jail and/or payment of a fine (not exceeding $1,000 in California). (*California Vehicle Code Section 23185 provides for $5,000 maximum fine for causing bodily injury while under the influence with a prior conviction.*)

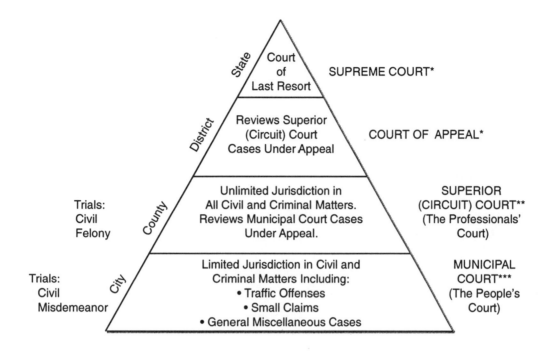

* = Revew Court—Trials not conducted
** = Limited opportunity for *Pro Per* representation
*** = Conducive to *Pro Per* representation in certain matters on trial

State Court System

• *Municipal Court also has jurisdiction over all civil (non-criminal) cases in which small amounts are sought.*

For example, in California, as of 1989, the maximum amount of money that can be claimed in such a case is $25,000. This may be a lot of money to the plaintiff, but it is relatively small in comparison to larger cases in which claims for hundreds of thousands, or even millions, of dollars are sought.

The Maximum Amount You Can Claim in Municipal Court

States vary in the maximum amounts of money (jurisdictional amount) allowable in Municipal Court. In California, for example, $25,000 may be sought, while in another state no more than $10,000 may be sought in trial.

You may obtain information about the jurisdictional amount allowed in your area by contacting your local Municipal Court clerk. If the amount you are claiming is beyond the figure allowed by law in your state, you may wish to change your demand to conform to local Municipal Court guidelines.

For instance, suppose you are seeking $30,000 in damages and you live in California; you may wish to waive $5,000 (just ask $25,000 in your complaint) to conform to the $25,000 maximum amount allowable in Municipal Court.

Why might it be beneficial to lower the amount you are seeking in order to have your matter heard in Municipal Court, rather than in Superior (or Circuit) Court? There are two basic reasons:

1. Municipal Court cases are usually resolved in much shorter time than those on the Superior Court calendar.

2. Municipal Court lends itself to *Pro Per* representation because it is "the People's Court."

If you had the choice, for example, of seeking $25,000 from Municipal Court, or $30,000 from Superior Court, would it be worth a possible wait of between two and five years to ask for the additional $5,000?

How to Contact Municipal Court
The fastest way to obtain information about the amount allowable in Municipal Court is to visit the courthouse in person. If you are unable to do this, you may call the courthouse; if all clerks are busy, you may be put on hold.

In the event you prefer to obtain your information by mail, call the courthouse and get the name of a specific individual to whom your letter should be addressed. You may pattern your written request around the letter which appears on the next page.

We suggest you enclose a self-addressed, stamped envelope (SASE) in which the clerk may enclose his reply.

Insight into Municipal Court
Municipal Court is divided into two main divisions: Municipal Court itself (consisting of three or more panels of judges who hear specific types of matters) and Small Claims Court. Although the descriptions given here are based on California's Municipal Court system, similar characteristics apply to all jurisdictions, beginning with the People's Court (Small Claims Court).

Introduction to Small Claims Court
As of January 1991, the maximum amount litigants could seek in Los Angeles Small Claims Court, a division of Municipal Court, was $5,000. Average time from date of filing to disposition of small claim matters is two months. Typical small claim cases include collection of compensation for service performed; bill collection; restitution

Proper name of individual
Clerk of the Municipal Court
Courthouse
Street address or P.O. box number
City, State, Zip Code

In re: Request for Information

Dear (Ms., Miss, Mrs. or Mr.) _____:
(person's last name)

I plan to file a lawsuit in the near future and wish to obtain information on the following matter:

(Fill in brief description of your case.)

What is the highest amount of recovery allowed by law in civil matters handled by the Municipal Court?

Your prompt response will be appreciated.

Sincerely,

Your name
(Optional: your daytime telephone number)

Letter Requesting Information
Re: Jurisdictional Amounts

for work left incomplete by contractors, laborers, or workmen; and a wide variety of other torts (civil wrongs): claims for damages, defaults, destruction of property, personal injury.

A large percentage of small claim cases is based on negligence, both of a private and professional nature. For further information, refer to Chapter 24, "How to Try Your Own Negligence (Personal Injury) Case."

The People's Court

The Small Claims Court division of Municipal Court is truly deserving of its nickname, "the People's Court," because:

- *Filing fees for small claims are so reasonable that just about anyone can afford them.* In California, the filing fee is fifteen dollars or thirty dollars if you file twelve or more cases a year (multiple filers). Other jurisdictions charge even less for filing claims; in cases of hardship, filing fees may even be waived or reduced.

- *Lawyers are not allowed to represent clients in small claim matters.* Therefore, Small Claims Court is the only court where a *Pro Per* must serve as his own legal representative. Can an attorney represent himself in Small Claims Court? Yes, provided he represents himself as either the plaintiff or defendant in the matter before the Bench.

The Defendant Has the Right to Appeal

In California small claims courts, the plaintiff may not appeal the judge's decision. The defendant is the only party to the action who may take the matter on appeal. This same rule also applies to most small claims courts outside California.

The court clerk in your local municipal courthouse can tell you whether plaintiffs in your area may appeal decisions in small claim matters; also, this information will be printed on the legal forms which must be filed in small claims cases.

The Judge's Participation

Small claims matters are decided by judges, not by juries. Unlike other judges who sit through trials conducted by litigants' counsel, a Small Claims Court judge may do most—if not all—the questioning of witnesses; he serves both as direct-examiner and cross-examiner of both sides. See Chapter 27, "How to Conduct Your Own Small Claims Court Case."

Introduction to Traffic Court

This division of Municipal Court handles traffic cases. In a small courthouse, one specific time, or courtroom, may be reserved part-time for traffic matter trials. In busy metropolitan courthouses, permanent traffic courts, which are separate arms of Municipal Court, operate full-time; some even hold night or weekend Traffic Court hearings.

The types of cases tried in Traffic Court fall into two categories:

- *Misdemeanors*—Misdemeanor traffic violations are punishable by imprisonment (in California for no more than one year in jail) and/or fine (in California, not exceeding $1,000) for such offenses as driving under the influence of alcohol or drugs, or for hit-and-run. Misdemeanors are criminal wrongs.

- *Traffic Infractions*—Traffic infractions include such offenses as illegal or incorrect parking, running red lights and stop signs, failure to stop for pedestrians, and tailgating.

Unlike Small Claims Court, which does not allow attorneys to represent clients, Traffic Court does allow attorneys to appear. In fact, in cases involving misdemeanors, legal counsel is recommended.

You May Qualify for a Court-Appointed Attorney

If you cannot afford a lawyer to handle your misdemeanor case, the court will appoint counsel to represent you; he will be paid by the county in which the matter is tried. After the case has been disposed, the court will conduct a hearing to determine your present ability to pay all or portions of the cost, or will order you to appear before a designated county officer who will make such a determination.

In both misdemeanor and traffic infraction matters, you may serve as your own legal counsel; the choice is yours. If you choose to appear as a *Pro Per*, you may be opposed by a city prosecutor who is a highly skilled trial lawyer.

Other Aspects of Municipal Court

"Muni Court" is the term by which judges and lawyers often refer to Municipal Court in general. Aside from small claim and traffic cases, which are special branches of Municipal Court, the wide variety of civil matters heard here include: landlord-tenant disputes; breach of contract lawsuits; wrongful termination cases; minor malpractice suits; personal injury claims; other torts (non-criminal wrongs).

Municipal Court also handles misdemeanor (criminal) matters; trials for major crimes (such as rape, mayhem and murder) are heard in Superior Court (also known as Circuit or District Court).

Municipal Court Panels

Groups of judges assigned to hear specific matters are called "panels." These panels are especially found in larger courthouses where the workload must be divided up in order to keep the cases moving through the system swiftly and efficiently.

In metropolitan Los Angeles, for example, Municipal Court is divided into three panels:

- *Civil Panel*—This is my usual assignment. We handle only civil trials and sometimes specially assigned criminal matters.

- *Criminal Panel*—This panel handles misdemeanor trials.

- *Preliminary Hearing Panel*—This panel handles only preliminary hearings in which the judge, sitting as a magistrate, considers evidence presented by the prosecution; if there is sufficient cause to believe that a crime, i.e. a felony, was committed and the defendant is guilty thereof, the magistrate "holds him to answer." The case is then transferred to the Superior Court, where the defendant is arraigned again and tried.

Self-Representation in a Criminal Matter

If your case will come before a criminal or preliminary hearing panel, I strongly discourage self-representation (*Pro Per*), because losing your case could mean incarceration (being sentenced to jail).

Your right to represent yourself is recognized by the United States Supreme Court; no court in the land will deny you that right. However, before you make a firm decision to serve as a *Pro Per* in a criminal case, consider the following:

- *You May Have A Right to Free or Low-Cost Legal Representation*
In a criminal case, the court will appoint an attorney to represent you, at no cost to you, if you have no funds; or an amount will be arrived at which you can afford to pay.

How to Address a Municipal Court Judge

When speaking to a judge of the Municipal Court, address him as "Your Honor" when court is in session, or "Judge Jones," "Judge Smith," or "Judge Williams" on other occasions. Judges are never addressed by their first names or nicknames, such as "Judge John," "Judge Bill," or "Judge Flash."

Once your case has been assigned to a specific judge, you should not write him letters for the purpose of telling him your side of the matter, attempting to convince him to take legal action on your behalf, or attempting to undermine your opponent.

If you try to influence the judge through correspondence, he will recuse himself (disqualify himself from the matter) because he can no longer render a fair and impartial decision. Nor can he give legal advice, so do not write and ask for it.

However, you may write to a judge for purposes other than those mentioned above; for instance, after your matter has been completely disposed in court, you may send him a thank you letter.

The proper way to address your correspondence to a judge of the Municipal Court is:

The Honorable (Judge's full name)
Judge of the Municipal Court
Courthouse, Division _____
Address
City, State, Zip Code

Dear Judge (Judge's last name) _____:

Introducing Superior (aka District/Circuit) Court

Superior Court is a higher court than Municipal Court. It serves the people of the county in which the court is located. If the county is large, there might be various branches of the Superior Court located in strategic places throughout the county; sometimes one central courthouse serves a broad area called a district and, therefore, is called "District Court" or "Circuit Court."

Different Courts May Share the Same Places

The Superior and Municipal Courts may or may not share the same District Court location. Judges are permanently assigned for a certain period of time, say a year. Also by assignment, some judges travel the "circuit" by going from courthouse to courthouse on their "rounds." A circuit is a specific territory, usually defined by north, south, east, and west borders, that covers a broad expanse of countryside.

Superior Court is the Place for Big Cases

Having the same location or circuit does not alter the fact that there exists a distinct division between the kinds of cases handled by the lower and higher courts. Although the laws of each state may vary slightly, basically every Superior Court has greater jurisdiction than Municipal Court, as follows:

- *Superior Court has unlimited trial jurisdiction in civil matters.*
  This means that in civil suits, there is no limit to the amount of money claimed. Cases involving hundreds of thousands—even millions—of dollars are heard in this court.

- *Superior Court also has unlimited trial jurisdiction in criminal matters.*
  This means that criminal matters heard in Superior Court are unlimited to the kinds of sentences that can be handed down. Since felonies (big crimes, as opposed to misdemeanors, which are smaller crimes) are tried here, everything

from maximum life imprisonment sentences to the death penalty can be given in this court.

The Professionals' Court

There is another major distinction between Municipal Court and Superior Court. Whereas "Muni Court" is called the "People's Court," Superior Court can be described as the "Professionals' Court." Here, as a rule, only attorneys try the cases for their clients; however, *Pro Pers* are allowed to try their own cases in Superior Court.

The Types of Lawyers You Might Meet

If you decide to try your own case in Superior Court, it is a good idea to know something about the types of lawyers you may meet in the courtroom. They include:

New attorneys who are still inexperienced in courtroom protocol and procedures; seasoned lawyers who know every tactic in the book (and some not in the book) for gaining judgment in their favor; in-house counsel representing their employers; corporate attorneys from big law firms; and attorneys in solo private practice.

Then there are the public servants, foremost among whom is the judge. Working for salaries that are less than the income of private practitioners, these dedicated men and women come in a variety of shapes, sizes, and personalities. You'll meet Prosecutors (District or City Attorneys) whose job involves representing "the People" in criminal cases; County Counsel who represent the county in civil cases; and Public Defenders, a unique group of attorneys on the county payroll who defend those persons charged with crimes who cannot afford to retain their own legal counsel.

The ADCs of Superior Court

In courthouses with heavy criminal calendars and a limited number of public defenders, you may also meet one or more alternate defense counsel, called "ADCs." The ADCs are private practitioners who regularly serve in court as defense counsel when the public defender is not available or there is a conflict. They are paid by the county for their professional services.

Miscellaneous Facts About Superior Court

What kinds of cases are handled in Superior Court? The answer is simple: everything that the Municipal Court cannot handle, both civil and criminal cases.

Note that criminal matters take precedence over civil cases. The welfare of "the People" of the state always has priority over the civil suits on the court calendar.

This explains why, as crime increases, civil suits become so backlogged on the court calendar that a case may not come to trial for one to five years from date of filing.

If you are considering trying your case in Superior Court, ask yourself whether it is really worth the long wait you will have to endure before you get to trial.

Relief is in sight, however, if age is on your side. Most cases filed by plaintiffs seventy years of age or older will be scheduled, upon motion, in as timely a manner as possible, so justice can be served while the parties are still alive.

How Appeals Are Reviewed

Superior Court, through its appellate department, reviews cases on appeal from Municipal Court. However, any cases under appeal from Superior Court may be reviewed by the Court of Appeal, which is the next highest court in the judicial system. But the Superior Court, on its own or upon motion of the party or the Court of Appeal itself, has to order that the case be transferred to the Court of Appeal before it can review the case on appeal to the Superior Court.

How to Correspond With a Superior Court Judge

If you wish to write to a Superior Court judge, your letter should be addressed as shown below:

> The Honorable (Judge's full name)
> Judge of the Superior Court
> Courthouse, Department _____
> Address
> City, State, Zip Code\

> Dear Judge (Judge's last name) _____:

If you wish to write to a Circuit Court judge, your mail should be sent to your local courthouse, where it will be held by the clerk and delivered to the judge when he arrives. Your letter should be addressed as follows:

> The Honorable (Judge's full name)
> Judge of the Circuit Court
> Circuit Court of (Name) _____ County
> Courthouse
> Address
> City, State, Zip Code

> Dear Judge (Judge's last name) _____:

Introducing the Court of Appeal

Each state Court of Appeal serves a district, which may include several counties in its territory. It may be the lower of two state appellate courts, and it performs distinctly different functions than the Superior Courts and Municipal Courts; it is "intermediate" or "in between."

Legal Think Tank
Unlike the lower courts, where judicial drama takes place, no courtroom trials are held in this court. As a member of the Bench once described it to me, "The Court of Appeal is a think tank."

All You Need to Know About the Court of Appeal
Unless you plan to appeal the judgment rendered in your trial, you will not need to be concerned with intimate details relating to the appeals court, which is distinguished by the following points:

- *The Court of Appeal reviews decisions handed down by Superior Courts for the purpose of reversing, altering, amending, or affirming the lower court's decision.* In most jurisdictions, three justices are assigned by the Presiding Justice to a case; one justice is assigned to write the opinion (decision) and at least one justice should concur with the opinion.

- *Judges who have been elevated to the Court of Appeal bench receive the title "Justice."* Address a justice as "Justice Jones," not "Judge Jones."

In making their decision, the justices, individually and then together, review carefully all aspects of a case after studying the paperwork associated with it and hearing the oral arguments of counsel.

If there is any possibility that you may want to appeal your case, once judgment has been handed down, keep your paperwork in good order by following the steps outlined in this book.

Countrywide Glance at Courts of Appeal
Every state has some type of appellate court, meaning a judicial body which reviews lower court decisions; however, the structure of the judicial system varies from state to state. The following summary, as explained in *Black's Law Dictionary*, sheds light on this matter:

The courts of appeal are intermediate courts in states having them, except in New York, Maryland, and the District of Columbia, where they are the highest appellate courts, meaning their decisions are "the last word."

In West Virginia, the supreme and appellate courts are combined; there, the "Supreme Court of Appeals" is the highest court in the state.

"Courts of Criminal Appeals" exist in Alabama, Oklahoma, Tennessee, and Texas; in Oklahoma and Texas, they are the highest state appellate courts for criminal matters. Also, "Courts of Civil Appeals" exist in Alabama, Oklahoma, and Texas; these are intermediate courts, not courts of last resort, for civil matters only.

California, the state which serves as a model for much of the material in this book, has a "Court of Appeal" that is an intermediate court; it reviews matters from lower (Municipal and Superior) courts, but is not the highest court in the state. The State Supreme Court holds that honor. It has the power to reverse, amend, alter, or affirm any decisions rendered by the Court of Appeal.

Should the need arise for you to appeal your case in court, your local court clerk can advise you regarding how the appeals courts are structured in your state, and also where to turn to set your appeal into motion.

How to Correspond With a Court of Appeal Justice

Correspondence to judicial officers of an appellate court should be addressed as follows:

> The Honorable (Justice's full name)
> Presiding Justice or Associate Justice
> Name of the Court
> District, Department, Division or Room Number
> Address
> City, State, Zip Code

> Dear Presiding Justice (Justice's last name) _____:

or

> Dear Associate Justice (Justice's last name) _____:

Introducing the State Supreme Court

The State Supreme Court serves the state in which it is located. Just as the United States Supreme Court is the highest judicial body in the nation, the Supreme Court of a state is the highest judicial body in that state. It, too, is a Court of Appeal.

The Court of Last Resort

The State Supreme Court is the "court of last resort" in matters under appeal from lower state courts, and its decisions are "the final word" in state-related judicial matters.

This court has been described as "holding the power to grant life or death," as has been demonstrated in states which have capital punishment. A decision from the Supreme Court can stay (halt) the execution of a convicted murderer awaiting execution on death row.

High Judicial Honor

Being appointed to the Supreme Court is the highest honor a member of the judiciary can receive. Those who sit on the Supreme Court are also called "Justices." There is one "Chief Justice" and all others are "Associate Justices."

How to Correspond With a Supreme Court Justice

The proper way to address correspondence to a member of the Supreme Court is as follows:

> The Honorable (Justice's full name)
> Chief Justice or Associate Justice of the Supreme Court
> Supreme Court of the State of (name state) _____
> Address
> City, State, Zip Code
>
> Dear Chief Justice (Justice's last name) _____:

or

> Dear Associate Justice (Justice's last name) _____:

The Courthouse—Heart of Your Community

Before closing this chapter, I would like to share a few more ideas about our courts. First, back in days of antiquity, a "court" was such an important place it was likened to the "heart" of a community, or "center" from which activity generated in relationship to the people of the area. Rulers, such as kings and emperors, "held court" and young men "courted" young women in the hopes of winning their undying affection. A "courtly" person is still considered an individual with regal demeanor.

Our courts today occupy an important place in the lives of everyone in our communities. Not only is justice carried out in the courts, vital statistics are often filed there. Records of births, marriages, divorces, and deaths may be on file in your local courthouse, along with tax records, records on property and other real estate ownership, and a variety of other public information pertaining to the community and those who live there.

Marriage licenses are issued in the courthouse and civil (non-religious) marriage ceremonies are performed by judges. Probate matters, divorces, child custody cases, and even records of adoptions are on "record" in the courthouse.

Courthouse Records—Open to the Public

A courthouse is like a vast depository of valuable information, open to inspection by those it serves: the public. If you are in need of vital statistics you do not know how to obtain, contact your local courthouse. If they do not have what you need, they should be able to tell you where to get it.

Miscellaneous Facts to Help You Win

When you try your own case in court, you will probably come before a judge. However, although their numbers are rapidly disappearing in the American judicial system, there is a slight chance the bench officer hearing your case will be a Justice of the Peace, a special type of judicial officer of the Municipal Court found in out-of-the-way areas having neither regular nor Circuit Court judges on the bench.

Your case may also be heard by an individual known as a "Judge Pro Tempore," or simply *pro tem*. These "temporary" judges, who may be court commissioners or other court-appointed officers, are fully authorized by law to serve in a judicial capacity.

If your case is already on the court calendar and awaiting trial, a final word of advice is in order: Do not correspond with the judge. To do otherwise would force the judge to recuse (disqualify) himself and, consequently, the trial of your case will be delayed.

Summary of State Courts

Before you can set your lawsuit into motion, it must be filed with the proper court, as summarized here:

Type of Matter	Court
Traffic: minor infractions*	Traffic Court/Municipal Court
Traffic: misdemeanor*	Traffic Court/Municipal Court
Civil Torts (small wrongs, usually seeking $5,000 or less in damages)	Small Claims Court
Civil Torts (medium wrongs, up to $25,000** being sought in damages)	Municipal Court
Misdemeanors (small crimes)*	Municipal Court
Civil Torts (big wrongs, no limit to amount of damages sought)	Superior Court
Felonies (big crimes)**	Superior Court
Appeal	Filed in court where trial was held; will be reviewed by next-highest court.

---

*Filed by the city or county prosecutor.

**Maximum allowed in California Municipal Court; amounts vary in different jurisdictions.

Notes

Chapter 6

How to File Your Case in Court

YOUR LEGAL MATTER cannot be tried in court unless it is a lawsuit.
A legal matter does not become a lawsuit until it has been filed in court. Therefore, if your case is not yet a lawsuit, it must be filed in court before it can be tried.

Filing the case is only the first step toward resolving the matter, however. A series of legal steps must then be followed which may result in resolution of the matter through trial—or one of the other means described in this section.

This chapter, which introduces typical legal forms used in civil suits like yours, covers the highlights of the process that follows the filing of a lawsuit. It is designed to familiarize you with the order and logic known as "due process of law" and give you insight into the process as you may make it work for you.

Filing the Civil Complaint

If you are the injured party who is seeking damages for the wrong you have suffered, you must file a form known as a *Complaint* with the court.

When your Complaint has been filed in court, you are known as the *Plaintiff*. The plaintiff is the party who brings suit.

The party against whom the Complaint is filed is known as the *Defendant*. The defendant is the party being sued.

The Complaint is the first legal form to be filed in your action. It is not the last, as you will see.

Introducing the Summons

The second legal form filed in a lawsuit is known as a *Summons*. It is filed along with the Complaint. A Summons is a court order demanding that the defendant file a response to the plaintiff's Complaint. Terms set forth in the Summons are determined by several factors which differ among various types of civil cases, as shown in these examples:

Unlawful Detainer—In an unlawful detainer case involving a landlord-tenant dispute which could result in eviction of the tenant, the defendant is given five days from date of service (the date he received the Summons and Complaint) to respond.

Miscellaneous Civil—In the majority of civil cases, except those involving small claims, the defendant is allowed thirty days from the date he received the Summons and Complaint to respond.

These examples are based on California law. Check the law in your own area to determine the length of time provided for the defendant to respond after date of service of the Summons and Complaint in your case.

In most types of cases, the Summons and Complaint, while served at the same time, are two separate legal documents. However, in the State of California, there is an exception:

Small Claims Cases—The Summons and Complaint are combined in small claims cases. The combination form orders the defendant to appear at a specified date, time, and place for the hearing (trial) of the matter; it also sets forth the plaintiff's complaint.

At the time small claims cases are filed in Los Angeles, the date of trial is set. However, in other types of civil matters, the date of trial cannot be set until the defendant has had the opportunity to respond to the Complaint.

Therefore, since a defendant is entitled to a thirty-day period in which to respond, the plaintiff must wait until that time period has elapsed before proceeding with plans to bring the matter to trial.

The Answer

The third type of legal paper involved in a lawsuit is the defendant's response to the Summons and Complaint he has been served by the plaintiff. His response is known as an *Answer*.

The defendant's Answer consists of two parts, with which every *Pro Per* (both plaintiffs and defendants) should be familiar. They are:

Denial—The first part of the Answer is known as the "Denial" or "General Denial." In his denial, the defendant denies the material allegations set forth in the plaintiff's Complaint. This means the defendant disputes the plaintiff's claim.

Denial by a defendant of a plaintiff's claim is standard procedure (even in cases in which the defendant might personally agree with the plaintiff's allegations). *The defendant's Denial is a challenge to the plaintiff to prove his claim.*

Defense—The second part of the Answer is known as the "Defense" or "Affirmative Defense."

In his defense the defendant *may introduce "new material"* (facts related to the matter which are not contained in the plaintiff's Complaint) in avoidance of, and/or in defense of, plaintiff's claim. However, he *may not seek damages for any injury, harm, or injustice he suffered.* This means that even if the defendant states he was an injured party, he may not ask for any compensation or restitution for injury or damages allegedly caused by the plaintiff.

Examples of Denial and Defense
The following example involves two neighbors who frequently borrowed gardening tools and other equipment from each other. The plaintiff took a stepladder from the defendant's shed while the defendant was out of town.

While climbing up to paint a trellis over his patio, the ladder collapsed and the plaintiff landed atop his new electric outdoor barbecue grill. It was smashed beyond repair. The plaintiff sued for the replacement cost of the broken barbecue grill.

The defendant's Answer consists of his general denial of the material allegations and the following affirmative defense:

Plaintiff had permission to borrow my gardening tools, not the ladder. It was defective when I bought it. He ignored the note taped to the top step: BROKEN—DO NOT USE. Plaintiff's own negligence was a substantial factor in bringing about the destruction of the electric outdoor barbecue grill.

Note that the defense contains a new material in defense and/or avoidance of the plaintiff's claim.

Since the defendant cannot seek damages in his Answer to the Complaint, does he have any legal recourse? Yes. He can file a *Cross-complaint*, which is a separate pleading. (In some states, the counterpart is a counterclaim which is part of the Answer.)

Introducing the Cross-complaint

In a Cross-complaint, the defendant countersues the plaintiff (or a third party; i.e., the electric barbecue grill manufacturer). This means the defendant files a Complaint (legally designated as Cross-complaint to differentiate it from the plaintiff's Complaint) against the plaintiff and serves him with the Cross-complaint, to which the plaintiff answers with a Denial and Affirmative Defense.

In a trial involving a Cross-complaint, the plaintiff tries his case against the defendant; then, temporarily becoming the plaintiff, the defendant tries his case against the plaintiff, who momentarily serves as the defendant.

The defendant in the matter involving the ladder filed a Cross-complaint. The court ruled for the defendant because the plaintiff had been negligent. The plaintiff was ordered to replace the defendant's ladder and to be responsible for the loss of his new barbecue grill.

A case with a Cross-complaint is a trial in which *both parties sue each other*. This is an especially valuable legal device for the defendant who believes he is entitled to damages from the plaintiff.

One Trial for Two Lawsuits

In a matter involving a Cross-complaint, one trial serves to settle both disputes which evolved out of the same basic issue; consequently, one decision is reached and one judgment is handed down by the court.

Does filing a Cross-complaint against the plaintiff relieve the defendant who has been served with a Summons and Complaint of the responsibility of filing an Answer? No. He should respond as already explained in this chapter.

For more information about countersuits, refer to Section IV.

Avoid Default

A Summons is an official order issued by the court for the defendant to respond to the Complaint within a specific period of time, and the defendant is bound to comply with it.

What are the consequences of non-response to a Summons? You risk losing the case. A defendant's failure to file an Answer on the date so ordered can result in the plaintiff winning "by default."

As you can see from the sample forms, space is provided for the defendant to summarize his defense succinctly. A lengthy detailed explanation is not necessary.

How Legal Documents Are Served

Legal documents should never be dropped casually in the mail, shoved under a door, or left in a mailbox. They should be served.

Service of legal documents is known as "service of process," and the people who perform this function are "process servers."

Details on process serving appear elsewhere in this chapter.

Just as the plaintiff must serve the defendant with the Summons and Complaint, the defendant must serve the plaintiff with his Answer. At this point, many *Pro Pers* find themselves confused by "legal red tape" based on the question:

What is Filed Where and by Whom?

Since several copies of a legal document are involved, you need to know what happens when a legal form is "filed" in court and these copies must be distributed.

"Filing" means registering or entering a legal matter into the court record. Here is how the system operates in Los Angeles; allowing for slight variations in different areas, the basic ground rules are the same in all jurisdictions.

Filing the Complaint—After the plaintiff has filled in the Complaint, he gives it to the designated court clerk, who affixes the Seal of the Court to the original, and signs, stamps, and dates it. The court retains the original Complaint and returns the copies to the plaintiff.

Filing the Summons—The plaintiff also gives the court clerk the completed Summons along with the Complaint. The clerk processes the Summons, then returns the original and all copies to the plaintiff. The plaintiff, through his process server, serves the defendant with the copy of the Summons and a copy of the Complaint. Plaintiff returns the original of the Summons, properly filled up by the process server, to the court.

Filing the Answer—The defendant serves the plaintiff with a copy of his response to the Summons and Complaint. The defendant should make a copy for his records. Defendant should file the original of his Answer with the Clerk of the Court. Attached to the Answer should be the proof of service of the Answer to the plaintiff.

When the plaintiff receives the Answer, *he should make an extra copy for his records.*

The Plaintiff's Choice

After the defendant answers the Complaint, the plaintiff makes the next move.

- *Discovery*—This legal term means *investigation for the purpose of discovering facts related to the opposition's side in the matter.* "Discovery" may involve sending interrogatories to the party, taking depositions, and inspecting the other side's proof: all the exhibits he plans to offer into evidence.

By employing this method, the plaintiff gets to know the other side's case—its strengths as well as its weaknesses. *The defendant may also wish to practice discovery of the plaintiff's side.*

The value of discovery is that both litigants become aware of each other's side in the lawsuit and, therefore, may be receptive to reaching a mutually satisfactory agreement without having to go to trial.

- *Trying the Case*—If the case is not settled out of court, the plaintiff now proceeds with setting the trial date for the purpose of having the matter resolved in court. He must file a form known in Los Angeles as a Memorandum to Set for Trial with the court. This request for a trial date may be known by another name in your area.

How to Cancel a Lawsuit

If you feel the defendant's Answer does not justify proceeding further with the lawsuit, you may be tempted to drop the matter entirely. Think twice! A defendant, disgruntled over being sued in the first place, may file a "Malicious Prosecution" suit against you charging that he was wrongly sued.

Unless you are very serious about your lawsuit, and intend to pursue it to its conclusion, it is better not to file it at all than to arbitrarily decide to forget the whole matter once the legal wheels are rolling.

The law does not forbid cancelling your lawsuit. To do so you must file a form known in Los Angeles as a Request for Dismissal. On this form you must state whether the case is being dismissed "With Prejudice" or "Without Prejudice," standard legal terms meaning:

With Prejudice—The matter is ended and cannot be refiled.

Without Prejudice—The lawsuit is cancelled but the matter can be refiled.

How to Request Judgment Without Trial

What recourse do you have if the defendant does not respond to your Summons within the established time limit? In Los Angeles, a plaintiff may file a form called *Request for Entry of Default and Court Judgment by Default,* asking the court to declare the defendant in default and to render judgment against the defendant without a trial. A similar form will be available in your area.

In addition to the form, the plaintiff must attach a *Declaration Under Penalty of Perjury,* stating that if he is called and sworn as a witness he can competently testify on his cause(s) of action, and then states precisely the factual and legal basis of his causes(s) of action, attaching the necessary exhibits.

Small Claims Court and Default

In most small claims courts, contrary to municipal, superior, and circuit courts, a defendant is not required to file an answer to the plaintiff's complaint; however, he is required to appear in court on the specified date. If the defendant is absent, the court will proceed to hear the plaintiff.

If the plaintiff fails to appear for the hearing, the court will dismiss the case.

Help is At Hand

At first glance, legal forms may seem confusing. However, today's legal forms are written in modified legalese, with step-by-step instructions on how to fill in the blanks. Several legal forms of the types introduced in this section appear in the back of this chapter.

Practice filling in these samples in pencil and read the instructions carefully to develop a feeling for, and understanding of, the same type of modified legalese which will appear on the forms involved in your lawsuit.

Today's legal forms assist *Pro Pers* in handling their own lawsuits without having to prepare complicated written pleadings; everything can be written in the spaces provided on some forms, while other forms offer multiple-choice questions that can be marked with the specifically applicable answers.

The forms provided as illustrations in this book are included to help you help yourself as a *Pro Per*. If you prefer not to mark the published forms, you may obtain copies of forms from your local court clerk. After practicing a few times, you will be ready to file the real thing with the court.

Where to Go

Now that you are acquainted with the basics of the lawsuit, your next step is to apply what you have learned by filing your case in court. Chapter 5, "How to Take Your Case to Court," explains where to file your type of legal matter.

If you have not yet read Chapter 5—and do not know where to file your case in court—we suggest you review it now. If you already know where to file your case in court, proceed with your study of this chapter.

The Cost for Filing

You must pay a filing fee when you file your Complaint. You will have to check with the clerk at the courthouse to find out how much the fee will be. In Los Angeles, for example, the filing fee for a small claims case is fifteen dollars. Such a fee may be more or slightly less in your area.

The forms you need are available at the courthouse. They are quite inexpensive, usually costing no more than a few cents apiece. (In California, small claims forms are free.)

In the event yours is a hardship case and you cannot afford the filing fee, explain your situation to the clerk. You may be eligible for a waiver of charges, which means certain things will be provided to you at no cost.

What to Do

When you have arrived at the court, go to the office of the clerk and explain to the person behind the counter, "I wish to file a Complaint and to buy the proper legal forms."

The clerk will ask for details. A lengthy explanation involving all the details about your case is not necessary. Stating the issue is sufficient. A few issues and their explanations are listed here as examples:

Issue	Description
Small Claim	A case in which damages being sought are $5,000 or less (according to California law)
Personal Injury	A case in which you have suffered injury to your body through an accident involving a vehicle, condition of the premises or acts of another person or persons.
Product Liability	A case in which a defective product has caused injury, damage or loss.
Unlawful Detainer	A case in which a tenant in your property has not paid the rent and you wish to start eviction proceedings.
Breach of Contract	A case in which someone with whom you have made an agreement has not fulfilled his end of the bargain.
Malpractice	A case in which someone who was supposed to perform competent professional services rendered less-than-satisfactory work, resulting in the plaintiff's damages

The clerk will give you the proper forms for both your Summons and Complaint. After you have filled them out and paid your filing fee, the clerk will date, sign, and stamp the documents with the Seal of the Court, distributing them as outlined in the beginning of this chapter. Your lawsuit has now been filed and you must serve the defendant with a copy of the Summons and Complaint (as previously explained).

How to Serve Documents

The legal term for delivery of documents is *Service of Process* and the people who perform this function are *process servers*. After a lawsuit has been filed, neither the plaintiff nor the defendant should casually drop important documents into the mail, shove them under a door, or stick them in a mailbox and hope they are received by the party for whom they are intended.

Introducing Proof of Service

You need proof that a document was served. The process server provides it on a form known as *Proof of Service*. Proof of Service appears on the back of many legal forms, including the Summons. The language on all Proofs of Service is basically the same, and since such proof accompanies service of every conceivable type of legal document, the Proof of Service is the most widely used single legal form in the country. You may create your own Proof of Service forms, if necessary, by patterning them around the sample shown in the back of this chapter.

Service by Mail

Hand-delivery of a document is the ideal way to effect service; however, other means are also sometimes necessary, including the mailing of documents. When a document is mailed, you need proof of service declaring the date it was mailed and by whom it was mailed. Send such documents by Certified or Registered mail, with a Return Receipt requested. The signature on the receipt is proof that the document was received by the individual who signed it.

Why is proof of service so important? It may be your only evidence with which to prove to the court you served—or attempted to serve—an important document to another party.

Answers to Complaints or Cross-complaints should be served by mail unless your jurisdiction provides otherwise.

How to Select Your Process Server

Any adult over the age of eighteen, who is a resident of your county and is not a participant in or party to your case, can serve papers for you. If such a private individual performs this service, draw up your own Proof of Service and have him sign and date it after he has served the paper(s).

If you prefer that a professional process server perform this important duty for you, look in your local Yellow Pages under "Process" or "Messenger" services. Also, firms specializing in legal services usually perform process serving.

Many of the larger courthouses have staffs of professional process servers on the premises. These uniformed officers, who include marshals and sheriffs, are experts at serving process. The court clerk can tell you whether the uniformed officers in your area perform *Service of Process*.

How Much Will It Cost?

You must choose your own process server and you are responsible for paying his fee. Find out how much you will be charged before you hire a professional process server; if one process server is too expensive, shop around. Many *Pro Pers* use nonprofessional individuals to serve process, often at little or even no cost. You may have a neighbor or acquaintance as your process server if allowed by law; however, we recommend the use of a professional process server whenever possible. The reason is clear: The "indicia of truthfulness" of an unbiased professional is greater than possible for a friend, neighbor, or relative who has done you a favor.

What Happens if Service Cannot be Completed?

Ideally, the process server hand-delivers a document to the party for whom it is intended. However, this is not always possible due to extenuating circumstances.

Or he may make several trips to the address of the person being served, only to find no one answers the door or the individual is always "out of the office" or "unavailable." Such experiences call for *substituted service authorized by the law.* The professional process server knows the alternatives to personal delivery, such as delivering a copy to a person other than the one for whom it is intended, and mailing a copy, or by publication, which is a complicated process. Because of space constraints, I will not discuss it here. Get at least a certified paralegal if not a lawyer to help you serve the defendant by publication.

He knows the proper wording to use on the Proof of Service form, regardless of the kind of process he serves. His expertise relieves you of the burden of attempting to use legalese on forms with which you are trying to work for the first time.

A Few More Forms Which May Be Helpful

There are four more forms about which every *Pro Per* should know. They will help you gain a better understanding of how a lawsuit progresses from beginning to end. Some of these forms may even be involved in your case.

All the examples in this chapter are listed by the names by which they are known in California. In some areas, legal forms are classified by form number rather than name. A list of forms by name and number is available for reference in the office of the court clerk, in the event you need this information for the forms applicable to your case.

- *Memorandum to Set Case for Trial*—This is the form the plaintiff files when requesting the court to set a date for his trial. (Defendant can also file this form.)

- *Clerk's Notice of Trial*—This is the court's notice to both the plaintiff and defendant that the case has been set for trial. The date, time, and place of the trial are specified.

• *Notice of Entry of Judgment*—This is the court's notice to the litigants which spells out the judgment awarded in a small claims case.

How to End Your Lawsuit

When the losing party has fulfilled his obligation to the winner, as ordered by the court, the court should be notified that the matter is satisfied.

• *Satisfaction of Judgment*—This form states that all obligations have been fulfilled. The loser has paid the winner. Judgment has been satisfied.

Summarizing the Lawsuit

Now that you have an inside view of the legal process, you are aware that a lawsuit has an opening, middle, and ending. The most dramatic—and unpredictable—portion of a lawsuit is the middle part, which involves a variety of forms.

Do not be concerned about which forms you may have to deal with as your lawsuit progresses. The clerk of the court can provide the proper form at the time it is needed.

As a starter, you are now ready to tackle your first legal forms. Turn to the Bonus Section at the end of this chapter and fill in both the Complaint and Summons. Remember to use a pencil so you can erase and start over if necessary.

When you feel satisfied with your effort, you are ready for the next big step—filing your own case in court and converting it from a legal matter to a lawsuit.

Most Common Legal Forms
(Bonus Section)

Eleven of the most common types of legal forms associated with civil lawsuits are included here. They are provided for your information only and should not be used as actual forms to be filed by you in court. You may obtain the proper forms you need from the clerk of the courthouse where your case is filed. The forms appear in the following order:

Name of Form	Description of Function
Complaint (pp. 53–55)	Plaintiff's claim. Basis of lawsuit. Notice to the defendant that he is being sued.
Summons (pp. 56–57)	Court's order to defendant to respond to Complaint.
Summons & Complaint (pp. 58–59)	Combined Summons & Complaint in small claim case. Trial date is specified.

Name of Form	Description of Function
Proof of Service (p. 60)	Process server's declaration that service was made.
General Denial (p. 61)	Defendant's answer to Summons and Complaint. Denies plaintiff's claim against him.
Request for Entry of Default and Judgment by Default (pp. 62–63)	Plaintiff's declaration that defendant defaulted by failure to respond. Request for court to render judgment.
Request for Dismissal (p. 64)	Plaintiff's request that the lawsuit be cancelled.
Memo to Set for Trial (p 65)	Plaintiff's request that the court set a trial date.
Clerk's Notice of Trial (p. 66)	Clerk's notice to plaintiff and defendant that the trial is now on the calendar.
Notice of Entry of Judgment (pp. 67–68)	Court's notice to plaintiff and defendant of its decision and judgment in a small claims matter.
Notice of Satisfaction of Judgment (p. 68)	Litigants' notice to the court that the terms of judgment have been fulfilled.

Note: To serve the public more efficiently, the Los Angeles Municipal Court is on the Internet and you can download these forms at no cost to you.

ATTORNEY OR PARTY WITHOUT ATTORNEY (NAME AND ADDRESS):	TELEPHONE:	FOR COURT USE ONLY

ATTORNEY FOR (NAME):

Insert name of court, judicial district or branch court, if any, and post office and street address:

PLAINTIFF:

DEFENDANT:

☐ DOES 1 TO _____

COMPLAINT—Personal Injury, Property Damage, Wrongful Death	CASE NUMBER:
☐ **MOTOR VEHICLE** ☐ **OTHER** *(specify):* ☐ **Property Damage** ☐ **Wrongful Death** ☐ **Personal Injury** ☐ **Other Damages** *(specify):*	

1. This pleading, including attachments and exhibits, consists of the following number of pages: _____

2. a. Each plaintiff named above is a competent adult
     ☐ **Except** plaintiff *(name):*
         ☐ a corporation qualified to do business in California
         ☐ an unincorporated entity *(describe):*
         ☐ a public entity *(describe):*
         ☐ a minor   ☐ an adult
            ☐ for whom a guardian or conservator of the estate or a guardian ad litem has been appointed
            ☐ other *(specify):*
         ☐ other *(specify):*

     ☐ **Except** plaintiff *(name):*
         ☐ a corporation qualified to do business in California
         ☐ an unincorporated entity *(describe):*
         ☐ a public entity *(describe):*
         ☐ a minor   ☐ an adult
            ☐ for whom a guardian or conservator of the estate or a guardian ad litem has been appointed
            ☐ other *(specify):*
         ☐ other *(specify):*

   b. ☐ Plaintiff *(name):*
       is doing business under the fictitious name of *(specify):*

       and has complied with the fictitious business name laws.
   c. ☐ Information about additional plaintiffs who are not competent adults is shown in Complaint—
       Attachment 2c.   *(Continued)*

Form Approved by the
Judicial Council of California
Effective January 1, 1982
Rule 982.1(1)

COMPLAINT—Personal Injury, Property Damage, Wrongful Death

CCP 425.12

76C551 - **CI 177JC** - (CR) - PS 6-85

COMPLAINT—Personal Injury, Property Damage, Wrongful Death   Page two

3. a. Each defendant named above is a natural person

☐ **Except** defendant *(name):*   ☐ **Except** defendant *(name):*

☐ a business organization, form unknown   ☐ a business organization, form unknown
☐ a corporation   ☐ a corporation
☐ an unincorporated entity *(describe):*   ☐ an unincorporated entity *(describe):*

☐ a public entity *(describe):*   ☐ a public entity *(describe):*

☐ other *(specify):*   ☐ other *(specify):*

☐ **Except** defendant *(name):*   ☐ **Except** defendant *(name):*

☐ a business organization, form unknown   ☐ a business organization, form unknown
☐ a corporation   ☐ a corporation
☐ an unincorporated entity *(describe):*   ☐ an unincorporated entity *(describe):*

☐ a public entity *(describe):*   ☐ a public entity *(describe):*

☐ other *(specify):*   ☐ other *(specify):*

b. The true names and capacities of defendants sued as Does are unknown to plaintiff.

c. ☐ Information about additional defendants who are not natural persons is contained in Complaint—Attachment 3c.

d. ☐ Defendants who are joined pursuant to Code of Civil Procedure section 382 are *(names):*

4. ☐ Plaintiff is required to comply with a claims statute, **and**
   a. ☐ plaintiff has complied with applicable claims statutes, **or**
   b. ☐ plaintiff is excused from complying because *(specify):*

5. This court is the proper court because
   ☐ at least one defendant now resides in its jurisdictional area.
   ☐ the principal place of business of a corporation or unincorporated association is in its jurisdictional area.
   ☐ injury to person or damage to personal property occurred in its jurisdictional area.
   ☐ other *(specify):*

6. ☐ The following paragraphs of this complaint are alleged on information and belief *(specify paragraph numbers):*

(Continued)   Page two

54

COMPLAINT—Personal Injury, Property Damage, Wrongful Death (Continued)   Page three

7. ☐ The damages claimed for wrongful death and the relationships of plaintiff to the deceased are
☐ listed in Complaint—Attachment 7 ☐ as follows:

8. Plaintiff has suffered
☐ wage loss
☐ hospital and medical expenses
☐ property damage
☐ other damage *(specify):*

☐ loss of use of property
☐ general damage
☐ loss of earning capacity

9. Relief sought in this complaint is within the jurisdiction of this court.

10. PLAINTIFF PRAYS
For judgment for costs of suit; for such relief as is fair, just, and equitable; and for
☐ compensatory damages
☐ **(Superior Court)** according to proof.

☐ **(Municipal and Justice Court)** in the amount of $_____
☐ other *(specify):*

11. The following causes of action are attached and the statements above apply to each: *(Each complaint must have one or more causes of action attached.)*
☐ Motor Vehicle
☐ General Negligence
☐ Intentional Tort
☐ Products Liability
☐ Premises Liability
☐ Other *(specify):*

_____   _____
(Type or print name)   (Signature of plaintiff or attorney)

SUMMONS
(CITACION JUDICIAL)

NOTICE TO DEFENDANT: *(Aviso a Acusado)*

YOU ARE BEING SUED BY PLAINTIFF:
(A Ud. le está demandando)

You have *30 CALENDAR DAYS* after this summons is served on you to file a typewritten response at this court.	*Después de que le entreguen esta citación judicial usted tiene un plazo de 30 DIAS CALENDARIOS para presentar una respuesta escrita a máquina en esta corte.*
A letter or phone call will not protect you; your typewritten response must be in proper legal form if you want the court to hear your case.	*Una carta o una llamada telefónica no le ofrecerá protección; su respuesta escrita a máquina tiene que cumplir con las formalidades legales apropiadas si usted quiere que la corte escuche su caso.*
If you do not file your response on time, you may lose the case, and your wages, money and property may be taken without further warning from the court.	*Si usted no presenta su respuesta a tiempo, puede perder el caso, y le pueden quitar su salario, su dinero y otras cosas de su propiedad sin aviso adicional por parte de la corte.*
There are other legal requirements. You may want to call an attorney right away. If you do not know an attorney, you may call an attorney referral service or a legal aid office (listed in the phone book).	*Existen otros requisitos legales. Puede que usted quiera llamar a un abogado inmediatamente. Si no conoce a un abogado, puede llamar a un servicio de referencia de abogados o a una oficina de ayuda legal (vea el directorio telefónico).*

CASE NUMBER: *(Número del Caso)*

The name and address of the court is: *(El nombre y dirección de la corte es)*

The name, address, and telephone number of plaintiff's attorney, or plaintiff without an attorney, is:
(El nombre, la dirección y el número de teléfono del abogado del demandante, o del demandante que no tiene abogado, es)

DATE: _____ Clerk, by _____, Deputy
(Fecha) *(Actuario)* *(Delegado)*

[SEAL]

NOTICE TO THE PERSON SERVED: You are served
1. ☐ as an individual defendant.
2. ☐ as the person sued under the fictitious name of *(specify)*:

3. ☐ on behalf of *(specify)*:

under: ☐ CCP 416.10 (corporation) ☐ CCP 416.60 (minor)
☐ CCP 416.20 (defunct corporation) ☐ CCP 416.70 (conservatee)
☐ CCP 416.40 (association or partnership) ☐ CCP 416.90 (individual)
☐ other:
4. ☐ by personal delivery on *(date)*:

Form Adopted by Rule 982
Judicial Council of California
76S818 - **CI1JC** (Rev. 1/84)(11)(OV)

(See reverse for Proof of Service)
SUMMONS

CCP 412.20

56

NAME AND ADDRESS OF ATTORNEY:	TELEPHONE NO :	FOR COURT USE ONLY:

ATTORNEY FOR (Name):

Insert name of court, judicial district or branch court, if any, and Post Office and Street Address:

PLAINTIFF

DEFENDANT

SUMMONS (JOINT DEBTOR)

CASE NUMBER:

NOTICE! You have been sued. The court may decide against you without your being heard unless you respond within 30 days. Read the information below.

If you wish to seek the advice of an attorney in this matter, you should do so promptly so that your written response. if any. may be filed on time.

¡AVISO! Usted ha sido demandado. El tribunal puede decidir contra Ud. sin audiencia a menos que Ud. responda dentro de 30 días. Lea la información que sigue.

Si Usted desea solicitar el consejo de un abogado en este asunto, debería hacerlo inmediatamente, de esta manera, su respuesta escrita, si hay alguna, puede ser registrada a tiempo.

1. TO THE DEFENDANT (Name):

You are hereby directed to file in this court, within **30** days after this summons is served on you, a written response to the Declaration or Affidavit accompanying this summons, giving any legal reason why you should not be required to pay the unpaid amount of: $ . . . . on the judgment rendered by this court on (Date): . . . . against: . . . .

Unless you do so. your default will be entered on application of the plaintiff and the court may enter a judgment against you for the unpaid amount due on the judgment, which could result in the garnishment of wages, taking of money or property. or other relief.

DATED: . . . . , Clerk, By _____ , Deputy

(SEAL)

2. NOTICE TO THE PERSON SERVED: You are served
   a. ☐ As an individual defendant.
   b. ☐ As (or on behalf of) the person sued under the fictitious name of: . . . . . .

   c. ☐ On behalf of: . . . .

   Under: ☐ CCP 416.10 (Corporation)   ☐ CCP 416.60 (Minor)
          ☐ CCP 416.20 (Defunct Corporation) ☐ CCP 416.70 (Incompetent)
          ☐ CCP 416.40 (Association or Partnership) ☐ CCP 416.90 (Individual)
          ☐ Other:

   d. ☐ By personal delivery on (Date): . . . .

A written response must be in the form prescribed by the California Rules of Court. It must be filed in this court with the proper filing fee and proof of service of a copy on each plaintiff's attorney and on each plaintiff not represented by an attorney. The time when a summons is deemed served on a party may vary depending on the method of service. For example, see CCP 413.10 through 415.50. The word "complaint" includes cross-complaint. "plaintiff" includes cross-complainant. "defendant" includes cross-defendant, the singular includes the plural

Form Adopted by Rule 982
Judicial Council of California
Revised Effective January 1, 1979

(See reverse for Proof of Service)

SUMMONS (JOINT DEBTOR)

CCP 989
76S838-CI3(8) 1/79 Rev.

57

Name and Address of Court:

SMALL CLAIMS CASE NO.

<table>
<tr>
<td>
</td>
<td>
</td>
</tr>
</table>

PLAINTIFF/DEMANDANTE *(Name, address, and telephone number of each)*:

DEFENDANT/DEMANDADO *(Name, address, and telephone number of each)*:

Telephone No.:

Telephone No.:

Telephone No.:

Telephone No.:

Fict. Bus. Name Stmt. No.   Expires:

☐ See attached sheet for additional plaintiffs and defendants.

PLAINTIFF'S CLAIM

1. Defendant owes me the sum of $ _____ , not including court costs, because *(describe claim and date)*:

2. a. ☐ I have asked defendant to pay this money, but it has not been paid.
   b. ☐ I have NOT asked defendant to pay this money because *(explain)*:
3. This court is the proper court for the trial because ☐ *(In the box at the left, insert one of the letters from the list marked "Venue Table" on the back of this sheet. If you select D, E, or F, specify additional facts in this space.)*

4. I ☐ have ☐ have not   filed more than one other small claims action anywhere in California during this calendar year in which the amount demanded is more than $2,500.
5. I ☐ have ☐ have not   filed more than 12 small claims, including this claim, during the previous 12 months.
6. I understand that
   a. I may talk to an attorney about this claim, but I cannot be represented by an attorney at the trial in the small claims court.
   b. I must appear at the time and place of trial and bring all witnesses, books, receipts, and other papers or things to prove my case.
   c. **I have no right of appeal on my claim,** but I may appeal a claim filed by the defendant in this case.
   d. If I cannot afford to pay the fees for filing or service by a sheriff, marshal, or constable, I may ask that the fees be waived.
7. I have received and read the information sheet explaining some important rights of plaintiffs in the small claims court.

I declare under penalty of perjury under the laws of the State of California that the foregoing is true and correct.

Date:

▶

. . . .
(TYPE OR PRINT NAME)

(SIGNATURE OF PLAINTIFF)

ORDER TO DEFENDANT

You must appear in this court on the trial date and at the time LAST SHOWN IN THE BOX BELOW if you do not agree with the plaintiff's claim. Bring all witnesses, books, receipts, and other papers or things with you to support your case.

TRIAL DATE / FECHA DEL JUICIO		DATE	DAY	TIME	PLACE	COURT USE
	1.					
	2.					
	3.					
	4.					

Filed on *(date)*:

Clerk, by _____ , Deputy

— The county provides small claims advisor services free of charge. Read the information on the reverse. —

Form Adopted by the
Judicial Council of California
(Rev. January 1, 1995)

PLAINTIFF'S CLAIM AND ORDER TO DEFENDANT
(Small Claims)

Rule 982.7, Cal. Rules of Court

76D176A3 **SC-5 JC** (Rev. 1-95)

(The space above is for the court's use)

INFORMATION FOR DEFENDANT

1. **What is the small claims court?** The small claims court is a special court in which disagreements are resolved quickly and cheaply. A small claim must be for $5,000 (*see below) or less. No person may file more than two small claims actions in which the amount demanded is more than $2,500 anywhere in the state in a calendar year. The person who sues is called a **plaintiff**. The person who is sued is called a **defendant**. Neither party can be represented by a lawyer at the trial, but both parties may talk to a lawyer about the case before the trial.

2. **What can you do if you are sued in the small claims court?**
   a. **SETTLE** — You may settle your case before the trial. If you do, be sure that the plaintiff files a dismissal form with the court. If you would like help in settling your case, ask the small claims advisor (see No. 5, below) to refer you to an alternative dispute resolution provider.
   b. **DEFAULT** — If you do not go to the trial, it is called a **default**. The plaintiff may win the amount of the claim and costs. The plaintiff may then be able to use legal procedures to take your money or property to pay the claim.
   c. **APPEAR AND CONTEST** — You may go to the trial and disagree with the plaintiff's claim. If you do, bring all witnesses, books, receipts, and other papers or things to prove your case. You may ask the witnesses in your case to go to the trial or, before the trial, you may ask the clerk of the court to issue a **subpena**. A subpena is a court order that requires the witness to go to the trial.
   d. **APPEAR AND REQUEST PAYMENTS** — You may agree with the plaintiff's claim, but you may be unable to pay the money all at once. You may then choose to go to the trial and ask the court to order payments you can afford.
   e. **POSTPONE** — If you live in the county where the claim was filed, the plaintiff must serve a copy of the claim on you *10 days before the trial*. If you live outside the county, you must be served *15 days before the trial*. If you did not receive the claim within these time limits, you may ask the court for a postponement.
   If you cannot attend the hearing on the date scheduled, write to the court before the hearing date and tell why, and ask the court to postpone the hearing. The court charges a fee to request a postponement.
   f. **CHALLENGE VENUE** — If you believe the plaintiff's claim was filed in the wrong court (see Venue Table, below), write to the court before the hearing date, explain why you think so, and ask the court to dismiss the claim.

3. **What can you do if you also have a claim against the person who sued you?** A claim against the person who sued you is called a **Defendant's Claim**. Ask the clerk for this form to file your claim. The claim must not be for more than $5,000.* If you received your copy of the plaintiff's claim *less than 10 days* before the trial date, you must serve the plaintiff with your claim *at least 1 day* before the trial date. If you received your claim *more than 10 days* before the trial date, you must serve the plaintiff with your claim *at least 5 days* before the trial date. The court will hear both claims at the same time.

4. **What happens after trial?** The court will deliver or mail to you a copy of a form called the **Notice of Entry of Judgment**. This form tells you how the case was decided. If you disagree with the court's decision, you may appeal the judgment on the plaintiff's claim. You may not appeal your own claim. If you appeared at the trial, you must begin your appeal by filing a **Notice of Appeal** and pay the required fees within *30 days* after the date the Notice of Entry of Judgment was mailed or handed to you at the time of the small claims hearing. If you did not appear at the trial, you must first ask the court to vacate or cancel the judgment. To make this request, you must file a **Motion to Vacate the Judgment** and pay the required fees within *30 days* after the date the Notice of Entry of Judgment was mailed to you. If your request is denied, you then have *10 days* from the date the notice of denial was mailed to file an appeal.

5. **How can you get help with your case?**
   a. **MINORS** — If you are under 18 years old, you should tell the clerk. You are too young to act for yourself in the case. You must ask the court to appoint someone to act for you. That person is called a **guardian ad litem**.
   b. **INTERPRETERS** — If you do not speak English, you may take a family member or friend to court with you. The court should also keep a list of interpreters who will interpret for you. You may choose an interpreter from the court's list. Some interpreters may be free and some may charge a fee. If an interpreter is not available, the court must postpone the hearing one time only so that you have time to get one.
   c. **SMALL CLAIMS ADVISORS** — The law requires each county to provide assistance in small claims cases free of charge. Here is some important information about the small claims advisor program in this county:

   Advisors are available Monday thru Friday, 8:30 AM to 4:30 PM at the County Hall of Administration, 500 West Temple Street, Room B96, Los Angeles 90012 or by calling (213) 974-9759.

VENUE TABLE

(The plaintiff must file the claim in the proper court and geographical area. This rule is called **venue**. The box on this page describes possible reasons for filing the claim in this court.)

If you are the plaintiff, insert the proper letter from the list below in item 3 on the other side of this sheet and specify additional facts for D, E, or F.

This court is the proper court for the trial of this case because

A. a defendant lives in this judicial district or a defendant corporation or unincorporated association has its principal place of business in this judicial district.
B. a person was injured or personal property was damaged in this judicial district.
C. a defendant signed or entered into a contract in this judicial district, a defendant lived in this judicial district when the contract was entered into, a contract or obligation was to be performed in this judicial district, or, if the defendant was a corporation, the contract was breached in this judicial district.
D. the claim is on a retail installment account or contract subject to Civil Code section 1812.10. *(Specify facts on the other side of this sheet.)*
E. the claim is on a vehicle finance sale subject to Civil Code section 2984.4. *(Specify facts on the other side of this sheet.)*
F. other. *(Specify facts on the other side of this sheet.)*

---

* The $5,000 limit does not apply, and a $2,500 limit applies, if a "defendant guarantor . . . is required to respond based upon the default, actions or omissions of another."

PLAINTIFF'S CLAIM AND ORDER TO DEFENDANT
(Small Claims)

PLAINTIFF (name):	CASE NUMBER:
DEFENDANT (name):	

PROOF OF SERVICE
☐ **Personal Service**   ☐ **Mail**

> A General Denial may be served by anyone at least 18 years of age EXCEPT you or any other party to this legal action. Service is made in one of the following ways:
> (1) Personally delivering a copy to the attorney for the other party or, if no attorney, to the other party.
>   **OR**
> (2) Mailing a copy, postage prepaid, to the last known address of the attorney for the other party or, if no attorney, to the other party.
> Be sure whoever serves the General Denial fills out and signs a proof of service. File the proof of service with the court as soon as the General Denial is served.

1. At the time of service I was at least 18 years of age and **not a party to this legal action**.

2. I served a copy of the General Denial as follows (check either a or b):

   a. ☐ **Personal service.** I personally delivered the General Denial as follows:
      (1) Name of person served:
      (2) Address where served:

      (3) Date served:
      (4) Time served:

   b. ☐ **Mail.** I deposited the General Denial in the United States mail, in a sealed envelope with postage fully prepaid. The envelope was addressed and mailed as follows:
      (1) Name of person served:
      (2) Address:

      (3) Date of mailing:
      (4) Place of mailing (city and state):
      (5) I am a resident of or employed in the county where the General Denial was mailed.

   c. My residence or business address is (specify):

   d. My phone number is (specify):

I declare under penalty of perjury under the laws of the State of California that the foregoing is true and correct.

Date:

▶

....
(TYPE OR PRINT NAME OF PERSON WHO SERVED THE GENERAL DENIAL)

_____
(SIGNATURE OF PERSON WHO SERVED THE GENERAL DENIAL)

982(a)(13) [Rev. January 1, 1987]

GENERAL DENIAL
(Proof of Service)

Page two

ATTORNEY OR PARTY WITHOUT ATTORNEY *(Name and Address)*:	TELEPHONE NO.:	FOR COURT USE ONLY
ATTORNEY FOR *(Name)*:		

Insert name of court, name of judicial district, and branch court, if any:

PLAINTIFF:

DEFENDANT:

GENERAL DENIAL	CASE NUMBER:

You MUST use this form for your general denial if the amount asked for in the complaint or the value of the property involved is $1000 or less.

You MAY use this form if:
1. The complaint is not verified, OR
2. The complaint is verified, and the action is subject to the economic litigation procedures of the municipal and justice courts, EXCEPT

You MAY NOT use this form if the complaint is verified and involves a claim for more than $1000 that has been assigned to a third party for collection.

(See Code of Civil Procedure sections 90–100, 431.30, and 431.40.)

---

1. DEFENDANT *(name)*:
   generally denies each and every allegation of plaintiff's complaint.

2. ☐ DEFENDANT states the following FACTS as separate affirmative defenses to plaintiff's complaint *(attach additional pages if necessary)*:

Date:

. . . .
(TYPE OR PRINT NAME)

▶

_____
(SIGNATURE OF DEFENDANT OR ATTORNEY)

If you have a claim for damages or other relief against the plaintiff, the law may require you to state your claim in a special pleading called a cross-complaint or you may lose your claim. (See Code of Civil Procedure sections 426.10–426.40.)

The original of this General Denial must be filed with the clerk of this court with proof that a copy was served on each plaintiff's attorney and on each plaintiff not represented by an attorney. *(See the other side for a proof of service.)*

Form Adopted by Rule 98.2
Judicial Council of California
982(a)(13)(Rev. January 1, 1987)
76G187 CI-176JC (11)(Rev. 1/87)(OV)

GENERAL DENIAL

61

CCP 431.30, 431.40

ATTORNEY OR PARTY WITHOUT ATTORNEY *(Name and Address)*:	TELEPHONE NO.:	*FOR COURT USE ONLY*

ATTORNEY FOR *(Name)*:

Insert name of court and name of judicial district and branch court, if any:

PLAINTIFF:

DEFENDANT:

REQUEST FOR ☐ **ENTRY OF DEFAULT** ☐ **CLERK'S JUDGMENT** **(Application)** ☐ **COURT JUDGMENT**	CASE NUMBER:

1. TO THE CLERK: On the complaint or cross-complaint filed
   a. On *(date)*:
   b. By *(name)*:
   c. ☐ Enter default of defendant *(names)*:

   d. ☐ I request a court judgment under CCP 585(b), (c), 989, etc. *(Testimony required. Apply to the clerk for a hearing date, unless the court will enter a judgment on an affidavit under CCP 585(d).)*
   e. ☐ Enter clerk's judgment
      (1) ☐ For restitution of the premises only and issue a writ of execution on the judgment. CCP 1174(c) does not apply. (CCP 1169) ☐ Include in the judgment all tenants, subtenants, named claimants, and other occupants of the premises. The Prejudgment Claim of Right to Possession was served in compliance with CCP 415.46.
      (2) ☐ Under CCP 585(a). *(Complete the declaration under CCP 585.5 on the reverse (item 4).)*
      (3) ☐ For default previously entered on *(date)*:

2. **Judgment to be entered**

	Amount	Credits Acknowledged	Balance
a. Demand of complaint	$	$	$
b. Statement of damages (CCP 425.11) *(superior court only)*†			
(1) Special.................	$	$	$
(2) General	$	$	$
c. Interest.....................	$	$	$
d. Costs *(see reverse)*	$	$	$
e. Attorney fees	$	$	$
f. **TOTALS**	$	$	$

   g. **Daily damages** were demanded in complaint at the rate of: $ per day beginning *(date)*:
3. ☐ *(check if filed in an unlawful detainer case)* **UNLAWFUL DETAINER ASSISTANT** information is on the reverse *(complete item 3).*
Date:

▶

. . . .
(TYPE OR PRINT NAME)   (SIGNATURE OF PLAINTIFF OR ATTORNEY FOR PLAINTIFF)

† *Personal injury or wrongful death actions only.*

FOR COURT USE ONLY	(1) ☐ Default entered as requested on *(date)*:
	(2) ☐ Default NOT entered as requested *(state reason)*:

Clerk, by: _____

(Continued on reverse)

Form Adopted by the
Judicial Council of California
982(a)(6) [Rev. July 1, 1996*]
CI-34JC

REQUEST FOR ENTRY OF DEFAULT
(Application to Enter Default)
62

Code of Civil Procedure, §§ 585-587, 1169

*See note on reverse.

3. **UNLAWFUL DETAINER ASSISTANT** *(Business and Professions Code sections 6400–6415)* An **unlawful detainer assistant**
☐ did **not** ☐ did for compensation give advice or assistance with this form. *(If declarant has received **any** help or advice for pay from an unlawful detainer assistant, state)*:
   a. Assistant's name: b. Telephone No.:
   c. Street address, city, and ZIP:

   d. County of registration: e. Registration No.:   f. Expires on *(date)*

4. ☐ **DECLARATION UNDER CCP 585.5** *(Required for clerk's judgment under CCP 585(a))* This action
   a. ☐ is ☐ is not on a contract or installment sale for goods or services subject to CC 1801, etc. (Unruh Act).
   b. ☐ is ☐ is not on a conditional sales contract subject to CC 2981, etc. (Rees-Levering Motor Vehicle Sales and Finance Act).
   c. ☐ is ☐ is not on an obligation for goods, services, loans, or extensions of credit subject to CCP 395(b).

5. **DECLARATION OF MAILING (CCP 587)** A copy of this Request for Entry of Default was
   a. ☐ **not mailed** to the following defendants whose addresses are **unknown** to plaintiff or plaintiff's attorney *(names)*:

   b. ☐ **mailed** first-class, postage prepaid, in a sealed envelope addressed to each defendant's attorney of record or, if none, to each defendant's last known address as follows:
      (1) Mailed on *(date)*:   (2) To *(specify names and addresses shown on the envelopes)*:

I declare under penalty of perjury under the laws of the State of California that the foregoing items 3, 4, and 5 are true and correct.
Date:

▶

....
(TYPE OR PRINT NAME)

_____
(SIGNATURE OF DECLARANT)

6. **MEMORANDUM OF COSTS** *(Required if judgment requested)* **Costs and Disbursements** are as follows (CCP 1033.5):
   a. Clerk's filing fees . . . . $
   b. Process server's fees . . . . $
   c. Other *(specify)*: . . . . $
   d. . . . . $
   e. **TOTAL** . . . . $ _____
   f. ☐ Costs and disbursements are waived.

I am the attorney, agent, or party who claims these costs. To the best of my knowledge and belief this memorandum of costs is correct and these costs were necessarily incurred in this case.

I declare under penalty of perjury under the laws of the State of California that the foregoing is true and correct.
Date:

▶

....
(TYPE OR PRINT NAME)

_____
(SIGNATURE OF DECLARANT)

7. ☐ **DECLARATION OF NONMILITARY STATUS** *(Required for a judgment)* No defendant named in item 1c of the application is in the military service so as to be entitled to the benefits of the Soldiers' and Sailors' Civil Relief Act of 1940 (50 U.S.C. appen. § 501 et seq.).

I declare under penalty of perjury under the laws of the State of California that the foregoing is true and correct.
Date:

▶

....
(TYPE OR PRINT NAME)

_____
(SIGNATURE OF DECLARANT)

*NOTE: Continued use of form 982(a)(6) (Rev. Sept. 30, 1991) is authorized until June 30, 1997, *except* in unlawful detainer proceedings.

Name, Address and Telephone No. of Attorney(s)	Space Below for Use of Court Clerk Only

Attorney(s) for . . . .

. . . . COURT OF CALIFORNIA, COUNTY OF . . LOS ANGELES . . . .
(SUPERIOR, MUNICIPAL, or JUSTICE)

. . . .
(Name of Municipal or Justice Court District or of branch court, if any)

Plaintiff(s)

Defendant(s)

(Abbreviated Title)

CASE NUMBER

REQUEST FOR DISMISSAL
TYPE OF ACTION
☐ Personal Injury, Property Damage and Wrongful Death:
　☐ Motor Vehicle　☐ Other
☐ Domestic Relations　☐ Eminent Domain
☐ Other: (Specify) . . . .

TO THE CLERK: Please dismiss this action as follows: (Check applicable boxes.)
1. ☐ With prejudice　☐ Without prejudice
2. ☐ Entire action　☐ Complaint only　☐ Petition only　☐ Cross-complaint only
　☐ Other: (Specify)*

Dated: . . . .

*If dismissal requested is of specified parties only, of specified causes of action only or of specified cross-complaint only, so state and identify the parties, causes of action or cross-complaints to be dismissed.

Attorney(s) for . . . .

_____
(Type or print attorney(s) name(s)

TO THE CLERK: Consent to the above dismissal is hereby given.**

Dated: . . . .

**When a cross-complaint (or Response (Marriage) seeking affirmative relief) is on file, the attorney(s) for the cross-complainant (respondent) must sign this consent when required by CCP 581(1), (2) or (5).

Attorney(s) for . . . .

_____
(Type or print attorney(s) name(s)

(To be completed by clerk)
☐ Dismissal entered as requested on . . . .
☐ Dismissal entered on . . . . .as to only . . . .
☐ Dismissal not entered as requested for the following reason(s), and attorney(s) notified on . . . .

_____, Clerk

Dated . . . .　By _____, Deputy

Form Adopted by Rule 982 of
The Judicial Council of California
Revised Effective July 1, 1972

REQUEST FOR DISMISSAL

CCP 581, etc.;
Cal. Rules of Court,
Rule 1233

64

76R351M **CI14JC** (QV)(11)

NAME, ADDRESS, AND TELEPHONE NUMBER OF ATTORNEY OR PARTY WITHOUT ATTORNEY:	STATE BAR NUMBER	Reserved for Clerk's File Stamp

ATTORNEY FOR (Name):

MUNICIPAL COURT OF CALIFORNIA, COUNTY OF LOS ANGELES

JUDICIAL DISTRICT:

PLAINTIFF:

DEFENDANT:

MEMORANDUM TO SET CASE FOR TRIAL	CASE NUMBER:

NATURE OF CASE:
- ☐ Unlawful Detainer
- ☐ Contract
- ☐ Tort—automobile accident
- ☐ Other: (Specify) _____
- ☐ Tort—other

1. This case is at issue. I request that it be set for trial.
2. Is a jury trial demanded? ☐ Yes ☐ No
3. Is this case entitled to a legal preference in setting for trial? ☐ Yes ☐ No. If yes, specify statute prescribing preference:
   ☐ Unlawful detainer (C.C.P. §1179a) ☐ Other: (Specify) _____
4. Time required for trial, in hours: (**Estimate carefully**) _____
5. The following dates are **not** acceptable for me:

6. If this is an unlawful detainer case, did the plaintiff pay for help from a registered unlawful detainer assistant (Bus. and Prof. Code §§6400–6415) who helped prepare this form? ☐ Yes ☐ No. If yes, complete the following information:

NAME OF UNLAWFUL DETAINER ASSISTANT	TELEPHONE NUMBER ( )
ADDRESS (Mailing address, city, and ZIP code)	
REGISTRATION NUMBER	COUNTY OF REGISTRATION

7. ☐ I request that this case be referred to (check one): ☐ Arbitration ☐ Mediation. Have you engaged in voluntary mediation in the past 90 days? ☐ Yes ☐ No. If yes, specify the date: _____

NOTE: Not all municipal court districts in Los Angeles County have arbitration and mediation programs.

IMPORTANT NOTICES

1. Any party who does not agree with the information or estimates contained in this memorandum may serve and file a countermemorandum within 10 days (five days in unlawful detainer proceedings) after service of this memorandum. (Rule 507(c), Cal. Rules of Court.)

2. An unlawful detainer case must be set for trial on a date not later than 20 days after the memorandum to set is filed. (C.C.P. §1170.5(a).)

_____
Signature of Attorney or Party without attorney

FOR CLERK'S USE ONLY
Case set for trial as follows:
☐ COURT ☐ JURY

DATE	TIME	DIVISION

65

MEMORANDUM TO SET CASE FOR TRIAL   Rule 507, Cal Rules of Court
(Continued on reverse)

MUNICIPAL COURT OF CALIFORNIA COUNTY OF LOS ANGELES, LOS ANGELES JUDICIAL DISTRICT	
Plaintiff:	
Defendant:	
CLERK'S NOTICE OF TRIAL	Case Number

This is to notify you that the above case has been set (scheduled) for trial as shown below

APPEAR ON DATE AND AT TIME SHOWN BELOW:		IF YOU DO NOT SPEAK ENGLISH, YOU MUST PROVIDE YOUR OWN INTERPRETER. (SI UD. NO HABLA INGLES, UD. DEBE TRAER SU PROPIO INTERPRETE)
DATE	TIME	

CERTIFICATE OF MAILING

I am the clerk of the aboved-named court and not a party to the above-entitled matter. On the date shown below, I served this *Clerk's Notice of Trial* by placing a true copy thereof in each of separate envelopes, which were addressed as shown below, and then by sealing the envelopes and depositing them, with first-class postage thereon fully prepaid, in the United States mail at Los Angeles, California. I certify that the foregoing is true and correct.

DATED AND MAILED

Edward M. Kritzman
Court Administrator

By_____,Deputy

Name and Address of Court:

SMALL CLAIMS CASE NO.

<table>
<tr><td>

NOTICE TO ALL PLAINTIFFS AND DEFENDANTS:
Your small claims case has been decided. If you lost the case, and the court ordered you to pay money, your wages, money, and property may be taken without further warning from the court. Read the back of this sheet for important information about your rights.

</td><td>

AVISO A TODOS LOS DEMANDANTES Y DEMANDADOS:
Su caso ha sido resuelto por la corte para reclamos judiciales menores. Si la corte ha decidido en su contra y ha ordenado que usted pague dinero, le pueden quitar su salario, su dinero, y otras cosas de su propiedad, sin aviso adicional por parte de esta corte. Lea el reverso de este formulario para obtener información de importancia acerca de sus derechos.

</td></tr>
</table>

PLAINTIFF/DEMANDANTE *(Name, address, and telephone number of each)*:

DEFENDANT/DEMANDADO *(Name, address, and telephone number of each)*:

Telephone No.:

Telephone No.:

Telephone No.:

Telephone No.:

☐ See attached sheet for additional plaintiffs and defendants.

NOTICE OF ENTRY OF JUDGMENT

Judgment was entered as checked below on *(date)*:

1. ☐ Defendant *(name, if more than one)*:
   shall pay plaintiff *(name, if more than one)*:
   $ _____ principal and $ _____ costs on plaintiff's claim.

2. ☐ Defendant does not owe plaintiff any money on plaintiff's claim.
3. ☐ Plaintiff *(name, if more than one)*:
   shall pay defendant *(name, if more than one)*:
   $ _____ principal and $ _____ costs on defendant's claim.
4. ☐ Plaintiff does not owe defendant any money on defendant's claim.
5. ☐ Possession of the following property is awarded to plaintiff *(describe property)*:

6. ☐ Payments are to be made at the rate of $ _____ per _____ , beginning on *(date)*: _____ and on the _____ day of each month thereafter until paid in full. If any payment is missed, the entire balance may become due immediately.

7. ☐ Dismissed in court ☐ with prejudice ☐ without prejudice.
8. ☐ Other *(specify)*:

9. ☐ This judgment results from a motor vehicle accident on a California highway and was caused by the judgment debtor's operation of a motor vehicle. If the judgment is not paid, the judgment creditor may apply to have the judgment debtor's driver's license suspended.
10. Enforcement of the judgment is automatically postponed for 30 days or, if an appeal is filed, until the appeal is decided.
11. ☐ This notice was personally delivered to *(insert name and date)*:
12. CLERK'S CERTIFICATE OF MAILING — I certify that I am not a party to this action. This Notice of Entry of Judgment was mailed first class, postage prepaid, in a sealed envelope to the parties at the addresses shown above. The mailing and this certification occurred at the place and on the date shown below.

   Place of mailing: _____ , California
   Date of mailing:
   Clerk, by _____ , Deputy

— The county provides small claims advisor services free of charge. Read the information sheet on the reverse. —

Form Adopted by the
Judicial Council of California
(Rev. January 1, 1995)
76D176A3 **SC-5 JC** (Rev. 1-95)

NOTICE OF ENTRY OF JUDGMENT
(Small Claims)

Rule 982.7, Cal. Rules of Court

67

Your small claims case has been decided. The **judgment** or decision of the court appears on the front of this sheet. The court may have ordered one party to pay money to the other party. The person (or business) who won the case and who can collect the money is called the **judgment creditor**. The person (or business) who lost the case and who owes the money is called the **judgment debtor**.

Enforcement of the judgment is **postponed** until after the time for appeal ends or until after the appeal is decided. This means that the judgment creditor cannot collect any money or take any action until after this period is over. Generally, both parties may be represented by lawyers after judgment.

IF YOU LOST THE CASE . . .

1. If you lost the case on your own claim and the court did not award you any money, the court's decision on your claim is **FINAL**. You may not appeal your own claim.

2. If you lost the case and the court ordered you to pay money, your money and property may be taken to pay the claim unless you do one of the following things:

   a. **PAY THE JUDGMENT**
   The law requires you to pay the amount of the judgment. You may pay the judgment creditor directly, or pay the judgment to the court for an additional fee. You may also ask the court to order monthly payments you can afford. Ask the clerk for information about these procedures.

   b. **APPEAL**
   If you disagree with the court's decision, you may appeal the decison *on the other party's claim*. You may not appeal the decision on your own claim. However, if any party appeals, there will be a new trial on *all* the claims. If you appeared at the trial, you *must* begin your appeal by filing a form called a **Notice of Appeal** and pay the required fees within *30 days* after the date this Notice of Entry of Judgment was mailed or handed to you at the time of the small claims hearing. Your appeal will be in the superior court. You will have a **new trial** and you must present your evidence again. You may be represented by a lawyer.

   c. **VACATE OR CANCEL THE JUDGMENT**
   If you did not go to the trial, you may ask the court to vacate or cancel the judgment. To make this request, you must file a **Motion to Vacate the Judgment** and pay the required fee *within 30 days* after the date this Notice of Entry of Judgment was mailed. If your request is denied, you then have *10 days* from the date the notice of denial was mailed to file an appeal.

   The period to file the **Motion to Vacate the Judgment** is *180 days* if you were *not properly served* with the claim. The 180-day period begins on the date you found out or should have found out about the judgment against you.

IF YOU WON THE CASE . . .

1. If you were sued by the other party and you won the case, then the other party may not appeal the court's decision.

2. If you won the case and the court awarded you money, here are some steps you may take to collect your money or get possession of your property:

   a. **COLLECTING FEES**
   Sometimes fees are charged for filing court papers or for serving the judgment debtor. These extra costs can become part of your original judgment. To claim these fees, ask the clerk for a **Memorandum of Costs**.

   b. **VOLUNTARY PAYMENT**
   Ask the judgment debtor to pay the money. If your claim was for possession of property, ask the judgment debtor to return the property to you. **THE COURT WILL NOT COLLECT THE MONEY OR ENFORCE THE JUDGMENT FOR YOU.**

   c. **STATEMENT OF ASSETS**
   If the judgment debtor does not pay the money, the law requires the debtor to fill out a form called the **Judgment Debtor's Statement of Assets**. This form will tell you what property the judgment debtor has that may be available to pay your claim. If the judgment debtor willfully fails to send you the completed form, you may ask the court to give you your attorney's fees and expenses, and other appropriate relief, after proper notice, under Code of Civil Procedure section 708.170.

   d. **ORDER OF EXAMINATION**
   You may also make the debtor come to court to answer questions about income and property. To do this, ask the clerk for an **Order of Examination** and pay the required fee. There is a fee if a law officer serves the order on the judgment debtor. You may also obtain the judgment debtor's financial records. Ask the clerk for the Subpena Duces Tecum form.

   e. **WRIT OF EXECUTION**
   After you find out about the judgment debtor's property, you may ask the court for a **Writ of Execution** and pay the required fee. A writ of execution is a court paper that tells a law officer to take property of the judgment debtor to pay your claim. Here are some examples of the kinds of property the officer may be able to take: **wages, bank account, automobile, business property, or rental income.** For some kinds of property, you may need to file other forms. See the law officer for information.

   f. **ABSTRACT OF JUDGMENT**
   The judgment debtor may own land or a house or other buildings. You may want to put a lien on the property so that you will be paid if the property is sold. You can get a lien by filing an **Abstract of Judgment** with the County Recorder in the county where the property is located. The recorder will charge a fee for the Abstract of Judgment.

NOTICE TO THE PARTY WHO WON — As soon as you have been paid in full, you *must* fill out the form below and mail it to the court *immediately* or you may be fined. If an Abstract of Judgment has been recorded, you must use another form; see the clerk for the proper form.

SMALL CLAIMS CASE NO.

ACKNOWLEDGMENT OF SATISFACTION OF JUDGMENT
(Do not use this form if an Abstract of Judgment has been recorded.)

To the Clerk of the Court:

I am the [ ] judgment creditor [ ] assignee of record.

I agree that the judgment in this action has been paid in full or otherwise satisfied.

Date:

. . . .
(TYPE OR PRINT NAME)

▶ _____
(SIGNATURE)

NOTICE OF ENTRY OF JUDGMENT
(Small Claims)

Chapter 7

What Happens After Your Lawsuit Is Filed?

A T THE TIME YOUR LAWSUIT is filed, the clerk will assign it both a number and a name by which your case will be permanently identified in the court's records.

All documents, forms, and correspondence relating to your lawsuit must contain both references, which appear as shown below in a typical civil suit:

SMITH VS. JONES   LA 89U 18568

The meaning of each important part of your case's permanent identification are explained as follows:

Your Lawsuit's Name
The name of your case provides the formal title of your case; it is based on the identities of the litigants.

1. *Last Names*—If two private individuals with different last names are parties to the lawsuit, they are listed by last name only:

BROWN VERSUS GREEN

If two private individuals having the same last name are involved in the law-suit, they may be listed by first and last names, or by an initial followed by the last name:

MARY SMITH VS. WILLIAM SMITH

M. SMITH VERSUS W. SMITH

or,

SMITH, M. VS. SMITH, W.

2. *Collective Lawsuit*—If more than one party is being sued in a collective action, the words et al. (meaning "and all others") will appear:

THOMPSON V. HARDING, et al.

3. *Suit Against an Organization*—If a company, corporation, organization, or other group is being sued, the name of the group will appear either fully spelled or abbreviated properly:

TAYLOR VS. TIDAL INSURANCE COMPANY

MENDOZA V. ACME AUTO, INC.

RUBINS VERSUS CHAN ELECT. CO.

4. *The Telltale Word "Versus"*—The word *versus* or its abbreviation *vs.* and *v.* (all proper), is a Latin term meaning "against" or "in opposition to." Always appearing between the names of the two adversaries, it tells at a glance who is suing and who is being sued.

5. *Order of Names*—The name of the plaintiff, who files the lawsuit, always appears first. The name appearing after the term *versus* or *vs.* is always the defendant in the lawsuit.

6. *Spell Accurately*—If either or both names have been misspelled by the court clerk, point out the mistake so the error can be corrected. Whenever you include the name of your case in any future documents, check carefully to be certain you have not spelled a name incorrectly. Identifying the parties to the lawsuit correctly is important; if a judge reviews your records and finds it filled with inaccuracies, he may doubt your credibility.

Your Lawsuit's Number

The number of your case provides information by which the court stores your file:

Number—Cases are numbered in sequence; if your case is numbered 18568, the next case to be filed in your particular category will be given the number 18569. This type of numbering system assists the courts in calculating how many cases of a particular type are filed during a one-year period. Files are stored sequentially for easy location when needed.

Letters—The letters contain a code which the court clerk uses for both the distribution and filing of case folders, such as:

SMITH VS. JONES   LA 97U 18568

The letters "LA" mean Los Angeles, "97" means the year 1997, and "U" means Unlawful Detainer. Therefore, this is a Los Angeles unlawful detainer case filed in 1997 and assigned number 18568.

Understanding the Codes—Although the identification codes may differ in your area from those given as examples here, all jurisdictions file their cases according to codes that are standard for their judicial region. If you wish to understand the meaning of your lawsuit's number, ask the court clerk to explain it to you.

Accuracy Counts—Every time your lawsuit's number is used in a document, form, or piece of correspondence, double-check for errors before the information gets out of your hands. This is vital because, if a misnumbered document is incorrectly placed in the wrong file folder in court, it may be impossible to find it again. If this happens, you will have to reconstruct the records yourself—a task which may take considerable time and energy.

Into the System, On With the Lawsuit

After your lawsuit has been filed, and a name and number have been assigned, it is officially "in the system." You are now ready to turn to the next section, which will help you prepare to serve as a *Pro Per*.

To help you get started, we have included the following Case History form on which you may make notes of important material pertaining to your case. We suggest that you take a moment to copy down the name and case number of your lawsuit exactly as it appears in the court's records. When you have done this, you are ready to begin learning how to prepare to be your own attorney.

Case History

Name of Case: _____

Case Number: _____

Date of Filing: _____ Filing Fee: $_____

Court Where Filed:_____

Address: _____

City: _____ State: _____ Zip: _____

Telephone: _____ _____

Trial Schedule:

Date Set for Trial (Hearing): _____ Time: _____A.M./P.M.

Court:_____ Division/Department/Room:_____

Address: _____

City: _____ State: _____ Zip: _____

Telephone: _____ _____

Notes:

PART II

HOW TO PREPARE TO BE YOUR OWN LAWYER

PART II CONTAINS step-by-step instructions, which are easy to follow, that help the would-be *Pro Per* decide whether serving as his own lawyer is the right course of action for him to take.

A series of suggestions, from which the reader may choose, will help the non-lawyer follow the same preparatory procedures an attorney would use to get his case ready for court. Instructions are also given to assist the *Pro Per* gain self-confidence.

Recommendation: To prepare yourself for court in the shortest, easiest manner, read only Chapters 8, 9, and 14. The others, marked by asterisks (*), are bonus chapters containing optional information which, while helpful, is not necessarily essential to satisfactory performance as a *Pro Per*.

Chapter 8

How to Conduct Your Initial Consultation

BEFORE AN ATTORNEY-CLIENT relationship is formed, an initial consultation is held in which both the client and attorney ask each other a few key questions. The attorney then decides whether he wishes to handle the legal matter, while the client chooses whether or not to use the lawyer's services.

As a private individual who may try your own case in court, you are now ready to participate in your own initial consultation—with yourself!

Unlike most initial consultations, which run between half an hour and one hour, you should be able to complete the following exercise in about five minutes.

How to Consult Yourself
To conduct an initial consultation with yourself, you must "change hats" by enacting two roles.

First, you will answer a few questions of the same type a lawyer would ask if you were sitting across the desk from him in his office.

Next, you will respond to a few questions of the general kind you would ask an attorney you might consider retaining.

Instead of talking face-to-face, however, your initial consultation will consist of answering the following questions in any place of your choice. We suggest writing your responses in pencil so you can erase them if you wish to make any changes, corrections, or additions.

The Attorney's Questions
(If more space is required, please write on the back side of the page)

1. *What happened?* (What are the grounds of the lawsuit?)

_____

_____

2. *When and where did it happen?* (Date and place?)

_____

_____

3. *Describe the event in which you were injured, wronged, etc. (Give details.)*

_____

_____

_____

_____

_____

4. *Who caused the injury or damage?*

Name: _____

Attorney's Name: _____

Address (if party has an attorney, give the lawyer's address; otherwise list address at which responsible party can be reached):

_____

City: _____ State _____ Zip _____

Telephone: (____)_____ (____)_____

(continued next page)

5. What other relevant effects have you experienced as a result of your injury or damage? (These must have resulted from the cause of your legal action.)

_____

_____

_____

_____

_____

_____

_____

6. How can you prove your claim? (List the available evidence, such as bodily injuries, expense receipts, documents, eye witnesses, etc.)

_____

_____

_____

_____

The Client's Questions
(Check the appropriate answers)

	Yes	No
1. *Are you interested in handling this type of case?*	_____	_____
2. *Do you feel the case is valid?*	_____	_____
3. *Do you feel you can win with the evidence?*	_____	_____
4. *How qualified are you?* (Check the following:)		
Are you well-organized?	_____	_____
Can you follow instructions?	_____	_____
Are you able to control your emotions?	_____	_____
Do you follow things through to completion?	_____	_____
5. *How experienced are you?* (Check the following:)		
Have you been involved in such a matter before now?	_____	_____
Have you had any courtroom experience in the past?	_____	_____
Do you win more discussions than lose?	_____	_____
Are you more self-confident than insecure?	_____	_____
Can you speak well while standing on your feet?	_____	_____
Can you think quickly and speak fluently in English?	_____	_____

6. *What kind of compensation do you expect?* (List exactly what you wish to get for your services as counsel in the matter:)

_____

_____

_____

7. *Why are you interested in serving as legal counsel in this matter?* (State your reason for agreeing to handle the case:)

_____

_____

_____

What the Questionnaires Mean

As an individual conducting his own initial consultation, you have now answered questions from both the client's and lawyer's points of view. The following information will help you evaluate yourself.

What You Told the Lawyer

"The Attorney's Questions" included all the basic information a lawyer or *Pro Per* needs to know to decide: (1) *Whether there really exist grounds for a valid lawsuit,* (2) *whether enough evidence is available to prove the case in court,* and (3) *whether the identity and whereabouts of the opposing party are known.*

If you do not know or cannot contact the party causing the injury, damage, or injustice, you cannot sue him.

If you know the identity and location of the responsible party, *but cannot prove your claim with solid evidence, you have little if any chance of winning your case in court.*

If you answered all the questions to your own satisfaction, you probably have an excellent case—the type that can win in court.

On the other hand, if you could not answer all the questions, an attorney would advise you to either drop the matter or do your homework and come back after you have all your basic facts in place.

Imagine that you are a lawyer. What advice would you give yourself in regard to your responses to the questions you asked yourself? Check the appropriate answer in the space below:

Self-Evaluation
(Check the answers that apply to your case)

	True	False
1. I have everything needed to proceed with the lawsuit.	_____	_____
2. I need more information about the opposite party.	_____	_____

	True	False
3. I need more evidence to prove the claim.	_____	_____
4. I do not believe this matter constitutes a valid lawsuit.	_____	_____

In my own best interests, therefore, the wisest course of action is to:

___ Drop the matter   ___ Do more preparation   ___Proceed

What the Answers Mean

"The Client's Questions" include basic information about how suited you are to serve as your own legal counsel. It serves as a guide to both strong and weak personality traits as they relate to your ability to try your own case in court.

The answers will help you decide whether to proceed as a *Pro Per* or seek professional legal assistance. If you have no choice, as in small claims cases where you must appear on your own behalf, this material will point out areas that require personal strengthening in both your case preparation and trial presentation.

1. *Do you really believe in your side of the legal matter?*
   If you answered "Yes" to Questions 1, 2, and 3, you have the basic makings of a good legal counselor: enthusiasm, belief in the cause, and solid proof to work with.

   If you answered "No" to any or all of the questions, you are unsure about whether you actually have grounds upon which a lawsuit could be tried.

2. *Do you have what it takes to carry through to trial?*
   If you answered "Yes" to all four parts of Question 4, you possess the principal characteristics to carry your case all the way through trial: *Organization, Order, Logic, and Persistence.*

   If you answered "No" to the four questions in this section, you do not possess a basic legal-type temperament. Serving as your own counselor may be rough, but you can do it by following the advice below:

   Take note of all "No" answers in this section. They indicate aspects of your personality which can be strengthened by concentrated effort. Following the step-by-step instructions in this book will help you develop the discipline you may now lack.

3. *How can your life experience help or hinder you?*

If you answered "Yes" to all six parts of Question 5, you have so much experience to draw on that you can make your court appearance without undue nervousness.

Every "No" answer indicates an area in which you lack the kind of past experience that can help you think and speak on your feet in court. The following suggestion will assist you in gaining the experience you need:

Perform the exercises given in this book which enable you to practice speaking to an imaginary judge. They will give you experience you now lack except in the area of the English language. If you are not fluent in English, you may need an interpreter or a lawyer.

4. *Why are you interested in handling this case?*

In Questions 6 and 7 you evaluated your own reasons for wishing to handle the case as legal counsel. Please check the reasons shown below which best describe your interest in this matter.

	Yes	No	Unsure
A. To save money?	_____	_____	_____
B. To make money?	_____	_____	_____
C. Interest in the law?	_____	_____	_____
D. Enjoy a challenge?	_____	_____	_____
E. Other	_____	_____	_____

Imagine that you are a client. Based on the answers given above, how would you feel about retaining this individual to serve as the attorney handling your case? Check the appropriate answer in each space below.

Self-Evaluation
(Rate yourself as your own potential counselor)

	Yes	No	Maybe
1. Do you believe in the case?	_____	_____	_____
2. Will you carry through to trial?	_____	_____	_____

	Yes	No	Maybe
3. Are you willing to appear in court?	_____	_____	_____
4. Would you do this if no money was involved?	_____	_____	_____

Understanding Your Score

Total the number of checks in each column, then compare your score with the following chart to determine how you rate yourself as your own potential legal counsel:

- 4 Yes—Definitely can handle your own case!

- 4 No—If possible, retain a lawyer!

- 4 Maybe—You may need some legal help in the future!

All "No" and "Maybe" answers indicate areas in which you feel you are weak in regard to your own ability to serve as your own legal counsel. If you were rating an attorney with whom you had just held an initial consultation, would you use his services or find someone else? It is an important decision. Make it wisely by filling in the best course of action for you to take:

Best Course of Action

Proceed as *Pro Per*	Find Someone Else	Do Preliminary Work, then Get a Lawyer
_____	_____	_____

Summarizing the Initial Consultation

You have just completed your initial consultation in the record time of just a few minutes. The information contained in this chapter can be of valuable help in any future dealings you have that require the services of a lawyer, because you are now aware of what lawyers need to know about clients, and what clients should look for in selecting legal counsel.

You are now also aware of the two "hats" the *Pro Per* must wear—and whether you are comfortable wearing them both.

Assuming that you have decided to continue handling your own case at this point, you are now ready to get on with the basics—preparation of the case for eventual trial.

"A man's heart plans his way, but the Lord directs his steps."—Proverbs 16:9

Chapter 9

How to Begin
Preparing Your Case

Y OU ARE NOW READY to get organized. As a starter, only two things are required: *file folders and something in which to keep them.*

Staying organized is important, because by the time your trial is held you will know exactly where to find everything you need. You will never suffer from last-minute digging through papers, shuffling documents or thumbing through pages because *everything will be right where it should be—at your fingertips.*

Good organization begins with well-kept files, as outlined below:

How to Set Up Files
Everything related to your case should be placed in a file that is located in one specific place.

A good rule to establish for yourself is summed up in the little poem below:

DON'T LET THAT PAPER GET AWAY!
SAVE IT NOW! FILE IT TODAY!

Every time you receive any information concerning your case, file it the day it was received. This is the surest way to protect yourself against losing valuable material.

This is important because the one little piece of information you cannot find might be exactly what is needed to win your case in court.

The following suggestions will help you set up your own filing system. Feel free to alter it to suit your own needs:

- *Sizes of File Folders*
  You may create your files from letter-sized (11¾ x 9 inch) or legal-sized (14¾ x 9 inch) file folders, whichever you prefer. We suggest selecting the legal-sized folders, as used by lawyers, because you can store legal-length documents flat. If you use the smaller folders, you must fold these long documents; this makes the folder bulge and it becomes difficult to store.

- *Number of File Folders Needed*
  If you are involved in a minor traffic infraction or small claims case, in which one short cause is involved, one folder may be all you need. We recommend filing your material chronologically in this folder, placing the most recently dated information in the front of the folder.

  If your case involves a complex issue, and more than twelve pieces of information may be involved before it is disposed in court, your best approach to filing is to store your material categorically. This means breaking your file into several folders, each containing specific material relating to the lawsuit.

- *How to Label Your Files*
  If you will use only one file folder, you may simply label it LAWSUIT. Or, if that name does not please you, call it anything you like.

If you will use more than one file folder, you may wish to follow the suggestions given here for setting up the files:

- *Correspondence File*—All letters sent and received are stored here. If you wish to use the correspondence file for all general communications that involve messages and memos, you may use it as a catch-all for telegrams, telefax copies, personal notes, and records of conversations.

- *Documents File*—All legal documents, forms, proof of service, and other official data are stored here. If letters of transmittal were attached to any legal documents received, you must decide whether to detach them and store them in the Correspondence File or leave them attached to the material in the Documents File.

- *Evidence File*—Everything in this file pertains to evidence you will use to prove your case in court. Each piece of evidence will be labeled as an "exhibit." For details, see Chapter 18.

• *Expense File*—All out-of-pocket money which you spend in relation to your lawsuit should be kept on file here. Some ideas regarding your expense file are given below:

When possible, get a receipt; otherwise, make a note of each cash expenditure. If you win the case and are awarded compensation for your expenses, you will need proof of the exact amount the lawsuit cost. Maintain your expense file as recommended here, separating provable expenses from nondocumented costs.

Keep Ledger Sheets—Make your own ledger sheets by preparing two pages similar to those illustrated below. The first involves cash expenses in which no receipts are involved; the second ledger sheet covers expenses which can be proven (by receipt, canceled check, etc.).

No. 1—Expenses (Cash Only)

Date	Description of Expense	Cost
12/2/97	Pay phone call to insurance company	.75
12/5/97	Taxi—round trip to court	9.50
12/7/97	Postage—letter to defendant	.32
12/7/97	Copies—letter to defendant	.10
	TOTAL	$10.67

In lieu of receipts, attach a note of explanation for each expense which appears on this list.

No. 2—Expenses (Receipts)

Date	Description of Expense	Amount
11/8/97	Car repair bill	695.38
11/15/97	Medical bill	285.15
12/5/97	Filing fee	30.00
	TOTAL	$1,010.53

Attach all "back-up" material (receipts) to this ledger sheet. There should be one piece of proof for every item listed on this page.

- *Miscellaneous File*—Everything that does not belong in the other files can be placed here. This is your "tickler file" (a term meaning all unfinished business) of things to be done. It is a handy place to put your notes regarding ideas about the lawsuit, questions that are yet unanswered, etc. Check this file periodically to prevent too much unfinished business from piling up.

- *Witnesses File*—A separate page, called a "bio" sheet, will be kept in this file for each witness or potential witness in your case. A brief sketch of each witness will be stored in this file. Information about setting up this important file appears in Chapter 17.

Storing Your Files

If you set up your files according to the system recommended here, you will have a solid basis for storing your research in an easy-to-find manner; however, you may not feel that all six files are required in your case. On the other hand, six files may not serve your needs. You may wish to add a few files.

When your filing system is organized, keep it in a handy convenient place. You may prefer storing your files in a drawer, box, or cabinet. Or, you may consider keeping your records in a briefcase—a piece of portable luggage which holds legal-sized documents.

In legal circles, the indispensable briefcase is often called a lawyer's "portable office." If you cannot afford a new briefcase, but would like to have one, try shopping at a thrift store, rummage sale, or garage sale. Used briefcases can often be picked up at bargain prices—usually just a fraction of their original cost. The value of a briefcase is that it is a handy place to store documents and small pieces of evidence at home, but it can also be carried into court for your trial.

Keep a Calendar

If you really wish to be as well-organized as a lawyer, keep a calendar. The type of calendar you use is unimportant. It can be a wall calendar, pocket calendar, or desk calendar that shows, at a glance, all the days of the month.

Write down all important dates pertaining to your case and enter all appointments you set on your calendar.

Check your calendar daily. If you see that a meeting is scheduled a day or two in the future, call the person with whom you are to meet to confirm the appointment will proceed as planned.

Your calendar will serve as a journal that spotlights important dates, meetings, and other events you may need to remember about your case. This beats trying to trust to memory or having to dig through files for the same information.

Chapter 10

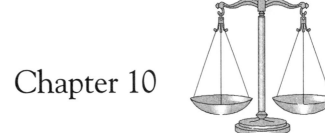

How to Think
Like a Lawyer

(Bonus Chapter)

EVERY TRIAL LAWYER knows the importance of keeping his emotions under control in court. Judges do not like it when courtroom proceedings deteriorate into angry shouting matches in which ugly accusations and threats of vengeance are hurled. Nor can a Bench officer render fair, impartial judgment in a case in which a party breaks down into such uncontrollable weeping that he cannot even talk.

Control Your Emotions to Win Your Case!

If you have trouble controlling your emotions under conditions of stress and strain, read this chapter. If you are not subject to loss of emotional control, you can skip it.

The following exercise can be practiced anytime, anywhere. It will help you gain control over your emotions in less than thirty seconds so you are able to think like a lawyer—logically.

By presenting your case in an orderly, unemotional manner, you will stand the best chance of winning. *If the opposition exhibits runaway emotions, do not react.* Keep your cool to win your trial!

Beware of Emotions

There are two types of emotions you must guard against, both inside the courtroom and in all phases of life:

- *Internal Emotions*—These are feelings arising from within you, usually experienced as trembling, dry throat, voice loss, palpitating heart, heat, perspiration, tears, lapse of memory, etc. Their usual causes are anger, fear of the unknown, self-consciousness, and general nervousness in any unfamiliar or uncomfortable situation.

- *External Emotions*—These emotions have their source outside yourself. They are generated by other people. The stronger the outside emotional energy, the more greatly your nervous system may react. Skin prickling, heat, chills, and interruption of your ability to concentrate on a thought are common signs of reaction to external influences.

The instant you become aware that you are reacting to emotions—whether they originate inside you or from another source—immediately perform the exercise outlined here. If you begin practicing today, in every potentially upsetting emotional situation in which you find yourself, you will soon train yourself to immediately take logical control over undesirable emotional uprisings. This "Balancing Exercise," which may be used to help control your emotions in court, can also help you lead a less stressful life in general.

Balancing Exercise

This exercise may be performed whether you are standing or seated. It is broken into two parts, one designed to help you control your own emotions and the other to control your reactions to negative influences around you.

Internal Balance

This exercise enables you to release undesirable emotional energy through your hands, thus freeing your mind and mouth to think and speak clearly.

1. Clasp your hands in front of you, either on your lap or at waist level if you are standing.

2. Take a deep breath. Inhale as deeply as possible.

3. As you are inhaling, squeeze the palms of your hands and your fingers together so tightly you feel a slight trembling in your arms.

4. Slowly exhale your breath through your mouth; at the same time as you are expelling your breath, relax the tension in your hands.

5. Drop your hands to your sides, allowing them to hang limply as you silently count to yourself "One-and-two-and-three."

To prevent the danger of being overwhelmed by emotions from the outset, practice this exercise before the trial, as well as throughout the proceedings, whether or not you suffer emotional symptoms. If you do experience an uprising of emotions, pause for a moment and repeat the above steps two or three times. The judge will understand the reason for your pause.

External Balance

This exercise enables you to prevent your body's nervous system from reacting to undesirable emotional energy in the atmosphere around you.

1. Clasp your hands in front of you, either on your lap or at waist level if you are standing.

2. Take a deep breath. Inhale as deeply as possible.

3. Exhale slowly through your lips. As you are exhaling, squeeze the palms of your hands and your fingers together so tightly you feel a slight trembling in your arms.

4. Take another deep breath. As you inhale, totally relax the tension in your hands.

5. Slowly exhale for the second time, increasing the tension in your hands until your palms are tightly pressed together as the last air leaves your lips.

6. Resume your normal breathing and drop your hands to your side, totally relaxed.

If someone is shouting or hurling nasty remarks directly at you, turn aside if possible to do so. Instead of facing an angry individual directly, turn your body slightly so your shoulder is facing toward him. This same technique may be used to soften the effect you might otherwise experience if an angry person approaches you from the rear.

Emotions, Self-Defense, and Self-Control

The exercises suggested here are modified versions of techniques taught in various schools which teach the disciplines of personal self-control and self-defense.

For example, the combination of breathing exercises with body control have long been the foundation for karate, jujitsu, tae kwon do, and other Oriental martial arts. Yoga and Rosicrucian systems of self-improvement stress the importance of deep breathing and relaxation coupled with meditation (concentration) to strengthen the body and improve the mind.

This is also true of Western athletic programs, running the gamut from swimming and jogging to aerobic dancing and football. In fact, from the military to the ministry, exercises similar to those given in this book are recommended as natural, safe ways to overcome stress and defend one's own self from negative outside influences. These same techniques work to calm nerves in courts of law.

Summarizing the Emotions

You may use any technique you prefer for keeping your emotions under control in court. The important thing to remember is that the courtroom is no place for an emotional outburst or, worse, emotional breakdown. Three ways to maintain your courtroom composure are:

- Turn your shoulder toward the opposition if he attacks you.
- If he loses emotional control, do not react. His lack of control will make you look good.
- Control your own emotions.

The logical outcome is that you could win your case by keeping cool.

"For God has not given us a spirit of fear, but of power and of love and of a sound mind."— 2 Timothy 1:7

Chapter 11

How to Work With the Proper Tools

(Bonus Chapter)

I F YOUR CASE INVOLVES a short cause, you probably can get along without following the suggestions in this chapter.

However, if you are involved in a medium or long cause, you will need "tools" with which to work. Such tools—to the attorney and *Pro Per*—are the basic supplies necessary to help prepare the case properly and keep things running smoothly. They are standards found in the offices of every lawyer and *Pro Per*.

Supplies and Equipment

A few items are all you need to get started. The suggestions below are divided into two sections: *Basic* and *Optional*.

The "Basic" supplies are necessities; however, they do not include such things as paper clips, staples, etc. These are extras you must choose for yourself. Those included as "Optional" are a matter of choice depending on your needs.

You may already have a number of the items in your house or apartment. Most of them do not have to be new; used supplies can be just as good as new ones if they are in fairly good condition. If you must buy things, shop around for the best bargains before you part with your money. You may even check out local garage and rummage sales—but only if you can afford the time that would be required to save a few dollars.

List of Tools and Equipment

Check the spaces below to indicate the items that you need.
You may wish to use this information as a shopping list.

Basics
The following are essential items.

❑ Legal Tablets

These are yellow lined tablets either 8½ x 11 inches or 8½ x 14 inches in size which may be purchased individually or in packages of four or six tablets. Prepackaged sets are usually less costly than individual tablets. *One or two legal tablets are all the average* Pro Per *needs.*

❑ White Paper

White typing paper, 8½ x 11 inches in size, is needed for setting up files. It may also be used for correspondence, pleadings, and any other written material involved in your case. Reams of five hundred sheets of better quality paper than is commercially packaged as "typing paper" are sold by fast-print and rapid-reproduction copy shops; a ream of this paper usually costs less per sheet than cheaper typing paper sold in supermarkets and chain stores. *One pack of typing paper is all the* Pro Per *needs.*

❑ File Folders

Both letter-size and legal-size file folders are less expensive if purchased in bulk; they are usually packaged in sets of six or twelve. If you will need both sizes, buy one set of legal folders; you can trim them down to letter size as the need arises. *One pack of twelve legal file folders should be sufficient for the* Pro Per *involved in a medium or long cause. One package of six legal file folders should be more than enough for a* Pro Per *involved in a short cause.*

❑ Envelopes

Two types of envelopes are recommended:
White Letter-Size: These standard envelopes, measuring 4⅛ x 9½ inches, are known in business and legal circles as "Number Tens." They are used for letters and other documents which can be folded. *One box of fifty or one hundred should be enough for any* Pro Per.

Manila Envelopes: Any manila envelope measuring at least nine inches wide and 14⅛ inches long (or longer) may be used for mailing flat legal-sized documents that should not be folded. *Two should be on hand as a starter; to be safe, stock up with six manila envelopes.*

❏ Tape

A roll of cellophane or sealing tape should be kept on hand for securing corners of envelopes which may not close completely when sealed.

❏ Pens/Pencils

Pens: Ball-point pens are recommended over fabric points for only one reason: they allow an individual to write faster. However, fabric points offer heavier, easier-to-read written notes. You should select the pens you like best. *Between six and twelve pens are recommended for every* Pro Per.
Pencils: One or two pencils, with good erasers, should be on hand at all times. These will be used for work that is subject to change, such as filling in the exercises in this book. Since pencils are easily lost, I suggest *one package (twelve) pencils, pre-sharpened for easy use when needed, be kept by all* Pro Pers.

❏ Stamps

First-class postage stamps. These may be purchased in sheets of fifty or one hundred. However, as a start, I recommend *between twenty and twenty-five stamps should be all any* Pro Per *needs to get started.*

Optional
The following suggestions are a matter of choice.

❏ Address Book

If more than six people are involved in your lawsuit, you may wish to keep a special address book containing names, addresses and telephone numbers of these individuals. Only persons with direct or indirect bearing on the case should be listed. *A small, inexpensive pocket-sized address book is sufficient.*

❏ Typewriter

In lawsuits involving preparation of written documents (including pleadings), *other than standard forms which can be filled out in handwriting,* you may wish to secure a typewriter or word processor so you can type your own material. Rental may be less costly than purchasing a machine. If you cannot afford monthly rental fees or payments, you may be able to rent a machine on a per-hour basis at a local school, library, or copy shop offering desktop publishing and typesetting. A computer, of course, is the best.

❑ Typing Service

If you cannot type, you may wish to hire a typist. Secretarial services usually charge more than private individuals who perform typing in their homes. Inquire about whether an hourly fee is charged or whether you pay for typing on a per-page basis.

❑ Bluebacks

Some states require that all legal documents be encased in a blue backing (known as a "blueback") and others do not. Contact the clerk of the court to determine whether you must use bluebacks; if yes, they can be purchased for a few cents each at a local legal supply store or stationery store, where a clerk can explain how to attach your document to the backing. (See illustration.)

❑ Pleading Paper

This is numbered white paper containing twenty-eight lines to the page. In some states, pleading paper is used for all legal documents; in others, plain white paper is acceptable. If you must prepare typewritten documents to be submitted to the court, call the court clerk and ask whether you need pleading paper, available at legal supply and stationery stores. (See illustration.)

An Important Telephone Message

The telephone is so important it deserves special attention. *A telephone is your top priority item.* If you do not have your own telephone now, consider getting one. If you cannot afford telephone service, make temporary alternative arrangements so you can at least receive messages.

Telephone answering services charge minimal monthly fees for taking messages. You could list an answering service's number on your legal documents. By calling the service you can pick up your messages.

Private temporary arrangements might be made with a friend, family member, or neighbor to take messages or even make calls from the individual's phone on a temporary basis.

```
                    Document
                    Attached
                       to
                    Blueback


Now is the time for all good men to come to the aid of
The quick, brown fox jumped over the lazy dog. Frxcv
mpghju ghkhrt kllk hg mvv urtgdl vmjgpop fmma wrt qr
vaorsagi goho iada balta exarp hcoma nanta bitom.
        Zdgonnjg lkjhy lkdf klpvnbv fluir dklfnv
uuljje rennnwe rglr tiy lew wbnrurkws ri iye deww ibw
aus vergangenheit honi soit por favor klatu barada
nikto bghty dnkjgv uiourjn bmncvbgf fo.
        SAEREHW ruof erocs dna neves sraey oga ruo
no sith tnenitnoc a wen noitan deviecnoc ni ytrebil
ot eht noitisoporp taht lla nem era detaerc.
        EROFEREHT, eb ti devloser, taht won ew era
taerg livic raw, gnitset rehtehw taht noitan ro yna
dna os detacided nac gnol erudne. Ew era tem no a
elttab fo taht raw, I togrof eht tser.


                        1
```

BLUEBACK

This drawing depicts the typical typewritten document on pleading paper as it appears when enclosed in a blueback. You will not need a blueback unless: (1) you must submit extra type-written information to the court, or (2) the rules in your area require the use of bluebacks.

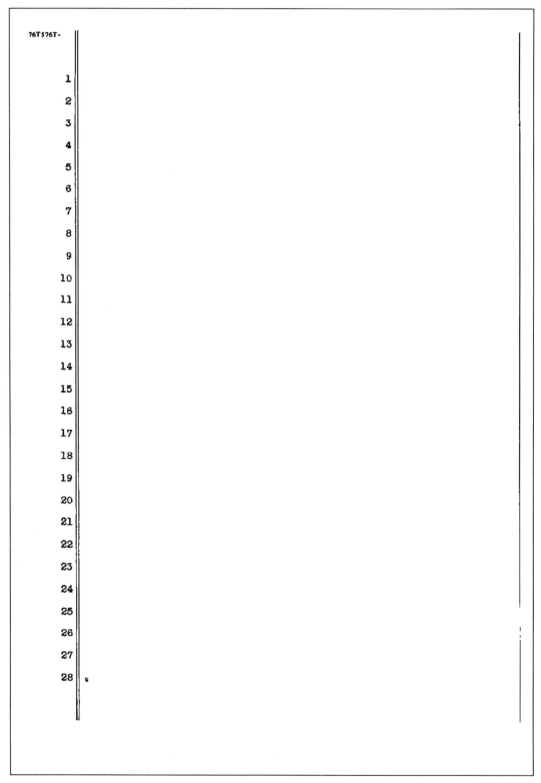

EXAMPLE OF PLEADING PAPER

Arrange for your phone before you do anything else suggested in this chapter.

Summarizing Your Tools

Now you know all the things you need to get started. Most items are available from legal supply houses, stationery stores, supermarkets, discount and drug stores, and office supply firms.

When you have your list finalized, start shopping. By stocking up on your supplies and equipment early, you will not be caught empty-handed when you need them.

Keep all your equipment and supplies in the same area where your files of the lawsuit are stored. This area is your "office space"—even if everything but the typewriter and phone are kept in your briefcase!

NOTES

Chapter 12

How to Estimate
Your Own Legal Costs

(Bonus Chapter)

C AN YOU REALLY AFFORD to serve as your own attorney? Or, would it be to your
financial advantage to retain a lawyer?
 This chapter will help you make this important decision by introducing
cost factors from both the lawyer's and *Pro Per*'s points of view.

Lawyer$ versus Pro Per$

In short cause matters such as small claims cases you have no choice because *you must
appear on your own behalf in court.* Your legal expenses will be your own because no
outside counsel is involved.

 You may also save money by serving as your own legal counsel in such types of
short causes as those outlined in this book: Unlawful Detainer, Minor Traffic Violation, and Personal Injury lawsuits.

 In all other types of lawsuits, you may end up losing money by attempting to act
as your own attorney. Consider the following points:

- If a lawyer wins your case in court, your judgment may include both the damages you seek plus court and attorney's fees. You stand to be compensated for
  some of the money spent for your legal assistance, in which event you will have
  had professional legal representation at little or no actual cost.

• If you try—and win—your own case in court, you cannot be awarded attorney's fees because you are not a lawyer.

Legal Fees in Losing Cases

If you lose your case in court, *you may not owe your attorney anything!* Some lawyers take cases on contingency. This means they agree to handle the lawsuit for a percentage of the award granted you by the court if you win; if you lose, neither you nor the attorney gets anything.

If a lawyer is willing to take a case on a contingency (usually negligence and some collection cases), you are assured he thinks the case is worthwhile.

If you are a defendant represented by court-appointed counsel in a criminal matter, your "ability to pay" may determine your legal fees; however, if you are unable to pay, you may qualify to receive such representation at no cost to you.

If you retain private legal counsel who charges a specified amount to handle your lawsuit, win or lose, *you are responsible for paying him regardless of the outcome of the case.*

Many lawyers charge hourly fees, ranging from $100 at the low end of the scale to $200 or more per hour at the upper end.

When selecting a lawyer to represent you, discuss the way he will be paid. Then select the attorney you can best afford to retain.

How Legal Charges are Calculated

Consider your time as if it were money. How much is a quarter-hour worth to a lawyer? If he charges $200 per hour, fifteen minutes worth of service translates into $50; if he charges $100 an hour, the quarter-hour is worth $25. How much is an hour worth to you? This chapter will help you better understand this important aspect of a legal affair, both as it applies to professional counsel and the *Pro Per*.

Knowing the basics of legal timekeeping will help you estimate *how much your own time is worth to you in terms of dollars and cents.*

Legal Time and Charges

Attorneys base their hourly charges on actual working time spent on a client's case. *Every minute counts.* To simplify accounting, legal timekeeping is based on segments of an hour, as follows:

The sixty-minute hour is divided into portions and billing is done according to the number of hours and segments thereof in which work is performed for the client. Each lawyer has his own system of timekeeping, usually based on one of the following systems:

$\frac{1}{30}$ hour = 2 minutes	$\frac{1}{6}$ hour = 10 minutes
$\frac{1}{12}$ hour = 5 minutes	$\frac{1}{4}$ hour = 15 minutes

An attorney's charges are prepared from time sheets on which he lists all time dedicated to his client during the month just ended. The lawyer does not wait until month-end to try recalling the exact amount of time spent on each client's behalf. *He keeps track of his time as he goes along, either by jotting it down on a notepad, desk calendar or special worksheet that he fills in just as regularly as a worker punches a time clock when he arrives and leaves his place of employment.*

If you have not been keeping track of your time since you first became involved in your legal matter, this chapter enables you to bring your records up to date in much the same way a lawyer does.

Timekeeping Made Easy

Breaking the hour into four quarters (fifteen minutes each) is the easiest, most effective approach to legal timekeeping. You may wish to use this same system to keep track of your own *Pro Per*'s time.

The example on the following page shows how charges, transferred from an attorney's time sheet to his statement, appear on the lawyer's bill.

Attorney's Statement

JOHN Q. SMITH, Esq.
10000 Ventura Blvd., Suite 100
Van Nuys, CA 91400

TO: Mrs. Donna Appleton   DATE: June 30, 1997
3321 N. Whitworth Street   RE: Appleton vs. Green
Van Nuys, CA 91401   Case No. NWC 100396

Itemized Expenses:

Telephone:
6/13/97   Donna Appleton   15 min.
6/14/97   William Green   15 min.

                                        ½ hr.

Conferences:
6/01/97   William Green   30 min.
6/04/97   Donna Appleton   30 min.

                                        1 hr.
Court:
6/05/97   Superior Court   2 hrs.

            Total Hours: 3½ hrs.

    Amount Due and Payable: $612.50

Fortunately, since you are both your own attorney and client you do not have to keep infinitely exact records of your time—unless you want to do so.

Nevertheless, *your time is worth money.* Whose money? Your money!

Are you really getting your money's worth by handling your own case? Fill in your own time sheet to find out just how much time and energy you have already put into your legal matter.

Scratch Paper
Use this space for figuring your costs to be included on your
Pro Per's Time Sheet (on next page)

Pro Per's Time Sheet

Fill in the amount of time you have actually spent working on your case, by category, starting with the date you first became involved in the legal matter. Estimate by quarter-hours of fifteen minutes each. Use scratch paper to calculate your figures, then write them below in pencil.

Time Period: Date Begun_____, 19____ to Today's Date_____, 19____

Service Provided	**Hours**	**Minutes**
Accounting	_____	_____
Conferences with:		
Adverse party	_____	_____
Witnesses	_____	_____
Lawyers	_____	_____
Other people	_____	_____
Evidence (gathering of)	_____	_____
Filing (your own files)	_____	_____
Mail (handling yourself)	_____	_____
Purchasing (supplies, etc.)	_____	_____
Reading	_____	_____
Telephone calls	_____	_____
Travel (transportation)	_____	_____
Other:	_____	_____

(Add your total hours and minutes:
sixty minutes equal one hour.)

Total Time:	_____	_____
	Hours	Minutes

Time Estimates Made Easy

How much is your time worth, figuratively speaking, as it relates to the minutes and hours you devote to serving as your own lawyer? The answer is simple: your *Pro Per*'s time is worth the amount you are paid by the hour for working.

If you earn $4.00 per hour, your *Pro Per*'s time is also worth $4.00 an hour. If you earn $10.00 per hour, your *Pro Per*'s time is also worth $10.00 per hour.

How to Figure Your Hourly Worth

If you are not paid by the hour, you can easily figure your hourly wage by dividing your gross (before taxes) income for one month by the number of hours you worked.

The average worker puts in twenty-two eight-hour workdays per month; therefore, he works 176 hours.

If you are collecting unemployment benefits, dividends, and interest from investments, pension funds, retirement pay, disability compensation, or welfare—or any other form of extraordinary income—you may wish to use the 176-hour figure to estimate how much your time would be worth if you were actually earning your monthly income from a regular job.

If you have no outside source of income, you must be your own judge of your hourly worth. I suggest basing your hourly net worth upon the minimum amount of money you would accept if you were to take a job.

Here are examples of various monthly incomes broken down to their hourly pay equivalents:

Hourly Income

Income per Month	No. Hours Worked During the Month	Hourly Rate of Pay
(Based on an average 176 hours worked during an ordinary month)		
$1000	176	$ 5.68
$1500	176	$ 8.54
$2000	176	$11.36
(Based on actual full or part-time hours worked during month)		
$ 500	40	$12.50
$1000	60	$16.67
$1500	160	$ 9.38
$2000	200	$10.00

How to Prepare Your Own Statement

When you have estimated your base hourly income, which may contain both dollars and cents (such as $4.55, $8.37, $15.65, etc.), write it below:

My Actual Income: $_____ per hour

You are now ready for your next step, in which you will convert your actual hourly income into the fees you would charge yourself for *Pro Per* services if you were a lawyer billing a client.

If you were actually going to bill yourself for the services you have rendered thus far as your own lawyer, the first thing you would do is simplify your accounting procedure by rounding your hourly fee to even dollars.

You may do this now, using this easy formula as it applies to your actual hourly income.

$.01 through $.49:	Delete the cents and leave the dollars.
	Examples: $4.35/hour = $4.00/hour
	$6.49/hour = $6.00/hour
$.50 through $.99:	Delete the cents and add one dollar.
	Examples: $4.55/hour = $5.00/hour
	$9.99/hour = $10.00/hour

This gives you the rate at which you can estimate both the value of service performed in your case in the past *and the amount every hour you put into the case in the future would be worth if you were being paid for your time.*

My *Pro Per*'s Rate: $_____ per hour

You may now prepare a statement for your own services by filling in the form which follows. If you wish to itemize your services on the statement, copy the applicable information from your time sheet. *To determine your total, multiply the total number of hours shown on your time sheet by the hourly rate which appears above.*

Statement

For *Pro Per* services performed between the dates of:

_____, 19___ and _____, 19___

_____ hours @ $_____ per hour

Itemized Breakdown of Services:

Date	**Description**	**Time**
_____	_____	_____ Min./Hrs.
_____	_____	_____ Min./Hrs.
_____	_____	_____ Min./Hrs.
_____	_____	_____ Min./Hrs.
_____	_____	_____ Min./Hrs.
_____	_____	_____ Min./Hrs.
_____	_____	_____ Min./Hrs.
_____	_____	_____ Min./Hrs.
_____	_____	_____ Min./Hrs.
_____	_____	_____ Min./Hrs.

Total Amount: $_____

Are You Too Expensive for Yourself?

Are you really saving money by serving as your own attorney? Or would it be less costly to retain a lawyer? Consider these facts:

• Most experienced attorneys handling cases similar to yours perform approximately ten times as fast as the average *Pro Per* who is handling his first legal matter himself. *This means you may be functioning at about one-tenth the speed of a lawyer; you may even go more slowly as case preparations become more complicated.*

- A lawyer knows the law—how to work within its framework, how to research it, and how to apply it to win a case in court—*while you are learning as you go.*

- An attorney has professional assistance: an accountant handles his finances; a secretary handles his correspondence and many phone calls; a paralegal does his research; a messenger picks up and delivers his legal documents. *You must do all these things yourself, plus prepare your presentation for court, all in your spare time.*

If one hour of a lawyer's time is, on an overall average, equal to approximately ten hours of a *Pro Per*'s time, what are those hours really worth to you?

Can you really afford to continue serving as your own lawyer? Or are you saving even more than you expected by handling your own legal matter? Here is how to estimate your money's worth:

How to Estimate Your Own Money's Worth

Using the suggested ratio of ten *Pro Per*'s hours to one attorney's hour of service, how does the time you are spending on your case measure up to the money your time is worth to you? You can arrive at the answer by following these steps:

1. Contact your local Bar Association to determine the average hourly fee charged by lawyers in your area. This is what you would pay for an hour of professional legal service in your case. Fill in the blank:

   Local Lawyer's Fee = $_____ per hour of work

2. Assuming you put in ten hours of your own time as a *Pro Per* to equal one hour of professional legal work, fill in the amount of money your ten hours would be worth if you were being paid. (Multiply your *Pro Per*'s hourly rate by ten, then fill in the space below: $_____ per hour x 10 = $ _____.)

   My Time is Worth $_____ for ten hours of work

3. Are you saving or losing the dollar equivalent of your time by serving as your own attorney? Compare numbers 1 and 2 above. You can readily see the difference, if any, between one hour of professional legal assistance and ten hours of your own time. Based on this figure, you must decide whether the money you are saving by serving as your own lawyer is really worth the time and effort required to do all the legwork—as well as suffer any associated stress and strain—in your own case.

Calculating Future Time

Are you willing to put as much time into further handling of your case as you have already devoted to it? Or would both your pocketbook and peace of mind be best served by retaining professional counsel?

The following chart compares the average number of hours a *Pro Per* can plan on putting into doing the things a lawyer can usually handle in one-tenth of the time.

Be your own judge as to whether or not you are really saving anything by serving as your own lawyer.

Time Comparison Chart
(The chart compares the average difference in time
required for a *Pro Per* and attorney to do the same things.)

Hours of Your Time is equal to	Hours of Attorney's Time
10	1
20	2
30	3
40	4
50	5
60	6
70	7
80	8
90	9
100	10

Easy Guide to Attorneys' Fees

For your convenience in estimating the amount of money a lawyer in your area might charge for performing legal services, the chart on the following page contains a breakdown of hourly legal fees currently being charged in different parts of the country.

Chart of Hourly Legal Fees
(Based on average fees charged across the U.S. in 1996)

Per Hour	No. Hours	Total	Per Hour	No. Hours	Total
$100	1	$ 100	$100	6	$ 600
$100	2	$ 200	$100	7	$ 700
$100	3	$ 300	$100	8	$ 800
$100	4	$ 400	$100	9	$ 900
$100	5	$ 500	$100	10	$1000
$125	1	$ 125	$125	6	$ 750
$125	2	$ 250	$125	7	$ 875
$125	3	$ 375	$125	8	$1000
$125	4	$ 500	$125	9	$1125
$125	5	$ 625	$125	10	$1250
$150	1	$ 150	$150	6	$ 900
$150	2	$ 300	$150	7	$1050
$150	3	$ 455	$150	8	$1200
$150	4	$ 600	$150	9	$1350
$150	5	$ 750	$150	10	$1500
$175	1	$ 175	$175	6	$1050
$175	2	$ 350	$175	7	$1225
$175	3	$ 525	$175	8	$1400
$175	4	$ 700	$175	9	$1575
$175	5	$ 875	$175	10	$1750
$200	1	$ 200	$200	6	$1200
$200	2	$ 400	$200	7	$1400
$200	3	$ 600	$200	8	$1600
$200	4	$ 800	$200	9	$1800
$200	5	$1000	$200	10	$2000
$250	1	$ 250	$250	6	$1500
$250	2	$ 500	$250	7	$1750
$250	3	$ 750	$250	8	$2000
$250	4	$1000	$250	9	$2250
$250	5	$1250	$250	10	$2500

Chapter 13

How to Sound Like a Lawyer

(Bonus Chapter)

I F YOU ARE INVOLVED in a short cause case, you need not be concerned with the question, "What is the right thing to say in court—and how do I say it?" All that is necessary is to *be yourself.*

This means common "garden variety" English is all that is required—or expected—by the judge.

In fact, down-to-earth everyday English is preferable in all types of cases, short causes as well as medium and long causes. There was a time when the more formal language known as "legalese" was standard in court, but this has changed.

While today's court proceedings are still conducted according to judicial and legal protocol, less legalese is used today than ever before. Although you do not need to speak in legalese, there are a few things you should know about the language of the law—particularly if you are involved in a medium or long cause which may involve considerable exposure to many unfamiliar terms.

Latin and the Law

Legalese is based on the Latin language. It is fairly easy to understand by individuals who use legal terms everyday. As happens in many other languages, legalese is based on combinations of terms.

For instance, *pro* means "for" while *persona* and *se* both mean "self." *Pro Per* is the term most widely used in the western United States while *Pro Se* is more common in the eastern states; both mean "for myself," which, loosely translated, is interpreted as "on my own behalf."

Another very common legal term is *pro bono*. Technically, it means "for good," but its popular meaning in legal and judicial circles today indicates "for free." If a lawyer handles a case free of charge, he is doing good by giving of his services.

As a *Pro Per* you will work as your own attorney on a *pro bono* basis.

Written Legalese

Legal documents are written in legalese.

Courtroom proceedings are based on rules and regulations inscribed in legalese.

All local, state, and federal codes, rules, regulations, statutes, and laws are worded in the language of the law.

All legal materials you may file with the court, or receive from the court, contain legal language.

It is far more important to understand the written legalese involved in your lawsuit than to speak the language of the law as fluently as a lawyer does.

Spoken Legalese

Lawyers speak legalese almost as if it was their native tongue. Non-lawyers cannot learn legalese overnight. There is no crash-course which will turn you into an instant expert in the language of the law.

However, you can integrate legalese into your everyday language by following three easy steps:

First, read this book. Underline each legal term you do not presently understand.

Second, refer to the glossary entitled "At Ease With Legalese," which appears in the back of Book Two. It contains explanations in everyday English of all the legal terms the average *Pro Per* needs to know about lawsuits, trials, and legal matters discussed in this two-volume set.

Third, after acquainting yourself thoroughly with written legalese as it is presented in this book, practice using some of the terms that most appeal to you in your daily language.

Begin by adding one new term to your vocabulary. After you have become so comfortable with your new legal word, add another, then another. When a legal term is so familiar that you use it automatically, it becomes a permanent part of your vocabulary and you are speaking legalese as a lawyer does—normally and naturally.

Summarizing Legalese

If sounding like a lawyer is important to you, then practice your legalese as outlined above. If not, forget it. In the event you brush up on legalese for the purpose of speaking like a lawyer during your trial, consider this idea: The use of legalese by a non-lawyer might backfire, making him appear pompous or trying to to cover up his ignorance by using big words. Nothing is better than being your own self!

Speak in legalese only if you are so comfortable with the language of law that it flows naturally. Otherwise, leave the legal language to the lawyers. Stick with the language you know best—everyday English.

"Yet the righteous will hold to his way, and he who has clean hands will be stronger and stronger."—Job 17:9

NOTES

(Use this space to list legal terms and their definitions as you may use them in court.)

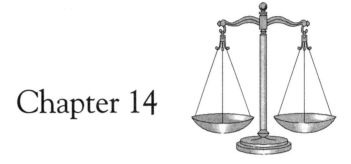

Chapter 14

How to Work Like a Lawyer

B Y APPLYING THE SUGGESTIONS you select for yourself from this Section, you have established your "base of operations" from which to serve as your own attorney throughout the lifetime of your lawsuit.

Your next step is to start working like an attorney, which means you should be prepared to alter your lifestyle to fit the important role you have elected to fulfill.

Must you make drastic changes? Probably not. However, you may have to do more than merely squeeze your lawsuit into your schedule—you may have to give it top priority billing in your life until it is disposed. This means working with the case in much the same way a lawyer would if he were representing you.

The Lawyer's Life
What are the three main differences that make the average attorney who is actively engaged in practicing his profession different from that of a non-lawyer? The brief chart below provides insight into this question:

Non-Lawyer	Lawyer
He works eight hours a day.	His workday is twenty-four hours in duration.
He works five days a week.	His work week is seven days long.
He leaves his work at work.	He takes his work home with him.

Does this indicate that attorneys never take breaks, stop to eat, watch TV or relax with friends and loved ones? No. It means that once a lawyer involves himself in a case, it remains "unfinished business" until the lawsuit is disposed.

Even if a lawyer does not carry his briefcase onto a tennis court, or into the bedroom at night, *he carries it in his mind.*

Unpaid Overtime

An attorney's thoughts are not regulated by a time clock, so he may awaken from a sound sleep because an important aspect of the case has presented itself in a dream. Or his workout at the gym might be interrupted by a phone call from a client who urgently needs to discuss the matter with legal counsel.

Unlike the average individual who is paid overtime wages for extra time spent doing the job, an attorney receives no overtime pay for thinking about a case. And since thoughts go with him everywhere, he literally works a twenty-four-hour day.

The *Pro Per*'s Life

A rule of thumb to remember is: *The more important the case is to the legal counselor handling the lawsuit, the more he will think about it; and the more complex the issues are, the more work must be done to prepare for trial.*

Are you willing to sacrifice some leisure time in order to devote the necessary minutes or hours—or even nights and weekends—required to do yourself justice in court? Are you really able to spare the time necessary to work like a lawyer by carrying the case around in your mind for twenty-four hours a day, seven days a week until it is disposed?

Making Your Commitment

When an attorney accepts a case, he makes a commitment to his client. By serving as your own attorney, you are making the same kind of commitment to yourself.

Are you prepared to make whatever sacrifices of personal time and energy are required to honor that commitment? Before answering, consider the following facts:

An experienced attorney, who successfully combines both his personal and professional lives, usually works on several cases at one time.

As a Pro Per, *you will handle only one legal case—your own.*

If you are committed to working like a lawyer in order to try your own case in court to win, proceed as your own legal counselor.

If not, get an attorney!

"But seek first the kingdom of God and His righteousness, and all these things shall be added to you."—Matthew 6:33

PART III

HOW TO PREPARE YOUR CASE FOR COURT

PART III CONTAINS point-by-point instructions about how to use the same thoroughness an attorney employs to tie together every aspect of a case before presenting it in court.

This section tells the *Pro Per* what he needs to take to court, and helps him learn how to find and organize his witnesses, evidence, and other facts facts so he stands the best chance of winning on the day of trial.

Recommendation: To prepare your case for court in the quickest, most efficient manner, read only Chapters 15, 17, 18, and 19. The others, marked by asterisks (*), are bonus chapters. If time permits, or yours is a complex case in which it is important that you understand the applicable law, also read Chapter 16. The remaining chapters are optional.

Chapter 15

How to Organize Your Research

Y OU ARE NOW READY to begin preparing your case for your ultimate presentation in court on your trial date. This means you are ready to organize your records and start filling your files with facts and figures, which may require doing a little—or a lot—of research.

You have already gained basic insight into how to organize your "office." Now you are ready to put that information to work.

Building Your Case Record

In Chapter 9, suggestions were given about how to set up a simple filing system consisting of six files. If you have not yet done so, please take the time to set up your files before proceeding beyond this chapter.

Your files constitute the storage place for the overall "record" of your case; it is actually the complete history of your lawsuit.

After your case has been disposed, you may wish to consolidate your various files into one—for easy storage. For the time being, however, it will be easier for you to build your case record by using the system of file folders described in Chapter 9 and illustrated in the following table.

119

Diagram of Case Files

1	2	3
Facts of the Lawsuit	**Follow-Up Filing**	**Figures of the Lawsuit**
Correspondence File	Miscellaneous File	Expense File
Documents File		
Evidence File		
Witnesses File		

Explanation of Columns:

Column 1: These files contain various facts relating to your lawsuit. The two top file folders contain documents concerning the legal action, the lawsuit. The two bottom files will be used for storage of facts from which to draw information for presentation during the trial; such facts will be used to prove your claim or disprove the opposition's case. *These are the files in which research is kept which can be used to win your case in court.*

Column 2: This is a "pending file" in which information that requires further action is kept temporarily. Everything that must be followed through to completion is filed here, including unpaid bills, incomplete research, and unanswered correspondence. When an unfinished piece of business has been completed, it is transferred into the appropriate folder under Column 1.

Column 3: This is a "figures" file in which nothing but information related to the expenses involved in conducting the lawsuit is stored. You may wish to think of it as your "accounting file" because you will use it for storage of all bills, receipts, cancelled checks, and other material concerning your expenses. You may draw upon data from this file to prepare your plea to the court that expenses such as court costs, attorney's fees, etc. be awarded you as part of the judgment you seek.

By filling these files with the appropriate information you gather from your research, you will be building your case record while, at the same time, getting together the proof you need to convince the judge he should hand down his decision in your favor and award you the judgment you seek.

This is known as "doing your homework."

How Much Homework is Required?

The amount of research remaining to be done depends on how much proof you already possess that can be used as favorable evidence during trial.

Generally, short causes like small claims and minor traffic cases demand much less homework than longer causes involving more than one issue, as is frequent in cross-complaints. Do you think you need to do any research? Evaluate your evidence to arrive at the answer.

Evaluation of Your Evidence
(Answer the questions in the spaces below. Simple one-
word responses are all that is required.)

1. List the physical and documentary evidence now in your possession which is unde-
niable proof that your claim is valid (or your opponent's is not):

_____
_____
_____
_____
_____

2. List the basic testimony of witnesses which proves your case's validity (or disproves your adversary's):

_____
_____
_____
_____
_____

3. Explain in your own words the law governing your type of lawsuit:

_____
_____
_____
_____
_____

Evaluating Your Evidence
If you had no trouble filling in the blanks, particularly numbers 1 and 3, you may already have all the evidence required for your trial. Little, if any, further investigation may be needed.

If you had to stretch your imagination to come up with any answers at all, you have little if any tangible proof to present in court. You must gather more facts in order to prove your case in court.

If you could not answer any of the questions, you have no evidence. Investigation should now be your top priority!

Insight into Investigation

There are three steps in investigation: *gathering of facts, organizing them, and putting them to use to prove your point.*

There are many ways to gather facts, starting with the information you already have in your possession. Are there any documents, contracts, letters, or other pieces of "paper evidence" in your file *which can be used to prove your case in court?*

Your investigative job is only half done when you have gathered evidence for your own files. In court you will offer your exhibits into evidence; they may or may not be accepted (refer to Chapter 34 in Book Two).

Concentrate on gathering only evidence that may be used to prove your case. In the event you are missing an important paper, agreement, or other document, many businesses, hospitals, public service, and state agencies will provide copies upon your request. Some may charge you a small fee for the service.

Assessing Your Own Needs

Before starting your research, you must assess your own needs. This will prevent you from gathering too many—or too few—vital facts. Start your evidence assessment by asking yourself questions. For instance:

Do you possess any x-rays, photographs, or recordings which can help prove your case in court? If not, can you acquire them?

Do you possess any nondocumentary type of evidence which can be offered as exhibits in court? For instance, a man won his case by producing the broken tail light from his car; it was streaked with blue paint from the defendant's automobile. A woman once produced the baseball that hit her on the head, causing a concussion; the signature of the man accused of causing the injury was written on the ball.

To supplement the facts you already possess, what outside research must be done? As a starter, consider the matter of eyewitnesses. Do you know the names of the people who witnessed the event in which you were involved? If no, you may have to search the area where the incident occurred to locate people who were witnesses.

When you have located potential eyewitnesses, did they see anything that could help you win your case in court? If yes, are they willing to testify on your behalf? The only way to find out is to talk with them. You may do this in person or by telephone, whichever is most convenient.

How Well Do You Know the Law?

Do you understand the law as it applies to your case? For instance, what do you have to do in order to raise the habitability defense in landlord-tenant cases? What is the law governing verbal (unwritten) contracts?

Many *Pro Pers* lose in court because they are unaware of the law that is applicable to their cases. They did not do their homework. They failed to find out the answers to such questions as:

Can a person be held in breach of contract if he fails to fulfill a promise? Or must every written agreement be signed by all parties thereto in order to be legally binding?

What is the law in your state covering personal injury accidents caused by uninsured motorists? What is the law in your town regarding the length of time a non-paying tenant can occupy a premises before the landlord has the legal right to evict him?

The matter of law for the layman is so important that a separate chapter has been devoted to it (see Chapter 16). *Finding the pertinent law in your case should occupy top position on your agenda of research to be done.*

Shortcut to Research

Cut your research efforts to a minimum by focusing on *physical evidence, documentary evidence, testimony of witnesses, and applicable law.* There is no need to overwork yourself. A few pieces of relevant information are far more valuable than a whole file of irrelevant facts.

Refer to the chart on pages 124–125 to gain an idea of the evidence you need to prove your case. You may, of course, gather more material if you wish. It is better to be overprepared than not prepared at all.

How Much Evidence Do You Need?

Admissible physical evidence, documentary evidence, and eyewitness testimony are the basics required to prove your case in court, but you must decide how much is enough. You can gauge the amount of evidence you need by the number of points you plan to prove in court. Each point should be based upon the law as it applies to your type of case, which is why it is so important to know the applicable law in your legal matter.

For example, a landlord sues a tenant for non-payment of rent on his apartment. This unlawful detainer case contains five basic issues: (1) there was a tenancy contract between the parties; (2) defendant did not pay his rent on time; (3) the defendant was served a three-day notice to pay his rent or vacate the premises; (4) defendant failed to pay his rent during the three-day period; (5) defendant continues to occupy premises.

If the defendant denies these allegations in his Answer, the plaintiff will have to prove all the facts, *because the law requires that all these matters occur before the defendant can be evicted.*

If the defendant admits in his Answer that all these facts are true but asserts the affirmative defense that his rental unit is not habitable, the defendant must prove that his unit is not capable of being lived in. *Here, the applicable law is the law on habitability.*

This means, for example, that if the defendant can prove that his apartment is crawling with cockroaches, the plumbing or heating does not work, or rain damage has created unhealthful living conditions, he may win. However, if he simply has not paid his rent (because he may be unemployed or short of cash), the landlord may win and the tenant can be evicted.

To avoid wasting time gathering evidence you may not be able to use, make your preparations in the following order:

Research the applicable law first.

Then investigate the facts you will present in court.

Planning Your Own Investigation

You must know what you are looking for before beginning your investigation into the facts for the purpose of gathering evidence. This list outlines the most common types of information presented as evidence in the four kinds of trials covered in this book: small claims, minor traffic infractions, unlawful detainer, and personal injury.

You can adapt this material to fit any type of case.

Most Common Types of Proof
(Factual evidence is listed by trial type.)

Type of Trial	Description
Small Claims	Advertisements (for items, services, etc.)
	Agreements, contracts, and letters of agreement (signed)
	Bills (for money owed)
	Documents (miscellaneous, including photocopies))
	Estimates (costs for service/labor to be performed)
	Eyewitness testimony
	Photographs and recordings
	Physical proof (damaged objects, weapons)
	Receipts (for money paid)
	Statistical data (details, descriptions))
	Warranties and guarantees (for merchandise and/or service)
Minor Traffic	Citation (copy of ticket, for reference in court)
	Documents (driver's and vehicle license, sales slip, registration, etc.)
	Eyewitness testimony
	Statistical data (measurements, traffic conditions, weather, visibility, etc., at scene of infraction)
	Photographs and recordings

Most Common Types of Proof
(continued)

Type of Trial	Description
Unlawful Detainer	Agreements, contracts (leases, rent receipts, etc.)
	Correspondence (letters, memos and notes)
	Documents (legal notices, answers and proof of service)
	Eyewitness testimony
	Photographs (exterior and interior of premises)
	Receipts (including checks for rent, security deposits)
	Rules (pertaining to use of premises)
	Statements (for money due)
Personal Injury	Correspondence (including memos, notes and messages)
	Bills (for money owed)
	Eyewitness testimony
	Expert witness testimony
	Insurance (claims, reports, etc.)
	Medical (evaluations, charts, laboratory reports, etc.)
	Physical proof (object causing injury)
	Photographs, x-rays, and recordings
	Receipts (for money paid)
	Statistical data (details at scene of the event; in a vehicular accident, speed at time of collision, distance car skidded before stopping, etc.)

Outlining Your Research and Investigation

You may use the following spaces to draw up your own research and investigation plan. Remember the following points:

- Research the law as it applies to your case.

- Investigate facts which will be admissible as evidence that prove your case according to the applicable law.

Avoid gathering irrelevant information—regardless of how interesting it may seem to you personally.

Research and Investigation Plan
(List the factual material to be gathered in the order of its importance to you.)

Three factors of primary importance:

1. _____

2. _____

3. _____

Secondary in importance:

4. _____

5. _____

6. _____

Other:

7. _____

8. _____

9. _____

10. _____

(Use a blank sheet if more space is needed)

Putting Your Plan into Practice

You are now organized and ready to start researching facts that will help you try your case. We suggest you start by researching the law(s) applicable to your matter; then, contact persons and places from which to gather evidence that will help you prove your case, or disprove your opponent's. For instructions about how to gather your legal facts, refer to Chapter 16, "How to Research the Law."

Chapter 16

How to Research the Law

(Bonus Chapter)

I F YOU ARE NOT AWARE of the law which applies to your type of legal matter, learn it! Learning the law may include finding out the speed limit on a street where a collision occurred or learning how the law looks upon auto repair shops that give a fifty-dollar estimate for fixing a car but end up charging more than one hundred dollars. The latter examples raises the question: is the customer bound to pay all the unexpected hidden charges, or does he owe only the fifty dollars he thought was due?

There are as many laws as there are kinds of lawsuits. In the types of cases discussed in this book, one law is usually all you are required to know. However, you may discover during your research that more than one law is pertinent to your case. In such an event, write down as much information as your research turns up.

A Few Examples
Here are a few examples of the kinds of questions *Pro Pers* are most likely to ask; one of them may describe your situation:

What is the law regarding a public walkway whose unmarked broken sidewalk caused a slip-and-fall accident? Can the city be held responsible?

Who is responsible if an injury occurs to a private party who falls in a hole in the ground, while cutting across property on which a "No Trespassing" sign is posted, after the owner of the property granted him permission to enter the premises?

In a two-car collision in which both drivers are uninsured, who is responsible for payment of car repairs? For medical expenses?

If a tenant withholds rent because the landlord has failed to repair a broken water pipe, and the tenant has had no hot water for more than a week, can the landlord evict the tenant for nonpayment of rent?

If a personal friend agrees to take pictures of a wedding for two hundred dollars, but the newlyweds do not pay him because they are not satisfied with the photos, can the photographer collect the money?

If a product which was advertised at a discount price is defective, can the purchaser demand his money back if he did not receive a warranty at the time he bought the item?

These are the types of questions every *Pro Per* asks. What are the questions you are asking regarding the law as it pertains to your case?

What Do You Need to Know?

If you have any unanswered questions about the law as it applies to your case, now is the time to sort them out. You may use the worksheet on the opposite page as an outline from which to conduct your research into the law.

Feel free to ask questions from both points of view—yours and your opponent's. The law also applies to him, although its influence on his side of the matter may be very different from the way it affects you.

A judge takes all aspects of the law into consideration. A well-prepared *Pro Per* should do the same.

Understanding the Law

Before beginning your research, an understanding of what you are looking for will help you find it more easily. Throughout this book, the word "law" refers collectively to all rules, regulations, statutes, ordinances, legislation, and codes enacted by legislative bodies or regulatory agencies legally empowered to set standards governing the conduct of the public-at-large.

The general purpose of every law is described in the Constitution of the United States: to insure domestic tranquility for both private and public sectors of the people.

Important Points of Law

In the two-hundred-year history of the United States, millions of laws have been enacted at the national, state, and local levels.

"Applicable law" may consist of a law or court decision, or combination of both.

The chance of your case being governed by a new law, or new appellate decision, is slim if not entirely nonexistent. Therefore, you may discover during your research that the same law has been amended or interpreted differently a number of times.

Outline of Law Questions
(Write your questions about the law as it applies to your case.)

_____

_____

_____

_____

_____

_____

_____

_____

_____

_____

_____

Notes:

Which version of a law or decision is the right one? *Generally, the latest version of a law or decision applies.*

Read your reference source carefully to determine whether the current version is retroactive; that is, does the current applicable version of the law or decision revert back to a date prior to its enactment? If so, the current version applies. Otherwise, the law effective on the date in question applies.

Introducing the Law Library

The best place to do your research is in a law library. Large cities usually have large law libraries which are open to the public; they contain vast collections of legal publications ranging from constitutional law down to local county ordinances.

Smaller communities or rural areas may not have public law libraries; however, many district courthouses allow attorneys and *Pro Pers* to do research in their law libraries. The bar association in your area might maintain a law library for member lawyers. You may be able to get permission to do your research in one of these facilities.

Public libraries usually contain a limited amount of reference material in their legal sections. While there is far less legal matter available in a public library, you might be able to find what you need. The reference librarian can answer your questions.

Preparing to Visit the Law Library

Before visiting the law library, prepare a list of items you wish to research. You may take the questions appearing in this chapter, or make up a new list.

Because it is easy to forget important points, this list will help you remember everything you came for. In this way, you can probably complete your research with just one trip to the library instead of two or three.

Take your own notebook and pens or pencils. If you think your research will take more than half a day, you might also take your lunch. Law libraries are quiet places at whose tables men and women engage in serious research into the law. Do not expect a cafeteria or snack bar to provide food or beverages, or a social gathering place for smoking cigarettes, drinking coffee, and chatting.

Other Law Library Tips

If you eat your lunch at the law library, do so outside or in any other area designated for this purpose. Never snack, chew gum, or sip on a beverage at a law library table.

Do not bring a cassette player or radio into the law library; even with the earphones on and the volume turned to low, the vibrations can disturb other people who are trying to concentrate on their research. Most important, your own concentration will be enhanced by leaving the entertainment outside.

Bring some pocket change. Most libraries have machines on which to copy pages of documents. The library provides this service, but you must pay for it. Everything else is free.

Last, is there a law library dress code? Many individuals may wear business clothing in the law library; others will be more casual. How casual is too casual?

Bathing suits, naked chests, and bare feet are definitely out. Shorts, depending on their cut and length, are questionable. Otherwise, dress according to your own taste.

How to Use the Law Library

Introduce yourself to the law librarian and explain who you are and what you need to accomplish. The librarian will tell you the layout of the library and the card files and other reference material.

In some law libraries, you must find your own material; in others, an assistant librarian may help you locate the specific information you need.

Search for the type of reference material you need by subject. For instance, if your legal issue revolves around an incident involving your car, look under "Automobiles" or "Vehicles." If an insurance claim is at issue, look under "Insurance."

Many of the legal publications are bound in shiny leatherette hard covers; others have soft covers. Some are large, some are medium-sized, and some are small. They all have one thing in common: legalese is the language in which all statutes, rules, regulations, ordinances, laws, and court decisions are written.

One Special Reference Book

There is one special reference book that beats all others for finding what you need quickly. Written in easy-to-understand language, it also contains only the most recent versions of laws.

This book, frequently referred to by members of the legal and judicial professions, makes fascinating reading for the *Pro Per* who knows little about the law but wants to learn.

Both current civil and criminal laws are included; most of the laws which are pertinent to the types of trials covered in this book are contained in the publication to which I recommend you refer when doing your research.

What is its title? I cannot tell you the answer because every area calls it by a slightly different name. Tell the librarian you wish to see a copy of your area's Criminal or Civil Jury Instructions Book.* If you look it up in the library files, it will be listed under the heading "Jury."

---

*In California the Criminal Jury Instructions Book is called "CALJIC" and the Civil Jury Instructions Book is called "BAJI."

Tips on Pockets

Law library books often contain jackets, called pockets, in the inside front and back covers. Updated versions of the law are stored in these pockets.

If information about your law is contained in these pocket parts, use it; it is the latest interpretation of the law or ruling currently on the record.

If no material relating to your pertinent law is contained in the pocket parts, the most up-to-date version appears in the body of the actual book.

How to Identify Your Research

Copy the information down exactly as it appears in the reference source from which you take it. Or, copy the page(s) on which it appears, if there is a copier available to you.

Do not attempt to interpret the law, or rewrite it into your own words, at this time. You can rework it later.

Identify each law separately. The following information should appear on every law or ruling gathered for your research files:

- *Name of the source* (code book, jury instruction book, vehicle code, etc.) from which you took the information. For example:

CALIFORNIA VEHICLE CODE

- *Identification of the law by name, number, and date.* Include all sections—indicated by the symbol §—and subsections. Abbreviations may be used to identify source material, as illustrated by the following citation of the California Vehicle Code:

Unattended Vehicle: Prima Facie Evidence; CVC ,41102 (d)
Amended by Stats. 1959 ПC 338, p. 2263, effective May 8, 1959

This is how a California appellate court citation would appear: *People v. Standard*, 181 Cal. App 3d 431 (May 1986)

This means the *People v. Standard* case can be found in volume 181, page 431 (rendered in May 1986), of the California Appellate Reports Third Series.

A Few Words About Legalese

Even if you select your area's jury instructions book as your principal source, a certain amount of legalese will appear in print. This is because legalese is the language of the law and cannot be avoided or entirely eliminated in writings dealing with law.

You may wish to take Book Two of this set along when doing your research. If you run across words or phrases you do not understand, consult the glossary in the back entitled "At Ease With Legalese." It provides easy-to-understand explanations of many terms you may run across in law books.

The law librarian can also lend you a legal dictionary to consult. If you cannot understand the dictionary's legal definition of a word, ask the librarian to explain it in ordinary English. You may, in fact, ask the librarian almost—but not quite—anything dealing with the letter of the law. Do not ask for free legal advice, because the librarian cannot give it.

Storing Your Research
When you have gathered your facts relating to applicable law, store them in a safe place for future reference. You may even wish to keep two copies, one in your lawsuit files and the other in this book, by using the handy form provided on the following page.

Record of Pertinent Law

(If more space is needed, attach a separate sheet.)

Reference Source   **Summary Description of Law/Ruling**   **Identification**

Chapter 17

How to Organize
Your Witnesses

Y OU ARE NOW READY to learn about organizing your witnesses. Whether you have several people testify for you in court, or you will be the only person giving testimony in your side of the case, you should familiarize yourself with the information in this chapter.

Only the basic facts you need to know about witnesses are covered here. You will learn more about working with witnesses in subsequent chapters of this book.

What Is a Witness?
A witness is an individual who observed something, or who possesses specialized knowledge, training, skill, or experience, or education regarding the issue being tried in court.

Most witnesses testify in person during the trial, after being sworn or affirmed to tell the truth.

Swearing Versus Affirming of Witnesses
Swearing of witnesses is based on an old Christian tradition that used to require laying one's right hand on a Bible when saying "I do" to the question asked by an officer of the court: *Do you promise to tell the truth, the whole truth and nothing but the truth, so help you God?*

In more modern times, the individual being so sworn raises his right hand as a symbol of his intention to be honest.

If a witness prefers not to be sworn in, he may ask to be affirmed. In this non-religious-based ritual, an officer of the court will ask the individual whose right hand is raised: *Do you affirm that the testimony you are about to give is the truth, the whole truth, and nothing but the truth under pain and penalty of perjury?*

The witness who has sworn or affirmed that he will tell the truth is legally bound to honor his promise to be truthful.

The swearing and/or affirmation of witnesses is always done before the examination portion of the trial begins. Witnesses may be sworn individually or in a group, depending upon the circumstances under which the case is being tried. For instance, in a small claims case, the judge may swear or affirm all parties to the action at one time; however, in a non-small claims personal injury trial, each witness may be sworn or affirmed separately.

Are Your Witnesses Willing?

Are the people you plan to use as witnesses willing to be sworn or affirmed in court? Explain to an individual you consider using as a witness the difference between the two, and ask whether he has any objection to being either sworn or affirmed. If he has no objection, proceed with your plan.

If he refuses to being sworn or affirmed, try to find someone else to serve as your witness.

Make Arrangements Early

Witnesses are not always willing or able to testify in court. Many people cannot afford the time to give personal testimony, others are afraid to appear on the witness stand, and some do not want to get involved in a legal matter.

A few may promise to testify, but after their initial enthusiasm wears off they may change their minds, get sick, or find some other reason for backing out at the last minute.

Introducing the Subpoena

In its infinite wisdom based on understanding human nature, the law provides inexpensive but effective protection for individuals whose trials depend on the testimony of witnesses.

The subpoena, a legal instrument you may use to order witnesses to appear in court, is so effective that lawyers refer to it as "trial insurance." Trial lawyers use the subpoena as a matter of course whenever a trial is to be held; a *Pro Per* may do the same.

Both witnesses and documents can be subpoenaed. Instructions on this subject are contained in Chapter 34 of Book Two.

Tips on Testimony
Testimony serves two important purposes during a trial. First, it fills the judge in on important facts relating to the case; second, it helps you prove your claim—or disprove your opponent's.

The only testimony your witnesses should give is that which helps prove the point you are trying to make. Irrelevant testimony should never be given. Testimony based on hearsay (refer to Chapter 37) should always be avoided.

Example of Testimony
Direct evidence and *circumstantial evidence* are two legal terms frequently associated with the testimony of eyewitnesses.

An example of direct evidence—meaning evidence which directly proves a fact—is illustrated by the eyewitness to an automobile collision who says, "I saw the defendant rear-end the plaintiff's car."

The eyewitness testifies: "I looked out the window. I saw the defendant's car behind the plaintiff's. There were no other cars in the street at that time. I was walking away from the window when I heard a loud crash. I ran downstairs and saw the damage to the plaintiff's car. I did not see the defendant or his car."

An example of circumstantial evidence—meaning evidence based on facts which allow the court to make a rational inference—is drawn from the above example in which the court infers, from the eyewitness's testimony, that the defendant was the person who rear-ended the plaintiff and then "ran" (left the scene).

Evidence in Chief
"Evidence in chief" is a legal term describing the entire case of each side, excluding the rebuttal or sur-rebuttal evidence.

The judge bases his decision on the direct and circumstantial evidence presented and the applicable law.

Are the people you are considering using as witnesses believable? They should be!

Good Character Counts
The judge trusts you. He also trusts that your witnesses are honest people.

All testimony—both yours and that of your witnesses—should always be truthful.

A witness who gives false testimony may be charged with "perjury" and the individual who secured his false testimony may be charged for "subornation of perjury." Both are serious crimes.

Some people can never admit they are wrong or do not know something. This type of person may be driven, under pressure, to bluff his way through the examination rather than honestly admit, "I am sorry, but I do not know the answer."

An individual of this kind may win in the game of poker, but when his bluff is called in court, you lose! If you must use a person of this type as a witness, be certain he understands the importance of telling the truth, the whole truth, and nothing but the truth.

Never ask a witness to lie for you, and never plan to put a known liar or individual of questionable moral character on the stand if you can avoid it. If you cannot avoid it, the risk you take is entirely your own.

Choosing Your Witnesses

You must select your own witnesses. This may require investigation, or you may already have the names of a number of people who are potential witnesses. However, your options may be limited to selecting the best from which you have to choose.

Types of Witnesses

The eyewitness and the expert witness are the two types of witnesses who appear most frequently to testify in cases such as yours; however, there are two other types of witnesses who may be beneficial during your trial, the perceptive witness and the information witness. Brief descriptions follow of the four types of witnesses.

The Eyewitness—As the name implies, an eyewitness is a person who saw the occurrence of an event which is the subject matter of a case.

The Perceptive Witness—This type of witness has gained his knowledge through personal perception based on one or more of his five senses. Examples of perceptive eyewitnesses include: a pedestrian who *saw* two cars collide in an intersection; a shopper who *felt* heat radiating from the rear of a store; a tenant who *heard* loud, abusing threats coming from the next apartment; a jogger who *smelled* gas escaping from a crack in the pavement; a consumer who *tasted* a strange flavor in his tap water. In most jurisdictions, this witness is included in the broad category of eyewitness.

The Information Witness—An information witness is a person who possesses relevant knowledge, inside information, related to a procedure, practice, habit, or other pattern of activity associated with the issue on trial.

Examples of Information Witnesses include a switchboard operator who testifies the company's phone lines open at 9:00 A.M., never earlier, so the defendant could not have placed his call at 8:15 A.M. as claimed; the personnel clerk who testifies that company policy is to fire people before they are fully vested, so no one ever receives full employee benefits; the neighbor who testifies that the retired woman on the corner walks her dog between 10:00 A.M. and 10:30 A.M. every morning except Sunday. Other information witnesses include the salesman who admits that overcharging customers is standard procedure in his company; the mechanic who admits his employer sells junkyard parts as "rebuilts" to unsuspecting customers; the tenant who testifies the landlord promises every new tenant that new carpeting will be installed, but never follows through once they have moved in.

Practice these principles when dealing with eyewitnesses, perceptive witnesses, and information witnesses:

- *Do not use a witness whose testimony is based solely on unfounded rumor, speculation, or gossip.*

- *Do not offer to give a witness a bribe (money) based upon an understanding that his testimony shall be thereby influenced.*

The fourth type of witness you may wish to consider is the expert witness.

The Expert Witness—This type of witness performs a special function in a trial in which unknown or unresolved factors exist. As an "expert," he must possess special knowledge, skill, training, experience, or education in a field related to the problem area about which he testifies.

The purpose of expert testimony is to give an opinion of what might have happened under a specific set of circumstances. For instance, a medical doctor testifies that a spinal injury could, indeed, occur as the result of the kind of accident suffered by the plaintiff; a mechanic testifies that engine malfunction could, in fact, have been the reason the defendant could not stop his vehicle; a handwriting expert testifies that the signature on the contested will may actually be a well-executed forgery.

An expert witness is not personally involved in the case on trial. He has neither witnessed anything nor does he possess inside information about the matter. As a rule, he is considered a neutral party who will give unbiased, honest testimony.

The law does not forbid payment of an expert witness for performing his professional services in court. Therefore, consider the following when deciding whether or not to use an expert witness during your trial:

- *Never expect an expert witness to volunteer his services as a good will gesture.* (Most expert witnesses either charge flat rates for making one-time courtroom appearances, or they collect an hourly fee for the time they put in.)

- *Before hiring an expert witness, find out how much he will cost. If you cannot afford him, do not hire him.*

How Many Witnesses Do You Need?

As a start, consider yourself your own best—or "key"—witness.

How many other witnesses do you need, if any? To estimate the number of witnesses in your case, perform the following exercise entitled "Witness Analysis."

Witness Analysis

(Check one answer that reflects how you feel about your case.)

_____ 1. My personal testimony is strong, but the physical and/or documentary evidence to back it up is weak.

_____ 2. All my evidence is strong except my testimony, which is too weak.

_____ 3. My testimony and the rest of my evidence support and prove each other.

_____ 4. I am unsure whether my testimony and the rest of my evidence support each other well enough to prove my case in court.

Scoring Yourself:

1. You need more evidence to corroborate your testimony, and/or call one or more witnesses to prove your case to the judge.

2. You may wish to call one or more witnesses whose statements may help supply facts now lacking in your own testimony; if no other witnesses are available, just tell the known facts sincerely and truthfully.

3. You are well-prepared to serve as your own "key witness." You can get by without another witness, although you may add one if you wish.

4. Do the exercises in Chapter 18; then re-take this quiz.

How to Find Your Witnesses

If your score indicates you could benefit by having one or more witnesses testify during the trial, you should begin your witness search now.

Start by interviewing everyone who knows anything about the matter. For instance, if a friend was a passenger in the car you were driving when the accident happened, talk first to him. If you have the names of other eyewitnesses, contact them next. Ask them to discuss what they witnessed.

How to Interview Witnesses

The difference between an interview and ordinary verbal discussion involving questions and answers is that the interviewer makes notes of all important points discussed. *Carry your notebook with you and write down everything potential witnesses tell you.*

If people give you "leads" about persons who may have witnessed something important, make notes and *follow up the leads by contacting the persons who may be of help to you.* If an accident occurred, visit the scene; talk with local residents, shopkeepers, and employees. Ask such questions as:

- *Did you witness anything on (give the date, time, location and brief description of the accident or other occurrence)?*

- *What details do you recall?*

- *What caused you to witness what happened?*

Even if your score on the previous page indicates that your testimony and evidence are strong enough to merit serving as your own key witness, without calling other witnesses to testify in court, we recommend interviewing all possible witnesses as suggested in this chapter.

If you should change your mind and decide to call witnesses to testify, your preliminary homework is already done. No last-minute legwork will be necessary. By following the system outlined below, everything you need in reference to potential witnesses will be neatly arranged in your personal case files.

How to Organize Your Witnesses

When you have completed your investigation, organize the material you have gathered and store it in your "Witnesses File" as suggested here:

1. *Prepare Witness Profiles*—Using the form shown on the following page, make up a profile sheet for each person who is a potential witness. Jot down the main facts about which he may testify, or explain the kind of information he possesses. You may write phone numbers, dates, or all other relevant information about the person on his profile sheet. *Make a separate sheet for each witness, including one for yourself.*

Witness Profile Sheet

(Create witness profile sheets by copying this form on 8½ x 11-inch white paper.)

Name:_____ (do not use nickname)

Address:_____

City:_____ State_____ Zip:_____

Telephone: (home)_____ (work) _____

Personal Information: Age_____ Occupation _____

Other _____

_____

_____

Description of What Was Witnessed (fill in details):

_____

_____

_____

_____

_____

Other Notes:

When you have finished drafting a profile sheet for each witness, including one or more key witnesses you wish to call, continue organizing your witnesses as outlined here:

2. *Rate Your Witnesses in Order of Importance*—Your key witness—your "Most Valuable Witness" (MVW)—is the individual whose testimony is most important in proving your case. In the upper right corner of your "Witness Profile Sheet," write "1-MVW." *He will be the first witness called to testify for your side.*

   Your next "Most Valuable Witness" is a person whose testimony also offers positive proof that your claim is true—or your opponent's is not true. Mark the upper right corner of his folder "2-MVW." *You may wish to call him as your last witness, for the purpose of ending your presentation with testimony that makes a strong impression on the judge.*

   If more than two witnesses will appear for your side, rank the remainder in descending order of importance by marking their profile sheets with the designation "W" (witness): 3-W, 4-W, 5-W. Each witness should have a rating. *They will be called to testify between your first and last witnesses.*

   Presentation of the opening and closing testimony of strong witnesses, and introducing weaker testimony during the middle of the examination phase of the trial, is a technique used by professional lawyers. The value of this strategy to a *Pro Per* like yourself is that you leave no "loose ends" dangling for the opposition to grab in an effort to instantly unravel your presentation by attacking your last witness. More about this winning strategy appears in Chapter 18, "How to Organize Your Evidence."

3. *Store Your Witness Profile Sheets*—When all your profile sheets have been ranked in order of the Most Valuable Witnesses, arrange them in the following sequence, starting with 1-MVW and ending with 2-MVW:

   1—MVW
   3—W
   4—W
   5—W
   2—MVW

Store the profile sheets in your "Witnesses File" folder. They are now arranged in the order they will be called to testify in court. You may refer to these profile sheets when drafting your "List of Witnesses" as explained in this chapter.

Notify Your Witnesses

If you have not yet done so, notify each individual selected as a witness that you wish for him to testify on your behalf and serve him with a subpoena.

If an expert witness will testify for you, also serve him with a subpoena.

Contact all your witnesses a few days before the trial date to confirm their plans to appear.

How to Prepare Your "List of Witnesses"

When your witnesses have been lined up, you are ready to make up your "List of Witnesses." We suggest writing in pencil so erasures can be made easily if changes are required before your day in court. Prepare your "List of Witnesses" by referring to the "Witness Profile Sheets" you have just prepared, as follows:

1. Write the name of the first witness in your file (1-MVW) on the top line of the "List of Witnesses." Write the name of the second witness on the second line, the third witness on the third line, etc., until your list is complete. *Your second most valuable witness (2-MVW) should appear at the bottom of the list.*

2. Starting with your first witness, and descending down the list, assign a number (if you are the plaintiff) or letter (if you are the defendant) to each name. Start with "1" or "A" at the top and continue down the list. *Your second most valuable witness (2-MVW) should be assigned the second number or letter.*

3. In the upper left corner of each "Witness Profile Sheet" write the number or letter appearing for each person on your "List of Witnesses." These profile sheets are for your information only. They will not be submitted to the court; however, the valuable information contained on them provides concentrated reference material from which to draw when preparing for trial.

What to Do With Your List

After completing your handwritten or typed "List of Witnesses," make three copies and store them in the front of your "Witnesses File." If you prepare your list by hand, print the witnesses' names in capital letters. Also write a fairly accurate estimate of the witness's direct examination. You can base your estimate on the number and kind of questions you will ask and the answers you expect to receive from the witness. Make allowance also for the speed with which you and the witness speak.

If the judge requests a list of your witnesses, give him a copy, give counsel for your opponent the second copy, and keep the other copy for yourself.

List of Witnesses

(Use pencil to fill in the spaces. Plaintiff's witnesses are numbered starting with "1" and defendant's witnesses are lettered starting with "A.")

Witness Number/Letter	Name of Witness
_____	_____
_____	_____
_____	_____
_____	_____
_____	_____
_____	_____
_____	_____
_____	_____
_____	_____
_____	_____

Summarizing the Witness

Testimony is so vital to a trial that trial lawyers make the organization of witnesses a top priority. This is what your opposition is doing, and it is what you must also do *now*. Because witnesses are so important, considerable attention is devoted to the subject in this chapter and throughout the book.

When you have completed the exercises contained in this chapter, you are ready to proceed with the next step in your trial preparations—organizing your evidence and preparing your "List of Exhibits," as explained in Chapters 18 and 19.

"That which is crooked cannot be made straight: and that which is wanting cannot be numbered."—Ecclesiastes 1:15

Chapter 18

How to Organize Your Evidence

N O MATTER HOW CONVINCING your side's testimony may be during the trial, you cannot win your case by words alone; you must also have physical and/or documentary evidence. *Evidence is your proof that everything you claim during the trial is true.*

You have already set up your evidence files; you are now ready to begin filling them with facts which prove your case, or disprove your opponent's.

How to Build Your Evidence File
Each piece of evidence that you will offer the court is identified as an "exhibit." The process by which you will "offer your exhibits into evidence" is explained in another section of this book.

This chapter will help you organize your evidence in the order in which you will present it in court. As a start, take inventory of all the evidence you now possess—or plan to acquire—regardless of the order in which you will offer it during your trial. Since your witness or witnesses will testify about specific exhibits, plan to present your evidence to coordinate with the order in which your witnesses will testify.

Order of Evidence
If you are serving as your own side's key witness, you should plan to present evidence which corroborates the topic(s) about which you testify. In cases in which *Pro*

Pers appear on their own behalf, the most valuable (most important) evidence is often that about which they testify; therefore, if this is applicable in your matter, you will be the first witness to testify and, consequently, your most important evidence should be presented first, during your testimony.

Conversely, if the most important evidence you plan to present will be offered at the time you call an expert witness, coordinate your presentation so this evidence will be presented at the time the expert witness takes the stand.

You may use this worksheet to draft a list of exhibits you will present as evidence.

Evidence List Worksheet
(List all of the exhibits you plan to offer into evidence. Please use a new line for each separate piece of evidence. It is not necessary to write items in order of importance; later you will prepare a final list from this worksheet.)

_____

_____

_____

_____

_____

_____

_____

_____

_____

How to Prepare Your Evidence File
Your next step is to prepare your evidence file.

Check your worksheet to be certain you have noted all exhibits you plan to offer in evidence. Then prepare an exhibit cover sheet for each piece of evidence you will present by numbering the exhibits in the order in which you plan to present them in court, using this sequence:

- *Plaintiff:* 1, 2, 3, 4, 5, and so forth.
- *Defendant:* A, B, C, D, E, and so forth.

When exhibit cover sheets have been prepared for all evidence listed on your worksheet, your file is complete. Use this system for preparing your evidence file, or devise your own method:

1. *How to Prepare Exhibit Cover Sheets*

    Using 8½ by 11-inch white paper, make up an exhibit sheet for each piece of evidence you plan to present in court. Write in the center of the page, about two inches from the top of the sheet, the plaintiff's number or defendant's letter of identification; also include a brief one-line description of the evidence so numbered or lettered.

    You may pattern your own exhibit cover sheets from those illustrated below, which involve a breach of contract case in which the plaintiff sued a building contractor who failed to finish a wall after cashing the plaintiff's down-payment check.

1

Photo of half-finished wall

2

Copy of signed contract

3

Plaintiff's canceled check for advance payment

2. *How to Put Your Evidence in Order*

    Use your exhibit cover sheets as suggested here, or create your own system of evidence record-keeping based on this one-page-per-exhibit method.

    DOCUMENTARY EVIDENCE

    The bulk of documentary evidence involves papers or copies of information. Paper clip each piece of documentary evidence to its cover sheet. Include a separate cover sheet for each bill, memo, receipt, medical record, letter or other document.

    If you wish to make any notes or jot down additional information about an exhibit, write on the exhibit cover sheet. Never write directly on a piece of evidence.

    You may fold paper evidence, as long as it is neatly done, to fit into your file; however, a photograph, x-ray, or other evidence which could be damaged by folding should be stored elsewhere if it does not fit into the file in its flat form.

Other Physical Evidence

Physical evidence cannot always be stored in a file folder; it may be too large, too oddly shaped, too heavy or simply non-storable (as an injury to a plaintiff's body). Regardless of the reason a piece of evidence cannot be placed in the evidence file, a cover sheet for that piece of evidence should be kept in the file as a record of the exhibit.

The place where a piece of non-filed evidence is stored should be clearly noted on the cover sheet so you will always be able to find it. For instance:

1
X-ray of spinal column
(In manila envelope in bottom drawer of chest in master bedroom)

2
Orthopedic brace
(Top shelf of linen closet)

3
Defective ladder
(In defendant's garage)

Missing Evidence

If a piece of evidence is missing, or you have not yet acquired it, make up an exhibit sheet anyway; however, in the upper right-hand corner, add this notation: INCOMPLETE.

Write your follow-up notes to yourself on the cover sheet. When you have followed through and filed the missing piece of evidence, make a new cover sheet for your exhibit.

When there are no "incomplete" sheets remaining in your file, you will have finished compiling your evidence and your exhibits are now a part of your research records.

How to Store Your Evidence

Arrange your exhibit cover sheets in sequential order. If you are the plaintiff, exhibit cover sheet number 1 should appear on top, number 2 directly behind it, with the highest number (last exhibit) at the back of the file. If you are the defendant, exhibit cover sheet A should appear on top, B should be behind it, and so forth. Store your "Evidence File" with your other case records.

How to Measure the Value of an Exhibit

Is there a yardstick by which you can measure the value of each bit of evidence you will offer during your trial? No. The importance of a piece of evidence cannot be gauged by size, shape, or impressive appearance. To appraise your own evidence, ask yourself this question: *Does it prove my case?* If yes, the evidence is valuable. The more strongly it proves your case, the more valuable it is as evidence.

A lawsuit was once won by a man who claimed his signature had been forged by proving he always dotted an "i" with a tiny star; the forger had simply made a dot. The plaintiff won with evidence the size of a pinhead!

Summarizing Your Evidence

Many *Pro Pers* assume that every exhibit they offer into evidence will automatically be admitted by the judge. This is erroneous, because the judge, on its own motion or ruling in favor of your opponent's objection, will exclude any exhibit which he finds inadmissible according to the Rules of Evidence. Therefore, you may wonder how much evidence you really need.

Since there is no hard-and-fast rule about minimum or maximum number of exhibits that can be offered into evidence, gather as much proof as you can. It is safer to have more proof than you need than to find yourself empty-handed on your day in court.

However, if only one or two pieces of evidence are available, use them. The quality—not the quantity—of proof is what counts. It is better to have one good piece of substantial evidence than ten exhibits that prove nothing.

Before proceeding to the next chapter, please put your evidence file in order as suggested in this chapter. You will need this information to prepare the list of exhibits which you will offer into evidence in court.

Notes

Chapter 19

How to Prepare Your List of Exhibits

THE COURT REQUIRES each side in a lawsuit to submit a list of exhibits during the trial. This list outlines all the things you are offering into evidence.

An exhibit list contains two types of identification which will be described in this chapter, as well as the order in which you plan to present each piece of evidence during the trial proceedings.

Making up your list of exhibits will be easy, since you already did the basic groundwork in Chapter 18, "How To Organize Your Evidence." If you have not yet completed the steps discussed in Chapter 18, please do so before continuing as suggested below.

Introduction to Courtroom Exhibits

As a litigant, you are responsible for your own exhibits. You must see that the exhibits you plan to offer into evidence are present in the courtroom on the day of your trial. If, for example, you will offer paperwork evidence, you can probably carry it into court in your file folder or briefcase; however, if large objects such as a dented car bumper or broken ladder are part of your evidence, you must arrange their transportation into court.

In lieu of the actual bulky items, you may present photographs which clearly reveal the bumper's dents or the ladder's broken rungs.

Substituting photographs for bulky exhibits is not mandatory. Nor are there any hard-and-fast restrictions governing the kinds of things which may be offered into evidence. If a large item will fit through the courtroom door, and you are capable of getting it into court, it will be allowed.

A chiropractor, on trial for professional malpractice, once brought his complete office set-up into the courtroom, including his desk, filing cabinets, and spinal manipulation table. Following the trial—which he won—the chiropractor gave the bailiff a spinal adjustment which corrected a painful condition in his lumbar area (lower back).

Dangerous exhibits are restricted, however. For instance, a party would not be allowed to offer a ticking homemade time bomb into evidence simply to prove such an object could explode. Let common sense be your guide about exhibits to be presented in court.

Beware of Missing Evidence

The court frowns on missing evidence; therefore, if an item appears on your list of exhibits, be certain it is present in the courtroom on your day of trial. If you have any doubt about whether you will be able to present a specific piece of evidence, omit it from your list of exhibits.

If one of your witnesses is supposed to bring a document, record, or other piece of valuable evidence to court, your surest way of making certain it arrives is to serve him with a *Subpoena Duces Tecum* (a written legal request, delivered by a process server, commanding that specified records be supplied to the court).

How to Identify Your Exhibits

To prevent a mix-up of the exhibits offered into evidence by both the plaintiff and defendant in a trial, the opposite parties identify their exhibits in the following manner:

Plaintiff's exhibits are numbered—Starting with the number "1" at the top of the List of Exhibits, all the plaintiff's evidence is outlined in the order in which he plans to present it during the trial. A brief descriptive summary is included for each exhibit. The following exhibit list illustrates the evidence offered by a plaintiff in a personal injury case:

"1"	Smashed bumper
"2"	Photo of broken windshield
"3"	Note—defendant's license plate number
"4"	Receipt for car repairs*
"5"	Hospital bill**

---

*Testimony of an automobile mechanic may be required during trial.

**Testimony of a doctor may be required during trial.

In this example, the plaintiff listed his two pieces of most valuable proof first (number 1) and last (number 5). The smashed bumper contained fragments of blue paint which matched the paint on the defendant's car, and the hospital bill proved he had been treated for lacerations of the forehead which were caused by striking the windshield when hit from the rear.

Defendant's exhibits are lettered—Starting with the letter "A" at the top of the List of Exhibits, all the defendant's evidence is outlined in the order in which he plans to present it during the trial. A brief descriptive summary is included for each exhibit.

The following exhibit list illustrates the evidence offered by a defendant in a slip-and-fall case in which the plaintiff sued the hotel, which defendant managed, for damages sustained when he cut across the lawn and fell into an open trench. The defendant, who claimed the grounds were off-limits to hotel guests, won his case with these exhibits:

"A"	Registration slip signed by plaintiff
"B"	"No Trespassing" sign from hotel grounds
"C"	"Keep Off The Grass" sign from lawn area
"D"	Photograph of trench at noon
"E"	Photograph of trench at night

In this example, the defendant proved the plaintiff had signed a disclaimer, which appeared in fine print on the registration slip, waiving the hotel's responsibility for injuries or losses sustained through entry into unauthorized areas. The photograph taken at night showed the trench to be well-lighted and clearly visible to individuals exercising prudence and caution.

Order of Evidence Presentation

Many trial lawyers save the next-best evidence for presentation last; this strategy is not mandatory, nor are we recommending that you save your next-best evidence for last. However, understanding this strategy may help you decide the arrangement of evidence for your trial.

Lawyers using this technique reason that opening and closing their presentations with strong proof of their clients' claims will influence the judge about the truthfulness of the matter, even if some of the evidence introduced during proceedings leaves room for doubt.

Saving the next-best evidence for presentation last is not a guarantee that the judge will render a favorable ruling; however, lawyers sometimes present the second-strongest evidence last in order to make a final impact on the judge.

Introducing Best Evidence in Sequence

Other lawyers prefer to introduce evidence in descending sequential order, starting with the strongest evidence and backing it up with all other evidence. This is the technique you may wish to use; it is a standard procedure in civil courts and should serve you adequately.

The reasoning of lawyers who prefer to present best evidence first is: the first impression makes the greatest impact on a judge.

If you were a judge, what arrangement of your evidence would most likely impress you?

Sequential Exhibit Arrangement

Sequential presentation of evidence is especially adaptable to personal injury cases in which numerous medical bills have accrued as the result of treatment necessitated by the accident in issue.

Two steps are required to arrange your evidence in chronological sequence:

1. Present your most valuable exhibits first; that is, plan to introduce one, two, or more exhibits that prove your case most strongly. For example, present a photograph of you in a body cast, and an x-ray showing that your legs, ribs, and arm sustained fractures from the accident.

2. Present corollary evidence in chronological sequence (by date):

    a. Start by showing evidence that originated at the time of the accident, or shortly thereafter. For example, present the bill for the ambulance that took you to the hospital.

    b. Proceed forward toward the present time, so the most recent exhibit will be presented last. For example, present your final medical bill last.

How to Prepare Your List of Exhibits

Using a pencil, prepare your "List of Exhibits" by completing these steps in the order suggested here:

1. *Review your "Evidence File"*—Review the "Evidence File" you prepared according to instructions in Chapter 18. The exhibit cover sheets should be arranged in the order you plan to present your evidence in court. If you feel the sequence should be rearranged, change the order of evidence in your file before proceeding.

2. *Renumber your "Exhibit Cover Sheets"*—Renumber the exhibit cover pages in your "Evidence File" so they conform to the order in which they are now

arranged. The reason for such markings is to identify each exhibit during the trial; therefore, you will assign each piece of evidence a separate "Plaintiff's Exhibit Number" or "Defendant's Exhibit Letter" by writing in capital letters, in the center of your exhibit cover sheet:

EXHIBIT "1"

or

EXHIBIT "A"

Examples of Exhibit Arrangement

Two examples are given to illustrate the manner in which a plaintiff and defendant arranged the presentation of their evidence during trial.

Plaintiff's Exhibits

EXHIBIT "1"
Smashed car bumper

EXHIBIT "2"
Photo of broken windshield

EXHIBIT "3"
Note—defendant's license plate number

EXHIBIT "4"
Receipt for car repairs

EXHIBIT "5"
Hospital bill

Defendant's Exhibits

EXHIBIT "A"
Registration slip signed by plaintiff

EXHIBIT "B"
"No Trespassing" sign from hotel grounds

EXHIBIT "C"
"Keep Off the Grass" sign from lawn area

EXHIBIT "D"
Photograph of trench at noon

EXHIBIT "E"
Photograph of trench at night

The last exhibit cover in your file should have the highest number or letter; this is the final exhibit to be offered into evidence in court.

How to Make Your "List of Exhibits"
You are now ready to make your "List of Exhibits" to be offered into evidence during your trial.

Copy the exhibit identification number or letter, along with the corresponding brief description, onto the form on the opposite page. Include only one number or letter per line. The exhibits should appear in sequential order, beginning with the first evidence you will introduce and ending with the last exhibit.

Summarizing Your "List of Exhibits"
When you have filled in your "List of Exhibits," make three copies and store them in the front of your "Evidence File" for handy access when you need them most—on your day in court.

You may give one copy to the opposing party, give one to the judge, and keep one for yourself.

List of Exhibits

(List exhibits in the order they will be offered into evidence in court. If you are the plaintiff, list your exhibits by starting with "1" and continuing until all exhibits have been assigned a number. If you are the defendant, list your exhibits by starting with "A" and continuing until all exhibits have been assigned a letter.)

Number/Letter   **Description**

_____   _____

_____   _____

_____   _____

_____   _____

_____   _____

_____   _____

_____   _____

_____   _____

_____   _____

(If more space is needed, attach a separate sheet)

NOTES

Chapter 20

How to Prepare Your Own Case Outline

(Bonus Chapter)

THE NEXT STEP, preparation of the outline of your case, is optional. We suggest that you participate in this easy exercise because it begins tying together your case for trial.

Preparation of an outline puts you through the same paces a lawyer must undergo when representing a client; however, instead of spending one or more hours on the project, you can complete your outline in approximately five to seven minutes.

Understanding the Outline

In professional circles, an "abstract" is a written excerpt of a longer piece of work. An abstract may be a condensed version of a complete presentation or only a highlighted part of a greater work.

An abstract differs from other types of written documents because general details (often irrelevant to the main points) are omitted; only particular points of interest are included.

The briefest type of abstract is an outline. This is what you will now prepare. Your outline will serve as the preliminary blueprint of your trial presentation.

Purpose of Your Trial Outline

A trial outline is like a recipe: it sets forth all the necessary ingredients, along with the order in which they are mixed so the final result turns out right.

Your outline brings together the numerous aspects of your lawsuit on which you have worked thus far; from this, you will have a working trial plan to which you can refer throughout the balance of your preparations.

How to Prepare Your Outline

Your preliminary trial outline is broken into seven divisions, each of which is self-explanatory. The order in which the divisions appear parallel the order in which the same information will appear in your oral courtroom presentation.

As you fill in each section, you will be familiarizing yourself with the general sequence of your forthcoming trial.

To fill in the blanks in the outline which follows, you may refer to information you have already written in the pages of this book, as well as from material now stored in your case files.

Trial Outline

(Fill in the spaces with brief answers; use as few words as possible
to describe the nature of each point.)

1. *Name and Number of Your Case:*

   _____   _____

2. *Issue* (describe the grounds of action):

   _____

3. *Complaint or Defense* (explain your position in the matter)

   _____

   _____

   _____

   _____

4. *Witnesses*—Witnesses' testimonies are presented to prove your case.
   In court, the first witness to appear will be your key—or most important—witness. Write his name at the top of the list which follows. In court, your second most valuable witness will be called to testify last. Write his name at the bottom of the list below. Then, fill in the names of all other witnesses who will testify for you, in descending order of importance.

You may refer to your "List of Witnesses" (prepared according to instructions given in Chapter 17) to complete this portion of your outline. If you are the *plaintiff*, use the left margin to *number* each witness (starting with "1" as your first witness). If you are the *defendant*, use the left margin to *letter* each witness (starting with "A" as your first witness). If you are the only person who will testify on your side's behalf, no number or letter is necessary.

This is the order in which your witnesses will be called to testify in court during your trial. If you plan to call an expert witness, his name should be included on this list.

Name   **Summary of Nature of Testimony**

_____   _____

_____   _____

_____   _____

_____   _____

_____   _____

_____   _____

_____   _____

_____   _____

_____   _____

5. *Evidence*—Documentary and physical proof, and the testimony of witnesses, are presented as evidence to prove your case.

   Please refer to the "List of Exhibits" you prepared in Chapter 19. Copy it here, using the left-hand margin for your identification numbers (plaintiff) or letters (defendant). *This is the order in which you will offer your exhibits into evidence during your trial.*

_____   _____

_____   _____

_____   _____

_____   _____

5. *Evidence (continued)*

_____   _____

_____   _____

_____   _____

_____   _____

_____   _____

_____   _____

6. *Pertinent Law(s)*—Write the law(s) applying to your case in the following spaces. Summarize the law(s) in as few words as possible. If not possible, copy the law(s) on a separate sheet of paper and attach it to this page. You may wish to recite the law(s) during the argument phase of your trial, although such citations are not mandatory.

Identification   **Summary of Meaning**

7. *Prayer for Judgment* (List everything you will ask be granted to you. Be specific. Spell out precisely what you are seeking.))

_____

_____

_____

_____

Summarizing Your Outline

Your outline is actually an abstract—a condensation—of everything important you have prepared up to this point. If you are your only witness, did you remember to list your own name on the outline? Were there any sections you could not fill in? If yes, you probably should do some more homework.

The outline summarizes everything you have prepared thus far; it also doubles as your lawsuit's road map to the future. We suggest making two copies: one for your file and one for your pocket (for ready reference).

NOTES

Chapter 21

A Review of
Your Research

(Bonus Chapter)

WHEN YOU HAVE COMPLETED all the applicable suggestions contained in this section, you have finished your case research. This means you are ready to move forward toward your trial.

Did you leave anything undone? The exercises contained in this section are listed below. If anything remains to be finished, follow through just as quickly as you can. If possible, do it now!

Research Checklist
(Check the following points which you have completed. Then
follow through on any research remaining to be finished.)

	Chapter	Description
___	15	Evaluation of Your Evidence
___	15	Research Plan (facts to be gathered)
___	16	Outline of Law Questions (re: your case)
___	16	Record of Pertinent Law (summary of laws)
___	17	Witness Analysis (case quiz re: witnesses)
___	17	Witness Profile Sheets (one per witness)

	Chapter	Description
___	18	Outline of Evidence (to be offered in court)
___	18	Storing Exhibits (make cover sheets for file)
___	19	List of Exhibits (evidence to offer in court)
___	20	Abstract (outline of your presentation)

Pulling the Pieces Together

This concludes your basic introduction to the courtroom trial in general. The information you have learned up to this point can be adapted to every type of trial—both short and long, civil and criminal.

You have learned so much about the law in the short time you have been working with this book that you are no longer a mere beginner of do-it-yourself lawyering. You are ready to become a practicing *Pro Per*!

If you completed the exercises in this section, you are ready to advance beyond the broad spectrum of legal generalities into your own courtroom trial specifics.

In the next section of this book, you will learn what makes your kind of trial unique—and how to slant your presentation to fit its format. Or, as the popular saying goes, you are now prepared to "pull all the pieces together."

PART IV

HOW TO TRY YOUR OWN CASE IN COURT

SECTION IV EXPLAINS the general procedure for all civil trials. It also offers individual guidance in trying four specific types of civil matters in court: negligence (personal injury) trials, unlawful detainer (eviction) trials, traffic infraction trials, and small claims court trials. The issues of each type of trial are presented, along with general laws pertaining to such matters. Each trial is condensed into a script outline form with instructions for what to say and do in court; the *Pro Per* may fill in blank spaces with his own words which fit his case.

The two bonus chapters in this section introduce the *Pro Per* to the true facts about courtroom drama, and help him become acquainted with courtroom personnel he may meet on his day of trial.

Recommendation: To prepare to serve as your own trial attorney in the fastest way, select one chapter which fits your type of case and concentrate on studying it as many times as necessary to prepare you for court. Choose from Chapters 24, 25, 26, and 27. Also read Chapter 28. If time permits, you may also find that the bonus chapters, marked by asterisks (*), are helpful as well as interesting.

Chapter 22

The Courtroom Drama and How It Works

(Bonus Chapter)

Are you a television fan who is captivated by the lights, action, and glamour of today's action-packed courtroom dramas? If your answer is "yes" and you have never actually witnessed a real trial before, you may feel you are expected to act like a "star" on your day in court.

In actual fact, however, the majority of courtroom trials are far less dramatic than those whose highlights are depicted on the screen.

Knowing the similarities and differences between a professionally produced teledrama and a real-life trial can help you win your case in court.

There's No Business Like Show Business
The old saying is true that there is no business like show business. It is also true that the best advice the *Pro Per* can follow is: *leave anything that resembles show business out of your presentation.* For example:

- *Speech*—You do not need to take speech or drama lessons in order to prepare for your oral presentation; nor would a "stage voice" help you in your delivery. All the exercises you need for coaching yourself in delivering a winning presentation are included in this book.

- *Gestures*—You do not need to perform gestures or deliver heart-rending emotional scenes to convince the judge of your sincerity. In fact, the more dramatic an individual becomes during his trial, the more he undermines his own credibility with the judge.

- *Wardrobe*—You do not need a special wardrobe—especially anything that resembles a costume—for your courtroom appearance. The only person unusually attired in court should be the judge, whose black robe is symbolic of his respected position.

Leave the show business aspects of a trial to the paid professional performers you see on the screen. *On your day in court, simply be yourself.*

Lights, Camera, Action

A familiar saying that applies to production of a filmed drama is "lights…camera… action." Here is how these terms apply to your type of trial:

- *Lights*—The courtroom is neither a stage nor a set which must be theatrically illuminated. The only lights in most courtrooms are those which are permanent fixtures. Therefore, do not expect to stand in a spotlight when making your presentation. Instead, be prepared to make your delivery under modern-day overheads or wall lighting most frequently provided through fluorescent tubing or bulbs.

- Cameras—Do not expect to be photographed, filmed, or taped during your trial. Although the judiciary has relaxed some rules pertaining to courtroom protocol over the past few years, most courts still ban cameras, camcorders, and sound-recording equipment during trials. Therefore, do not attempt to bring unauthorized recording or film equipment into the courtroom. However, if you would like a picture of yourself as a personal memento, ask the clerk if you may have your photo taken in the courtroom during a recess or after your trial has ended. Some jurisdictions are more permissive than others.

- *Action*—Unlike professionally filmed or taped shows, in which the action is directed by a person working from the sidelines, your trial will be directed by the judge participating actively in the action.

These are the major differences between a theatrically produced courtroom drama and the sitting for a real trial. There is one aspect of both a teleplay and a trial that is similar: *both follow a script format.*

One Act in Five Scenes

Just as a play has one or more acts, which are broken into separate scenes, a trial also has separate and distinct parts. For this reason, a trial can be compared to a one-act play with five scenes: *opening, examination, arguments, decision, and appeal.* They are explained in this chart:

Five-Part Trial

(This chart summarizes the five parts of a trial. They
are listed in the order they occur during proceedings.)

Part	Meaning	Description of Action
I	*Opening* (start of proceedings)	The court is called to order, all parties are sworn or affirmed and the litigants approach the counsel table. If the plaintiff will make an opening statement, he delivers it now. The defendant may also make an opening statement now, or reserve it until later when he puts on his case. If no opening statements are given, the judge now instructs the litigants to proceed.
II	*Examination* (introduction of evidence)	The plaintiff's witnesses take the stand to tell what they observed or know about the issue. After direct examination by plaintiff's counsel or *Pro Per*, each witness may be cross-examined by the defendant. When plaintiff has finished presenting his case, he offers the exhibits in evidence. If the defendant objects to one or more of plaintiff's exhibits, the objectionable exhibits are argued by both parties. The judge rules for the admission or exclusion of plaintiff's evidence. With the admission of his exhibits, the plaintiff "rests." The defendant may now make his reserved opening statement. The defendant's witnesses take the stand to tell what they observed or know about the issue.

Part	Meaning	Description of Action

| II | *Examination* (continued) | After direct examination by defendant's counsel or *Pro Per*, each witness may be cross-examined by the plaintiff. |

When the defendant has finished presenting his case, he offers the exhibits in evidence. If the plaintiff objects to one or more of defendant's exhibits, the objectionable exhibits are argued by both parties. The judge rules for the admission or exclusion of defendant's evidence.

With the admission of his exhibits, the defendant "rests."

(rebuttal and surrebuttal)

Plaintiff may now rebut (challenge) specific portions of the defendant's presentation by: (1) introducing rebuttal physical and/or documentary evidence; (2) calling rebuttal witnesses. Plaintiff conducts direct examination of rebuttal witnesses; defendant cross-examines them. Plaintiff may re-direct examine the rebuttal witnesses; defendant may re-cross examine them.

The plaintiff offers rebuttal exhibits in evidence. Both parties argue these exhibits and the judge rules for the admission or exclusion of plaintiff's rebuttal evidence. The plaintiff then "rests."

Defendant may now rebut (challenge) specific portions of the plaintiff's rebuttal evidence by: (1) introducing sur-rebuttal evidence; (2) calling sur-rebuttal witnesses. Defendant conducts direct examination of sur-rebuttal witnesses; plaintiff cross-examines them. Defendant may re-direct examine the rebuttal witnesses; plaintiff may re-cross- examine them.

The defendant offers sur-rebuttal exhibits in evidence. Both parties argue these exhibits and the judge rules for the admission or exclusion of defendant's sur-rebuttal evidence. The defendant then "rests."

Part	Meaning	Description of Action
III	*Arguments* (case summation and prayers for judgment)	(Optional: Opening and closing arguments are presented in jury trials and in complex cases which require more than a short period of time for hearing. In short civil matters, such as small claims cases or short matters that are tried and disposed the same day, arguments are not required.) The plaintiff delivers his opening argument in which he attempts to convince the court he should win the case based on the evidence and the applicable law. The defendant delivers his argument by attempting to convince the court he should win the case as shown by the evidence and the law. The plaintiff then delivers his closing argument, rebutting defendant's interpretation of the evidence and the law, and prays to the court that the decision and judgment be rendered in his favor.
IV	*Decision* (findings made upon conclusion of trial)	The court's ruling is handed down: In a court trial, the court decides and renders judgment. In a jury trial, the jury decides who wins and the court renders the judgment. The court's decision is final, unless the case is taken on appeal (Step V).
V	*Appeal* (litigant's action for reversal of court's decision)	(Optional: If one of the litigants contests the court's decision by appealing it, the matter remains undisposed until the appellate court's final decision has been handed down.)

Like an Inverted Pyramid

A trial may be visualized as an inverted (upside-down) triangle whose broad base is at the top and whose apex (point) is at the bottom.

Your trial will proceed according to this geometrical pattern, starting with a broad, wide beginning and narrowing down to specifics upon which the court bases its decision and hands down judgment. This same illustration can be applied to stage or screen plays whose action narrows down to the final scene in which all conflict is resolved.

Note in the diagram on the next page how the courtroom action becomes more and more condensed as the proceedings progress from beginning to end. You may wish to place this outline on the counsel table during your day in court and refer to it as your trial road map during the proceedings.

The diagram included here is for a typical non-jury civil trial. In the event your case will be heard by a jury, the panel rather than the judge will "deliberate" the case and reach a decision. The authority rests with the court to impose the judgment or sentence.

Key Words You Need to Know

The only people justified in memorizing their courtroom presentations are professional actors who must follow their scripts. A *Pro Per* should not memorize testimony or arguments; however, you may memorize key courtroom language in order to make a favorable impression on the judge.

Since courtroom protocol includes usage of a few standard terms, which have long been traditional parts of judicial/legal language, you may wish to memorize the following courtroom dialogue. These ten words are the most commonly spoken legal terms in trials.

The easiest way to learn them is by writing each term on a separate three-by-five-inch card. Memorize one card at a time. Then practice making up sentences in which you speak these words aloud. The more you become familiar with them now, the easier it will be to integrate them into your courtroom language on your day of trial.

Chart of Trial Dialogue

(Memorize the following key words or phrases,
then use them during your trial.)

Word or Phrase	Meaning
Counselor	Proper form of address to be used when speaking to a lawyer.
Your Honor	Proper form of address to be used when speaking to the judge.
The defendant The defense	Proper way to refer to the defendant when the plaintiff addresses the judge during trial; however, "the defense" is the proper term the defendant uses to refer to his own side when addressing the judge or opposing counsel during trial.

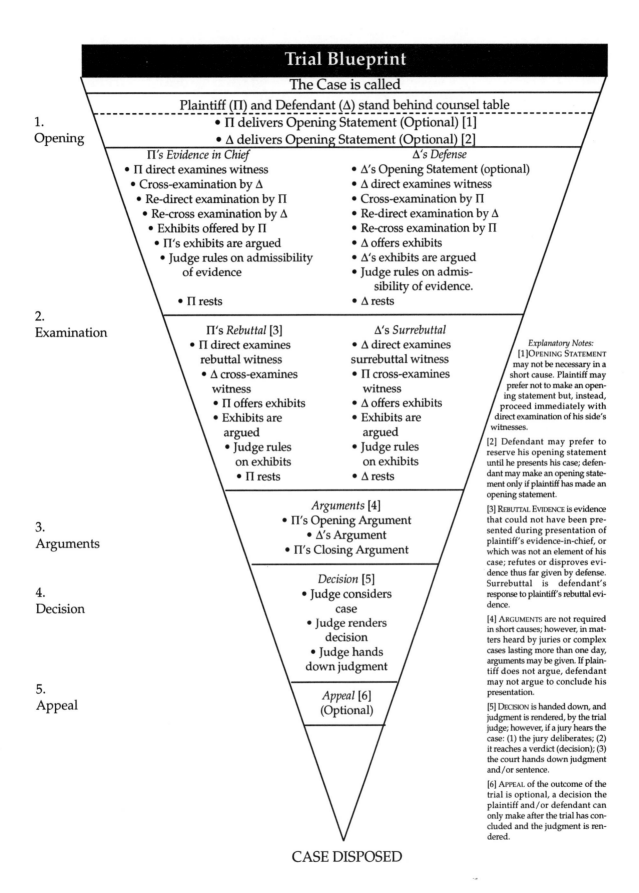

Trial Blueprint

The Case is called

Plaintiff (Π) and Defendant (Δ) stand behind counsel table

1. Opening

- Π delivers Opening Statement (Optional) [1]
- Δ delivers Opening Statement (Optional) [2]

Π's Evidence in Chief
- Π direct examines witness
- Cross-examination by Δ
- Re-direct examination by Π
- Re-cross examination by Δ
- Exhibits offered by Π
- Π's exhibits are argued
- Judge rules on admissibility of evidence

- Π rests

Δ's Defense
- Δ's Opening Statement (optional)
- Δ direct examines witness
- Cross-examination by Π
- Re-direct examination by Δ
- Re-cross examination by Π
- Δ offers exhibits
- Δ's exhibits are argued
- Judge rules on admissibility of evidence.

- Δ rests

2. Examination

Π's Rebuttal [3]
- Π direct examines rebuttal witness
- Δ cross-examines witness
- Π offers exhibits
- Exhibits are argued
- Judge rules on exhibits
- Π rests

Δ's Surrebuttal
- Δ direct examines surrebuttal witness
- Π cross-examines witness
- Δ offers exhibits
- Exhibits are argued
- Judge rules on exhibits
- Δ rests

3. Arguments

Arguments [4]
- Π's Opening Argument
- Δ's Argument
- Π's Closing Argument

4. Decision

Decision [5]
- Judge considers case
- Judge renders decision
- Judge hands down judgment

5. Appeal

Appeal [6]
(Optional)

CASE DISPOSED

Explanatory Notes:

[1] OPENING STATEMENT may not be necessary in a short cause. Plaintiff may prefer not to make an opening statement but, instead, proceed immediately with direct examination of his side's witnesses.

[2] Defendant may prefer to reserve his opening statement until he presents his case; defendant may make an opening statement only if plaintiff has made an opening statement.

[3] REBUTTAL EVIDENCE is evidence that could not have been presented during presentation of plaintiff's evidence-in-chief, or which was not an element of his case; refutes or disproves evidence thus far given by defense. Surrebuttal is defendant's response to plaintiff's rebuttal evidence.

[4] ARGUMENTS are not required in short causes; however, in matters heard by juries or complex cases lasting more than one day, arguments may be given. If plaintiff does not argue, defendant may not argue to conclude his presentation.

[5] DECISION is handed down, and judgment is rendered, by the trial judge; however, if a jury hears the case: (1) the jury deliberates; (2) it reaches a verdict (decision); (3) the court hands down judgment and/or sentence.

[6] APPEAL of the outcome of the trial is optional, a decision the plaintiff and/or defendant can only make after the trial has concluded and the judgment is rendered.

The plaintiff	Proper way to refer to the plaintiff when the defendant addresses the judge during trial. Also, the correct way for the plaintiff to refer to his own side when addressing the judge or opposing counsel during the trial.
Objection	A one-word statement indicating plaintiff objects to the defendant's questioning of a witness, or that the defendant objects to the plaintiff's questioning of a witness. Also, a term meaning the party objects to an exhibit being introduced or offered by the opposition.
No objection*	A term indicating that one side does not oppose testimony or an exhibit being offered by his adversary. Consequently, the testimony or exhibit is admitted.
Submitted	A term used by one side to inform the court that this party has said everything that needed to be said in support of, or in opposition to, a motion or objection made by the other party and now asks the court to rule on the motion or objection.
Nothing further	A term used by a party to advise the court he has completed his examination of a witness.
Plaintiff rests	A term used by the plaintiff to indicate he has completed a phase in the proceedings. He rests when the examination of his side's witnesses is finished and his exhibits are admitted in evidence; he also rests when his rebuttal is ended.
Defense rests	A term used by the defendant to indicate he has completed a phase in the proceedings. He rests when he has finished the examination of his side's witnesses and his exhibits are admitted in evidence; he rests when his sur-rebuttal is finished.

---

*"No objection" is a term often used incorrectly in courtroom movies and TV shows. For example, the plaintiff makes a motion. In response, the defendant says, "No objection." The court record now shows that the defendant did not disagree with the plaintiff; therefore, if the defendant should later take issue with the subject of the plaintiff's motion, he may not be allowed to do so because his "no objection" response literally meant: *I do not oppose.*

The correct—and safest—response would have been, "Submitted, Your Honor." This tells the court: *I have already said everything I intend to say at this time; therefore, I request the court to rule.* This approach allows the defendant to say something further about the subject in issue when it comes up again.

To protect your position during your trial, stick with the phrase "Submitted, Your Honor" and eliminate "No objection" from your courtroom dialogue.

How to Practice Trial Dialogue

In the privacy of your home or office, practice mixing and matching the key courtroom terms on the foregoing chart by making up your own sentences. Stand on your feet and speak up. Here are a few examples to help you get started. You may fill in the blanks with words which fit your own case:

Introduction
(Given at start of trial while standing at the counsel table.)

> *Your Honor, my name is* (your name) _____.
> *I am the (plaintiff/defendant).*

Making an Objection
(Stand up. State your objection and reason for objecting.)

> *Objection! Plaintiff's question is irrelevant.*
> *Objection! Defendant is leading the witness.*

Response to Opposition's Objection, Motion, or Argument
(Advises the court you have nothing more to say and asks the court to rule on the objection, motion, or argument.)

> *Submitted, Your Honor.*

Ending Examination of Witness
(When you have finished questioning a witness.)

> *Nothing further, Your Honor.*
> *No further questions, Your Honor.*

Resting
(When you have completed the presentation of your case, you rest; the other party now takes the floor.)

> *The plaintiff rests, Your Honor.*
> *The defense rests, Your Honor.*

The Pros and Cons of Television Dramas

Would watching television courtroom dramas be beneficial to your trial preparations? This may depend upon why you are watching such programs. Consider these facts:

Since the end of World War II in 1945, America's court calendars have become increasingly backlogged as litigation becomes a way of life. Increased population, as well as rising crimes and civil torts, are responsible for many of these court cases; however, television has also contributed to this increase by educating people about justice through the entertainment medium.

The popularity of two post-World War II series provided more pro-court publicity than all combined legal, judicial, or political campaigns generated between 1776 and 1957, the year Perry Mason made his television debut.

America's Most Beloved Defense Attorney

Between 1957 and 1965, more than three hundred black-and-white episodes of *Perry Mason* were filmed. Based on characters created by Erle Stanley Gardner, actor Raymond Burr starred as the indomitable defense attorney, who was assisted by his loyal secretary, Della Street, played by actress Barbara Hale.

Although the characters and crimes were different in every episode, the basic plot line was the same for every script: an innocent person, accused of a crime based on circumstantial evidence, was represented by Perry Mason. During a preliminary hearing or in trial, the prosecution almost pinned the guilt on the defendant; however, through his own private investigation into the facts, combined with his expert cross-examination of witnesses, Perry Mason caused the real guilty party to confess. The charges were subsequently dropped against the accused.

Perry Mason became the most famous lawyer of history, and while he never really existed he continues to be the world's most beloved defense attorney!

Thirty years after the series made its debut, Burr and Hale continued performing in *Perry Mason* television movies, which followed the same basic format that has held three generation of viewers armchair captives to courtroom drama.

Realistic Trials on Television

The most popular nonfictitious television courtroom show of the last quarter of the twentieth century is *The People's Court,* a nationally syndicated daily production featuring retired Los Angeles Superior Court Judge Joseph A. Wapner.

In this program, Judge Wapner hears civil matters which have been diverted from the public court calendar into his studio courtroom. These cases are disposed on camera and then filed with the court having jurisdiction.

Because of the authenticity of the judge's rulings, and his over-the-air explanations of applicable laws upon which his decisions are based, the viewing public has become both litigation-oriented and law-conscious. Instead of taking the law into their own hands, more people today are taking their unresolved disputes to court than ever before.

A forerunner to *The People's Court* and several other similar productions was the popular daytime show, *A Day in Court,* filmed live in Hollywood at the same time the weekly segments of *Perry Mason* were first captivating prime-time viewers.

A guest judge, sitting behind the bench on the CBS set, heard fictitious cases enacted by unknown actors and actresses who made up their lines while the cameras rolled. Shortly before the filming started, the performers were handed typewritten plot outlines with character sketches of the people they would play. Based upon the few facts they were given, each person improvised his lines as the proceedings progressed.

The spontaneity—and, therefore, the believability—of the performers, who often stuttered and stumbled over their lines, catapulted Southern California into its love affair with litigation, both dramatized and nonfictional. Los Angeles is one of the litigation capitals of America.

Has the public's interest in television courtroom dramas decreased over the past thirty years? No. It has increased. In 1990, the popular series, *L.A. Law,* based on the soap-opera format in which miniscenes involving several characters and subplots are shown in one segment, was one of the most highly rated programs on prime time network television.

Did Television Influence This Book?

Wanda Sue Parrott, who assisted me in writing this book, was studying creative writing in Hollywood between 1958 and 1962; she held part-time odd jobs, one of which was as a bit player in motion pictures and television. One of her first speaking roles was on *A Day in Court,* at which time she played an eyewitness to a crime that never really happened. It was also her first exposure to the courtroom scene. Intrigued with law, she became a professional writer and part-time *Pro Per,* handling all her own legal matters for more than the past quarter century.

Her journalism career began with *The Seaside News-Sentinel* in Monterey, California, in 1964. She later spent seven years with *The Los Angeles Herald Examiner* and two years with *The Valley News* (a subsidiary of *The Chicago Tribune*) before establishing her own publishing firm in 1980.

Between editorial assignments, Wanda has filled several short-term positions in the law enforcement/legal and judicial fields, including: plainclothes undercover detective, police stenographer, legal secretary, and assistant to Joetta L. Moore, executive judicial secretary of the Van Nuys Branch of the Los Angeles Superior Court.

Wanda helped me convert my thoughts into easy-to-understand English, when it would have been far simpler to write a book for judges, lawyers, and law students. Despite her background as a *Pro Per,* her attendance at countless civil and criminal trials, sitting on two jury panels, and participation in several community legal committees in the San Fernando Valley area of Southern California, Wanda never lost her ability to explain legal procedures in non-legal language.

Wanda's love for the law began with one appearance on *A Day in Court.* It lasted a lifetime!

Did television influence this book? Yes, but only indirectly. If Wanda had never been exposed to the television courtroom, maybe she would not have become a *Pro Per*—and *How to Try Your Own Case in Court—and Win!* might still be an incomplete manuscript, or would have been written by me as a book for lawyers.

Does this imply I heartily endorse television courtroom dramas as a way for you to learn to try your own case in court—and win? No!

Summarizing the Courtroom Drama

There are three reasons I am biased against television courtroom series. First, they are overdramatized. Second, they are unrealistic. Third, they contain procedural inaccuracies which could mislead you—and cause you to lose your own case in court.

So, whether or not you can benefit from watching television courtroom shows depends entirely on your reason for watching such programs. If you like good entertainment, such programming can provide it. Or if you wish to familiarize yourself with the court trial, or to test yourself on how well you understand what you have learned in this book, you may profit from watching such presentations.

However, if you are planning to imitate a trial lawyer like Perry Mason, switch channels!

Chapter 23

Introduction to Key Courtroom Figures

(Bonus Chapter)

I f you have never been in court before, you should become acquainted with five courtroom figures you may meet on your day in court.

The most important individual you will encounter in the courtroom is the judge; however, he is not the first officer of the court with whom you will deal. Instead, the first two courtroom personnel with whom you will speak are the court clerk and the bailiff.

This chapter explains the roles they play in the overall courtroom proceedings. Advice is also offered about how to make a winning impression on these two individuals upon whom the judge relies both professionally and confidentially.

Introducing the Court Clerk

Often considered a "judge's third hand," the clerk assists the judge in whose courtroom he is assigned by being responsible for all paperwork related to his court's activities. He also informs the judge about all courtroom business, including relaying messages, handling telephone calls, and confiding information to the judge about the behavior, attitudes, or other conduct of litigants and other parties in the courtroom.

The clerk usually remains in the courtroom when the judge is in his chambers or on recess. If you must deliver a pretrial message to the judge, the clerk will convey it to him.

A few things about which you should be aware are outlined below:

- *Check in Early*—Arrive between fifteen and thirty minutes early and check in with the court clerk. Let him know you are present. Also, check the court calendar, which may either be posted on the courtroom door or is in the clerk's possession, to be certain your case is listed.

- *Advise Him If You Leave*—If you must visit the rest room or make a telephone call, or otherwise step out of the courtroom, tell the clerk where you are going and how long you will be gone. Then be certain you return on time. If the clerk is busy, hand him a note; print your name and the message. If you do not, the following may happen: if you are the plaintiff, the judge may dismiss the case; if you are the defendant, the judge may hear the plaintiff in your absence and render judgment against you.

- *Keep Your Business to Yourself*—Do not "bend the ear" of the clerk or attempt to get "buddy-buddy" by running through a pretrial recitation of your side of the legal matter. Keep your business to yourself and let him concentrate on his.

Practice good manners by observing the following common courtesies to enhance your courtroom etiquette:

- *Refrain from Asking for Opinions*—The clerk gives your case file to the judge prior to the trial so he can read through it to familiarize himself with the matter you will be trying. The clerk may also have glanced through the pleading. Never ask for the clerk's opinion on your case, or one similar to yours.

- *Questions You Should Never Ask*—A court clerk cannot give legal advice, so never ask for it. However, he does have the authority to suggest where you may go or what you may do in an emergency. If you must ask questions, confine them to topics of a nonlegal nature. Two other questions you should never ask are: "May I use your telephone?" and "May I have a cup of your coffee?" Last, never pry into the judge's personality or private life or ask, "Is he fair, tough, or middle-of-the-road?"

- *Make Patience Your Virtue*—Nothing makes a person more uncomfortable than to have someone pacing up and down, drumming his fingers, muttering under his breath, or constantly checking his watch if an appointment is running late. If your trial does not begin on time and you cannot wait, approach the clerk calmly and tell him your situation. He will advise you about what to do. Even if you must reset the trial date, you will have done so courteously without subjecting him to unpleasant pressure, which he may report to the judge.

Summarizing the Court Clerk

Although the clerk may appear as a low-key figure in courtroom proceedings, he is actually entrusted with high-powered responsibilities, which include swearing and affirming of witnesses, preparation of "minute orders" (highlights of a trial), and serving as confidante to the judge.

Stay on his good side and the clerk might not say anything about you to the judge; however, get on his bad side and you can be certain the judge will hear about it and, therefore, will have an adverse impression of you before your trial even begins.

Introducing the Bailiff

The bailiff is usually, although not always, a uniformed, armed officer, whose main responsibility is maintenance of order in the courtroom and security for persons assembled therein.

The bailiff often assists the court clerk; however, there are specific responsibilities with which a court clerk never helps a bailiff, such as bringing prisoners into a courtroom to serve as witnesses and escorting jurors to and from the jury room.

A few things you should know about bailiffs include:

- *Nonuniformed Officers*—Some courts employ "civilian bailiffs" who wear regular business clothing while on duty. Along with their main duties of maintaining courtroom order and security, they admit people in and out of the courtroom. They also answer questions about the court and judicial procedures. In this way, they serve the judge by acting as hosts or guides; also, bailiffs may function as public relations representatives of the court system.

- *Civil versus Criminal Courts*—In most civil trials, only one bailiff is present in a courtroom. Criminal cases often require the presence of several uniformed officers during a trial. In a civil court requiring only minimum security, one bailiff may serve several courtrooms at a time by dividing his time among them.

Summarizing the Bailiff

The courtroom bailiff is usually a congenial individual. To stay on his good side, do not ask him to run errands for you, make phone calls on your behalf, or bring you a cup of coffee. The bailiff is present in the courtroom to be of service, *not to act as a servant.*

Along with the court clerk and bailiff, there is another courtroom figure who may be involved in your trial, the court reporter.

Introducing the Court Reporter

A court reporter is not an official "officer" of the court. He reports courtroom proceedings and may also take depositions. The court reporter prepares word-for-word transcripts of the proceedings.

Most of today's court reporters work on portable machines called stenograph machines similar to typewriters; however, the operator can touch several keys at the same time. Their tapes are later transcribed on computers or typewriters. Software now on the market transcribes the tapes simultaneously.

The main difference between a court reporter and a stenographer is that the "steno" takes his own notes in shorthand, often writing between 180 and 225 words per minute or faster. Stenos are rare in court today.

In Superior Court trials, a court reporter is always present; however, in the types of civil cases tried in many Municipal Courts, the minute order prepared by the court clerk is the only record of the trial that is required.

A few things you should know about court reporters follow:

- *Who Makes the Decision* to have or not have a court reporter? That is often the question in court. The judge who will hear the case decides whether or not to use the services of a court reporter.

- *Who Pays the Reporter?*—Some courts retain a staff of court reporters, while others retain them on a temporary or part-time basis. Reporters assigned by the court are paid by the jurisdiction in which the court is located.

- *Can You Bring Your Own Reporter?*—If the court is not going to use the services of a court reporter, but you want a transcript of your trial, can you bring your own reporter? Yes, but you must pay for his services.

Summarizing the Court Reporter

In most trials of the types outlined in this book, the services of a court reporter are not necessary. However, in the event you wish to use a reporter, you may contact your local Bar Association for references or check the "Legal" listings in your Yellow Pages for court-reporting services. Or a "steno" may be available through a local employment or temporary job service agency.

Do not attempt to tape record the trial for the purpose of having a transcript prepared later. No recording equipment is allowed in most courtrooms. In California, with the court's permission, you can tape record for your own personal use only.

Introducing the Judge

The judge is the key courtroom figure. His job is summed up in three words: *dispensation of justice*. Vested with authority none of the other courtroom personnel possess, his is a fourfold power:

- *The Power to Make Rulings*—A "ruling" is the establishment of a rule or guideline decided by the judge during the course of a trial. The judge's rulings represent the official position of the court and should not be contested by the parties to an action. Three of the most frequent rulings are:

1. RULING ON MOTIONS: A motion is a request for the court to grant a favor, usually to the party making the motion. After considering the motion, the judge grants it or denies it. If you must make a request during the trial, state it as a motion. For example: *Your Honor, I move that the witness be excused.*

2. RULING ON EVIDENCE: After hearing both parties argue an exhibit that has been introduced into evidence, the judge makes his ruling. If he admits an exhibit into evidence, it is allowed into the case record and may be taken under consideration for the purpose of reaching a decision. Exhibits not admitted into evidence will not be considered in reaching a decision, but they are part of the case file.

3. RULING ON WITNESSES: The judge may rule that one witness be excused while also ruling that another witness be recalled for further testimony.

The judge's rulings constitute "court orders" and participants in a trial should abide by them. Failure to honor a ruling could result in a "contempt of court" finding against the party who refused to obey the court's order.

- *The Power to Render Decisions*—A judge does not "cast judgment" on people; he hears the testimony and considers the evidence presented during the trial and then makes a decision. His decision is based both on the evidence and the law. He may decide "for" the plaintiff or "for" the defendant. The decision upon which the outcome of your case is based is actually the main "ruling" made by the judge. If he decides in your favor, you win. If he rules for the opposition, you lose. If he decides there was not enough evidence to constitute a case, he will find for the defendant. The judge's decision stands unless it is reversed or modified through "appeal."

- *The Power to Hand Down Judgment*—The judge has the power to state precisely the rights and obligations of the parties by spelling out exactly how the injury, damage, loss, or other injustice shall be resolved. If monetary compensation is sought, the judge outlines how much is to be paid, to whom it shall be paid, and by whom it must be paid.

- *The Contempt Power*—To maintain order, the judge has the power to cite in contempt of court any person who disrupts the proceedings. The judge will then order the bailiff to put that person in jail.

Some of the most frequently asked questions about judges are included here. Knowing the answers will relieve you of the temptation to raise these questions with the court clerk and bailiff:

Q. *How Does a Judge Get His Job?*
A. By public election or through appointment to the Bench by the governor of the state. In California, the governor appoints only lawyers who have been certified as qualified by the State Bar Commission on Judicial Nominees Evaluation (Jenny Commission). Each state has its own rules regarding how judges get their jobs.

Q. *How Does a Judge Take Office?*
A. After being appointed to the Bench, an individual must be sworn into office by a person authorized to administer the oath, following which the new judge is qualified to wear the robe which symbolizes the high honor conferred upon him.

Q. Is a Judge "Titled"?
A. When speaking to the judge, address him (or her) as "Your Honor." When writing to a judge, his proper name should be preceded by the "The Honorable," as shown here:

The Honorable John Jones
Judge of the Municipal Court

Informally, however, you may refer to Judge Jones or Judge Smith.

Q. *Were All Judges Formerly Lawyers?*
A. In most places the answer is yes. However, in some remote areas of the country, a disappearing breed of judges known as "Justice of the Peace" still exists. These "justices" may or may not be licensed to practice law; however, they are duly authorized to perform a number of legal duties which include, but are not limited to, performing civil marriage ceremonies and hearing cases in court.

Q. *Can Judges Practice Law?*
A. When he takes his oath of office, a judge exchanges his right to practice law for the privilege of dispensing justice. While serving in a judgeship, an individual is not allowed to practice law; however, after his retirement or resignation from the Bench, he may re-enter the legal profession.

Although the judge possesses greater knowledge of the law than most other courtroom personnel, you should never ask him for legal advice. As a dispenser of justice, the judge is a neutral party. As a neutral party, he is not allowed to give legal advice.

An Inside Look at the Judge's Chambers

The judge's "chambers" are more than just an office. Here he has his library of law books, along with his desk, chairs, and other furniture, which may include a couch and table. Whether his chambers consist of a large apartment-sized suite or one tiny room, this is his private space which may be decorated with paintings, potted plants, or throw rugs that reflect his own personality.

Some judges' chambers contain refrigerators, microwave ovens, stereos, and television sets. Others contain little more than is required to conduct business.

Most judges' chambers have a private bathroom, which may or may not contain a shower.

You may be called into the judge's chambers to discuss your case or to participate in a conference with the opposing party. In such a situation, you will have the opportunity to enter into informal, relaxed discussions about your legal matter. While in the judge's private quarters, practice the same good manners you would use as a guest in another person's home.

How Much Liberty Can You Take?

If you are wearing a suit, do not remove your coat just because the judge may take off his robe when inside his chambers.

Some judges are more informal than others. If a judge put his feet up on the desk during your meeting, should you lean back and also put your feet up? Definitely not. Keep your feet on the floor.

Can you smoke in his chambers? Not unless he invites you to do so. In California, smoking is not allowed in the courthouse.

How much liberty can you take in the judge's chambers? You must set your own standards. An easy way to do this is to avoid saying and doing anything which invades his privacy.

For example, regardless of how relaxed you feel in the presence of the judge, here are three ways to avoid invasion of his privacy: *avoid asking if you can use the judge's restroom by visiting the facilities provided by the court before you enter his chambers; do not request permission to make a phone call on his private telephone; never inquire about how much money he makes.*

While his salary is a matter of public record, it is a private matter to the judge. If you really want to know how much judges make in your area, check with the local office of your state's judicial council, bar association, or court clerk.

How Judges Are Paid

Individuals who leave private law practices to serve on the Bench usually take sizable cuts in pay. Most practicing attorneys earn considerably more money than the judges who hear their cases in court.

Such lawyers are in *private practice* while judges are *public servants* whose salaries are paid by the taxpayers whom they serve.

Although salary scales vary among the many jurisdictions across the country, most are based on a sliding scale. For example, municipal court judges earn less than superior court or circuit court judges, while justices of the highest court of appeal receive more than the other judicial officers in the state.

How to Help the Judge Help You

By tailoring your presentation to suit the judge's temperament, you can increase your chances of winning by helping him perform his job with ease and proficiency.

There are three basic judicial temperaments, and the judge who hears your case will possess one of them:

- *The Objective Judge*—Temperamentally "tough," he may appear insensitive. The best way to make your presentation to this type of judge is through the application of logic. Concentrate on the facts, underemphasize the emotion, and keep your own feelings in check.

- *The Subjective Judge*—Temperamentally "kind," he may appear sensitive. The best way to make your presentation to this type of judge is to avoid overly dry dullness. Inject a few colorful words to create an image, or briefly describe an action or sensation. Be careful not to be too long-winded or to get swept up in your own emotions.

- *The Imperturbable Judge*—Temperamentally "even," he may appear unpredictable. The best approach to a presentation made before a judge of this type is through a fairly even mix of logic and feeling. You may spice up the facts with a few brief emotion-stirring descriptions, but guard against letting your own feelings become dominant in court.

If you cannot "read" the judge—that is, intuitively perceive whether he is objective, subjective, or imperturbable—do not guess at his temperament, because you may be wrong.

Instead, stick with the facts and avoid strategies designed to appeal to the judge's emotions. When in doubt, let logic win out.

Summarizing the Judge

Regardless of his own temperament, the judge who hears your case will attempt to render a fair decision and judgment based on the pertinent law and evidence presented during the trial.

The judge is the most important courtroom figure. There remains one other important courtroom figure upon whose presence effective communication with the judge may depend: the *interpreter.*

Introducing the Interpreter

An interpreter is an individual who speaks two or more languages fluently and who is able to verbally translate courtroom proceedings as they occur so that the judge and litigants and/or witnesses understand each other.

If you are not fluent in English, you need the services of an interpreter during your trial.

Some courts supply interpreters; others require that you bring your own interpreter into the courtroom. Check with the court clerk before your date of trial to find out whether you must supply your own interpreter. If the court supplies the interpreter, make your arrangements early so you will be assured the interpreter will be available for your trial.

If you must bring your own interpreter to court, plan this important aspect of your trial early.

Where to Find Interpreters

Professional interpreters are listed under "Languages" in the Yellow Pages of most telephone directories.

Also, teachers or advanced students of foreign languages sometimes work as interpreters; they may be contacted through local private language schools or through the foreign language departments of local high schools, colleges or universities.

If you cannot locate an interpreter through the Yellow Pages, your local Bar Association may be able to refer you to individuals who may be of service. Also, the court clerk may give you one or more names to call.

Can a personal friend or acquaintance serve as your interpreter? Yes, provided *he neither has any interest in, nor any involvement with, your lawsuit.*

Summarizing the Interpreter

If you are fluent in the English language, you do not require the services of an interpreter. However, if you intend to call a witness who is not fluent in English, you need an interpreter.

When you check in with the court clerk on the day of your trial, notify him that you have brought your own interpreter and give him the interpreter's name.

Final Words About Courtroom Personnel

This concludes your introduction to the key courtroom personnel you may expect to meet during your day in court. Your next big step is to meet them in person as you enter the courtroom and try your own case to win!

Introduction to Your Own Trial

The next four chapters give step-by-step instructions about how to try your own case in court. Each chapter covers one of the types of trials best suited for trial by *Pro Pers.*

Regardless of which type of trial you will conduct as your own legal counselor, there are four things you should know which will complete your pre-trial training: *venue, jurisdiction, peremptory challenge,* and *judicial recusal.*

Insight into Venue and Jurisdiction

Venue means "location."

Jurisdiction means "the court's power."

For example, accident cases are usually tried in the court which has jurisdiction over such matters in the venue where the accident occurred, even if the parties to the action live elsewhere. This means that if a tourist from Hawaii and a resident of San Diego, California, are involved in an accident in Los Angeles, the trial will be held in Los Angeles. In California, the action may be filed in the county where the injury occurs or where the defendant resides.

Sometimes, however, a "change of venue" results in the matter being moved to another courthouse in a different judicial district. For example, a change of venue may occur in a widely publicized criminal matter, in order for the defendant to receive a fair hearing.

Changes of venue are seldom, if ever, granted in the types of civil matters covered in the next four chapters. For example, a party in an unlawful detainer suit (eviction proceeding) may not request a change of venue simply because he has moved out of the area and finds it inconvenient to return to the locality in which the court has jurisdiction.

If you are the defendant in a civil matter, and you live outside the judicial district where the trial is scheduled, you must go to court—because the court will not come to you. If you fail to appear, you will be in "default" and the plaintiff will win.

There are exceptions to the venue rule, however. A change of venue may be granted if the plaintiff or defendant files a *Motion for Change of Venue* with the court where the plaintiff's complaint was filed. Such a motion must be based on one of these grounds:

Grounds for Motion for Change of Venue

1. A fair and impartial trial cannot be held in the court where it is now scheduled.

2. The convenience of witnesses and the ends of justice would be better served by a change of venue.

3. The court does not have a judge qualified to act in this matter.

For instance, if the judge assigned to hear your case is the brother of the defendant, and no other judge is available to hear the matter, a change of venue may be granted. This leads back to the key courtroom figure in your trial: *the judge.*

How to Exercise Peremptory Challenge

As a litigant, you have the right to exercise "peremptory challenge." This means you may request the removal of the judge assigned to hear your case because you believe he may be prejudiced against you or otherwise biased.

Timeliness is of utmost importance in exercising peremptory challenge. As soon as you become aware of the identity of the judge assigned to hear your case in court, you should file your motion (*Affidavit of Prejudice*) requesting the removal of the judge.

It is not usually necessary to state your reasons for believing the judge is prejudiced. The clerk of your local court will provide you with the proper form. Simply tell the clerk, "I want to file an affidavit of prejudice."

Introducing Judicial Recusal

Finally, there is another method by which the judge assigned to hear your case may be removed. In "judicial recusal," the judge recuses himself!

Why would a judge remove himself from his assignment to hear your case? He may feel he is biased and, therefore, unable to render an impartial decision. Or he may have a personal interest in the matter that causes him to believe justice would be best served if another judicial officer heard the case.

If the judge assigned to hear your matter recuses himself, you may or may not be given a reason for his recusal. When you arrive in court, your case will be tried before another judge.

Notes

Notes

Notes

Chapter 24

How to Try Your Own Negligence Case

(Personal Injury)

More cases involving negligence are now tried in civil courts than five years ago. If your case involves an injury or damage, and fits any of the following descriptions, this chapter will help you with your trial.

Definition of Negligence

Negligence is *the failure to use reasonable care while performing an act; participating in an action, event, or other condition; or otherwise doing something which a reasonably prudent person would not do under similar circumstances.* There are two broad classifications into which all matters involving negligence fall, one of which describes your case:

- *Negligence*—Any type of negligence other than professional malpractice. Both professional and nonprofessional persons may be liable for this type of negligence.

- *Professional Negligence*—Also known as "professional malpractice," this type of negligence occurs while a professional person is engaged in the performance or practice of his professional line of work.

The legal yardstick by which the court measures a defendant's liability in this type of case is the degree or extent of his "comparative negligence" and the plaintiff's "contributory negligence." In other words, what is the amount of the defendant's negligence compared to the plaintiff's contributory negligence?

For example: the defendant's negligence is found to be seventy percent (70%) and the plaintiff's negligence is thirty percent (30%). If the plaintiff's damages amounted to $20,000, he gets only $14,000 (plaintiff's 30% contributory negligence, $6,000, is deducted from $20,000).

Introducing Duty of Care

To arrive at a defendant's degree of negligence, if any, the judge determines the defendant's "duty of care" and evaluates his observance of this duty of care in light of his act or omission resulting in plaintiff's damages. The usual duty of care is: *that care a reasonable, prudent person would observe under the same or similar conditions.*

For example, a man looked out his kitchen window and saw that his yard was on fire. He thought the fire was not big enough to do any harm, and it would burn out by itself. By not doing anything, he did not do what a reasonable, prudent person would do under the same circumstances (exercise standard duty of care; i.e., putting out the fire).

If the same man ignored the fire after becoming aware of it, allowing it to burn out of control and destroy his neighbor's home, he would be negligent and, therefore, liable for his neighbor's damages.

In a professional malpractice case, the standard of care is measured by the action a reasonable, prudent professional would exercise under the same or similar conditions in his field of practice.

For instance, a plaintiff-patient sued her dentist for professional malpractice. The dentist, who did not check the patient's file before filling her tooth, administered an anesthetic to which she was allergic. Although the anesthetic was commonly used by all dentists in the area, and the defendant used it on most of his patients with no side effects, the court found he had failed to exercise the standard of care commonly practiced by other local dentists who routinely check patients' files before, not after, giving treatment.

The Other Side of Negligence

Negligence is not measurable solely by something a person did. It can also be measured by something a person could have done or did not do.

For instance, most drivers slow down at blind curves. However, the defendant in a personal injury case disregarded the posted road signs; instead of slowing down, he sped around several dangerous curves, crossing the center dividing line at a high rate of speed. His negligence was found to be the proximate cause of an accident that could have been avoided if he had exercised a reasonable, prudent person's care while driving under dangerous conditions.

Introducing Negligence Trials

There are six types of negligence matters most frequently tried in civil courts. Five come under the general heading of "negligence" and the sixth is "professional negligence." Read the following descriptions to determine which category best describes your case.

I. Negligence

- PERSONAL INJURY—As the name implies, this type of case involves injury or damage sustained by one's person (body, mind, or emotions). In California and most other areas, the term "P.I." commonly refers to legal matters involving vehicular accidents resulting in injury or damage. The automobile is the vehicle most often linked to P.I. cases; however, any "over the road" (OTR) vehicles may be involved in P.I. matters, such as buses, trucks, vans, motorcycles, and any other motor-driven modes of transportation associated with street, road, or highway traffic.

- LAND OWNERS AND OCCUPANTS—This type of injury case involves claims filed against owners and occupants of property or premises whose failure to exercise ordinary and prudent care in the use, management, or maintenance of such property or premises resulted in harm or damage to a guest or user. For example, a guest sued the owner of the farm for negligence after he fell into a dry cistern and broke both legs; the owner had neither cleared debris away from the well nor posted notice of its existence. In another case, a man was injured when the roof of the house he was visiting fell in on him; the occupant had not treated the house for termites, although he was aware of their presence, and the timbers collapsed.

- SLIP AND FALL—This type of lawsuit is filed by a plaintiff who has slipped, fallen, and injured himself and/or damaged his personal property in a public place. For instance, a woman slipped and fell, sustaining a brain concussion, on an icy street; a leaky water hydrant had not been repaired by the city utility company although the seepage had been reported by several people. Slip-and-fall cases may also occur on private property. A man slipped on the uncarpeted stairway of a Las Vegas casino and broke his back; the hotel's proprietor had failed to cordon off the staircase or post warning signs during renovation of the premises.

- ACCIDENT—This general label is a catchall for various accidents that fall outside the specific injury-or-damage-related cases listed here. For example, a bank customer walked into a glass door, smashing his nose and cutting his eyes so severely surgery was required to remove the splinters from his broken eyeglasses; he won his case by proving the door, which looked as if it were open, bore no markings or signs inside or outside the glass. In another case, a woman won her lawsuit by proving negligence on the part of the county, which operated a public equestrian trail. While riding her horse, the animal stepped on a live electric wire and was electrocuted; the woman fell with the horse, hitting her head on a rock. The court awarded judgment for both personal injuries and damages (loss of the horse and general damages for pain and suffering) sustained as a result of the accident).

- PRODUCT LIABILITY—This type of matter involves injury or damage sustained by persons who use products that are defective, dangerous, or otherwise the cause of harm. For example, a plaintiff won his lawsuit against a bottled water company by proving that, when he attempted to place the large jug in his cooler, it broke, severing his thumb. In court, he won by producing the bottle, through which a large hairline crack ran the length of the container. In another product liability case, the plaintiff won by proving that the manufacturer of a line of electric toasters used uncovered wiring in its elements; her toaster had caught fire, burning her face and hair so badly that she required plastic surgery on her lips and nose.

II. Professional Negligence

- PROFESSIONAL MALPRACTICE—This type of case involves injury or damage sustained by the client or patient of a professional practitioner. For instance, a tax accountant failed to prepare his client's income tax returns correctly and caused an investigation by the Internal Revenue Service, which revealed the client was liable for thousands of dollars of unpaid taxes. Or a dentist extracted a patient's incisor, which could have been saved, without first taking an x-ray to determine the condition of the tooth; because of the needless extraction, expensive bridgework was required to fill in the gap in the patient's mouth. Also called "professional negligence," these negligence cases involve claims against professionally licensed persons in such fields as accounting, dentistry, law, medicine, and psychology/psychiatry.

In these cases the issues are "liability" and "damages." To prove the defendant's liability, the plaintiff should show that: (1) the plaintiff was negligent; (2) the defendant's negligence was the "proximate or legal cause" of the injury, loss, or damage. Further details are given in this chapter.

Insight into Negligence
If you are the plaintiff, you must be able to prove that the defendant was negligent. Strong and convincing evidence is best: testimony corroborated by documentary and

physical evidence. Tangible evidence that can be seen or touched makes excellent proof in this type of matter. You may also call expert witnesses whose opinions support your contention.

If you are the defendant, you must be able to prove you were not negligent. Support your position with as much documentary and physical evidence, and testimony, as you can gather. You, too, may call one or more eyewitnesses to testify in your defense.

Regardless of whether you are the plaintiff or the defendant, remember these points when trying your own case in court:

- Do not call the adverse party a liar during court proceedings, even if you know he is not telling the truth.

- Instead, concentrate on building a solid, believable case that supports your position.

After hearing all the evidence, the judge will reach his decision and award judgment.

Introducing Proximate Cause

A standard legal term applicable to negligence matters is "proximate cause." A proximate cause of injury, damage, loss, or harm is one which, in natural and continuous sequence, produced the injury, harm, damage, or loss, and without which cause the injury, harm, damage, or loss would not have occurred.

When a jury will decide a case, the judge gives the jurors instructions on the legal points to consider during deliberation. Proximate cause is always considered in negligence matters. The jurors are instructed to ask themselves, "Has the conduct of the defendant caused the plaintiff's loss?" If your negligence case is heard by a judge, rather than a jury, he will contemplate this same question before reaching his decision.

Proving Proximate Cause

In the types of cases covered in this chapter, the plaintiff must prove by "a preponderance of the evidence" that:

- The defendant's negligence proximately caused the plaintiff's damages.

- The plaintiff's injuries and other damages did not exist before the occurrence and only came about because of the defendant's negligence.

A proximate cause may not necessarily be an accident, but may be the reason the accident occurred. For example, a plaintiff, who sustained serious injuries and destruction of his automobile in a head-on collision with a runaway truck, won his case by proving the proximate cause was the trucking firm's failure to service the big rig after it completed a cross-country haul. As a result, the truck's brakes failed and the driver lost control, crossing the center divider and smashing into the plaintiff's oncoming car.

An expert witness, testifying on behalf of the plaintiff, stated that if the truck had been serviced, its brake fluid would have been replaced; therefore, the brakes would not have failed and the driver probably would not have lost control.

A witness employed by the trucking firm testified that the company had recently initiated a cost-cutting program in which trucks were serviced every twenty thousand miles rather than after every cross-country trip.

Because the plaintiff was able to prove his accident resulted from the defendant's negligence, the proximate cause, he was awarded damages for both his personal injuries and property damage.

How to Time Proximate Cause
This hypothetical time frame outlines the sequence of events considered in the determination of a proximate cause.

Sequence of a Proximate Cause

- BEFORE—The proximate cause precedes the accident or mishap.

- DURING—The proximate cause causes the accident to occur.

- AFTER—Injury and other damage brought about by the accident.

If you are the plaintiff, winning your negligence case in court depends on how convincingly you establish the proximate cause of your damages. However, while establishment of proximate cause goes a long way toward helping you win, it is not enough; you must also convince the judge that the opposition's negligence was the proximate cause of your loss or damages.

If you are the defendant, your possibility of winning is greatly enhanced if you can prove you were not negligent; that is, you must prove you were neither irresponsible nor responsible for any actions contributing to the proximate cause.

Legal Cause
When two or more causes may have brought about the injury, the cause (called "legal cause") that is a substantial factor in bringing about the injury is used instead of proximate cause. For example, in a three-car collision, the second car bumped the first car lightly, but hit it hard the second time because the third car was going very fast when it rear-ended the second car. Here, the legal cause of the first driver's injury is the third driver's negligence.

(Note: In California, the state Supreme Court found, in *Mitchell vs. Gonzales* 54 C3 1041 [December 1991], the *"But for"* test of causation [Proximate Cause] to be *obsolete*, and ruled that the *"Substantial factor"* test [Legal Cause] *should now be applied in all California cases.)* Our California Jury Instruction BAJI 3.76 states: "The law defines cause in its own particular way. A cause of injury, damage, loss or harm is something that is a substantial factor in bringing about an injury, damage, loss or harm."

Introducing Comparative Negligence

The judge takes every aspect of a case into consideration before rendering his decision and handing down judgment. One of the factors he considers is "comparative negligence," in which the extent and degree of the plaintiff's negligence is subtracted from the plaintiff's total damages.

Here is how comparative negligence may affect the outcome of your trial. If, in the judge's opinion, the defendant is proven by the plaintiff to be totally negligent, his decision will be for the plaintiff. The defendant loses. He must make the plaintiff "whole." This means he must restore the plaintiff to his former condition, plus compensate him for his pain and suffering, in an approximated monetary value determined by the judge.

If the judge is not convinced the defendant was negligent in any manner, he will find for the defendant. The plaintiff loses. The defendant is not ordered to make any restitution to the plaintiff.

In the event the judge finds that both parties were negligent, he will apportion his decision and consequent judgment between the litigants. When both parties are ordered to share a percentage of the responsibility, the judge makes a "comparative negligence" decision.

What is a comparative negligence decision? It is a decision in which the percentages of negligence are divided between the litigants. For example, in a personal injury case, the judge found the plaintiff thirty per cent (30%) negligent and the defendant seventy per cent (70%) negligent. If the judge finds that the plaintiff was contributorily negligent, and the plaintiff's negligence contributed to the defendant's negligence which brought about the proximate or legal cause of the plaintiff's injury, here is what you can expect:

1. The total damages sustained by the plaintiff will be determined.

2. The plaintiff's percentage of negligence will be subtracted.

3. The balance will be the amount awarded to the plaintiff.

Introducing the Prevailing Party

In matters involving negligence, the "prevailing" party wins. Does this mean the prevailing party is always the party with the smallest percentage, if any, of contributory negligence? No.

For example, the plaintiff in a personal injury case was seeking $10,000 in damages. However, the court found that the plaintiff was eighty per cent (80%) negligent; that is, his negligence contributed to the defendant's negligence which was the proximate cause of the accident.

Although the plaintiff prevailed in this hypothetical case, the defendant was only ordered to pay the plaintiff $2,000 in damages, or twenty per cent (20%) of the original damages sought by the plaintiff.

Introducing Statutes of Limitations

If you wait too long to file your complaint, you may be out of luck. Every area has "statutes of limitations," which govern the length of time a plaintiff may file his lawsuit after an accident or any other cause of action has occurred.

For instance, in most areas the statute of limitations for filing a personal injury (P.I.) suit is one year. If, for example, a car accident occurred on October 31, 1991, but the plaintiff waited until November 1, 1992, to file his civil claim in court, the statute of limitations would have run out. In other matters, the statute of limitations may be two, three, or four years.

Therefore, if you are the plaintiff, you must file your complaint within the time period allowed, following the occurrence which gave rise to your cause of action.

To determine the statute of limitations applicable to your case, check the following publications at your local law library; it is possible they are also available in the reference section of your public library: *for civil matters check your state's Code of Civil Procedure, and for criminal matters check your state's Penal Code.*

Introducing the Demurrer

If you are the defendant against whom the plaintiff files a complaint after the statute of limitations has run out, you may file a demurrer to the complaint. This form, available from the courthouse where the plaintiff's complaint was filed, notifies the court that the plaintiff's complaint was filed after the statute of limitations had run out. What advantage, if any, is there in filing a demurrer? Quite simply this: the defendant prevails!

Exceptions to Statutes of Limitations

Perhaps, as a plaintiff, you have a valid reason for not filing your complaint before the statute of limitations ran out. Were you sick, incapacitated, or receiving special treatment that was required after you sustained the damage for which you now wish to sue the party who caused your injury? Were you a minor when your injury occurred, although you now have attained majority status? Is there any chance you might still file your lawsuit, although the statute of limitations has run out? You may qualify as an "exception" under the rules governing statutes of limitations in your area.

Most states have limited specific exceptions to statutes of limitations; they spell out specific conditions under which extensions may be granted. To determine whether your legal matter qualifies as an exception to your area's statute of limitations, check your state's Code of Civil Procedure or Penal Code.

How to Settle Without a Trial

If you and your opponent agree that you would prefer not to take your matter to trial, you may arrange a "settlement conference" with the judge scheduled to hear your matter in court. The purpose of such a conference is to discuss the matter in the privacy of the judge's chambers.

With the judge serving as a mediator or arbitrator, you and the adverse party lay your cards on the table and enter into a discussion aimed at reaching a mutually satisfactory agreement to both sides. If such an agreement is reached, the matter will be duly recorded by the court clerk and the case will be taken off the calendar or dismissed.

Because the settlement conference enables the litigants to avoid going to trial, it is a quick and inexpensive way to dispose the matter in less time than would be required by going to trial.

In Los Angeles, civil cases are first referred to ADR (Alternative Dispute Resolution). The court orders litigants to attempt to settle their matters before trial. Your area may have the same requirement.

The clerk of the court where your case was filed can advise you of the rules applicable to settlement conferences and arbitration/mediation procedures in your area. In both arbitration and mediation, a court-appointed official or volunteer helps litigants resolve their differences and reach an agreement.

If you and the opposition should settle the matter privately between yourselves, out of court, the plaintiff should file a report with the court clerk; your case will then be removed from the court calendar or dismissed. However, if you are not able to reach an agreement by using any of the methods outlined here, your matter will go to trial. There, the judge makes the decisions you and the opposition were unable to achieve.

Tips on Winning Your Negligence Trial

In a negligence trial, half the battle consists of proper preparation and the other half involves proving your case to the judge. The following pretrial tips and techniques slash legal red tape by telling you exactly what is required for putting together a winning presentation.

The specific types of cases already introduced in this chapter are included. If your case does not fall under one of the categories outlined here, I suggest you either follow the advice given for "Accident Cases" or construct your own general outline based on the suggestions you feel are most applicable to your matter.

Insight into Personal Injury Cases

The majority of P.I. cases involve one or more types of insurance: insured and/or uninsured motorist; health; accidental death and dismemberment; medical; life; Medicare, etc. One or more insurance settlements may be involved in your P.I. matter, depending on the nature of the accident and extent of damages and injuries sustained by you or the other party.

If you are covered by insurance, the accident should be reported immediately. Whether you are the plaintiff or defendant, make copies of all reports in writing. If you call your agent to report the accident, follow up the telephone conversation with a written memo recalling the key issues you discussed. If you meet with your agent, or the insurance firm's lawyer, make notes of the topics you discussed. Keep copies of all communications with your insurance carrier in your file. You may never need them; however, in the event the insurer defaults and you file suit against the insurance carrier, you will need this information as evidence.

If you are not covered by any insurance, or your insurance carrier fails to defend you or honor the policy under which you are covered, I suggest you contact an attorney who specializes in P.I. matters. Explain your situation to the lawyer and ask if he would be willing to handle your case on a "contingent basis." Lawyers handle contingency cases only for plaintiffs in matters in which the defendants' liability is clear. If the lawyer agrees to take your matter "on contingency," he will receive a percentage of the settlement money. P.I. lawyers often take as much as forty per cent (40%) of settlements if the cases are litigated in court; otherwise, they may charge thirty-three and one-third percent (33⅓%) of settlements reached out of court.

For example, in a $100,000 settlement reached in court, a P.I. attorney received $40,000 plus costs of the suit. His client paid no money out of his own pocket. In another $100,000 settlement, however, the attorney received $33,334 for a matter settled out of court. Consider these facts:

- An attorney willing to work on contingency believes the case has such an excellent chance of winning that he is willing to take a risk by representing you.

- A lawyer unwilling to take your matter on a contingent basis may not believe you stand much chance of winning. He may offer to handle the case for a fee, meaning you pay out-of-pocket as the matter proceeds. In such an event, you are the person taking the risk. If you lose, you will not recover your legal fees; however, the lawyer has been paid for his professional services.

Contingent fee arrangements may not be feasible for an attorney, particularly if only a small amount of money stands to be recovered. Even if he is convinced you stand an excellent chance of winning, his time and professional services may exceed the compensation he would receive by taking a percentage of your settlement. In such an instance, the lawyer may agree to take your case only if you agree to pay his fees.

Representation by a lawyer is entirely out of the question if your P.I. case will be heard in small claims court, where the law requires both plaintiffs and defendants to appear as *Pro Pers*.

Issues in Personal Injury Trials
Whether you are represented in your P.I. matter by an attorney or yourself, your trial presentation must include one or more of these issues:

P.I. Plaintiff
As plaintiff, you must prove by a preponderance of the evidence:

- There was an accident.
- The party being sued (defendant) was negligent.
- The defendant's negligence was the proximate or legal cause of your injuries and damages.
- The injuries and damages you sustained.

P.I. Defendant
As defendant, you must prove in your affirmative defense:

- There was no accident.

Or, if you admit there was an accident, you must prove:

- You were not negligent.
- You were not responsible for the plaintiff's injuries/damages; or
- Plaintiff was contributorily negligent.

Or, if taking issue with plaintiff's claim of harm, prove:

- Plaintiff's injuries and damages are not what he claims.

For instance, if you know the plaintiff broke his arm after the accident, not during it, as he claims, you must be able to disprove his contention that you caused his injury. Or, if the plaintiff's rear fender was already crumpled at the time your car smashed into his, you must be able to prove you were not responsible for this portion of his damages.

Insight into Land Owners and Occupants Cases

In this type of case, the plaintiff sustained injuries from a condition on privately owned land or in privately owned premises because:

- The occupant did not exercise ordinary care in its use, management, or maintenance; or

- The owner did not exercise ordinary care in its use, management, or maintenance.

For example, if you were shopping in a store where merchandise was improperly maintained by the proprietor, and you were struck by a top-heavy shelf which suddenly fell over, the proprietor would be the defendant in your lawsuit. Although he leases the premises from the property's actual owner, he is responsible for exercising ordinary care in the operation of his business. However, in cases of this nature, it is often the best practice for a plaintiff to include the lessor (property owner) as co-defendant in the lawsuit.

For instance, if you were shopping in a store when fire broke out, caused by substandard wiring throughout the building, here is how this lawsuit should be handled:

1. First, you should sue both the owner and occupant for your injuries and/or damages by naming them as co-defendants in your lawsuit. An example is:

    John Smith, Plaintiff, versus Alan Greene and William Wright, Defendants

2. Second, the proprietor-tenant of the business may then sue the owner-landlord, who failed to exercise ordinary care in the maintenance of his building, for indemnification and, in addition, the tenant should also sue the landlord for his (tenant's) own losses and damages.

Instead of filing two separate lawsuits (one against the shop owner and the other against the owner of the building), by naming them both defendants you need file only one complaint. Copies of your complaint must be served to both parties according to the instructions given in Chapter 6, "How to File Your Case in Court."

As plaintiff bringing suit against the owner of the shop, your only concern is the step you should take. You need not be concerned about whether the proprietor-tenant does or does not file his own lawsuit against his landlord.

Instead of receiving injuries or damage in or on private property, if you were in a public building or on public land when the injury or damage occurred, the defendant in your lawsuit would be the city, county, state, or federal agency whose duty of care includes use, management, or maintenance of the land/premises. For example:

John Smith, Plaintiff, vs. County of Kern

Issues in a Land Owners and Occupants Case

Whether you are represented in your land owners and occupants case by an attorney or you are appearing as a *Pro Per,* your trial presentation must include the following:

Land Owners and Occupants Plaintiff

As plaintiff, you must prove by a preponderance of the evidence:

- The owner/occupant did not exercise reasonable care in the use, management, or maintenance of the land/premises, resulting in the harmful or dangerous condition;

- Defendant's negligence proximately or legally caused your injuries while you were at, in, or on his land.

- The nature, degree and extent of your injury and other damages.

The land owner did not exercise reasonable care if he had notice of the dangerous condition or the dangerous condition had existed long enough for a reasonable person to discover it, fix, or remove it, or give warning to foreseeable land users.

Land Owners and Occupants Defendant

As defendant, you must prove either or all of the following, depending on the evidence:

- Plaintiff sustained his injuries/damages elsewhere, not on your property or in your premises.

- You had exercised ordinary care in the use, management, or maintenance of the land/premises, and the conditions were safe at the time the plaintiff claims he suffered his injury or damage.

- The plaintiff was contributorily or solely negligent.

- You did not have notice or sufficient time to learn about, repair, or remove the harmful or dangerous condition.

- The plaintiff did not sustain any injury on your property or in your premises; or

- The plaintiff's injuries and/or damages were not as serious as claimed.

Insight into Slip and Fall Cases

In this type of case, the plaintiff sustained injuries or damages from slipping and falling on private or public land. The conditions in this type of case are similar to those in a land-owners-and-occupants matter in which the plaintiff sues the party responsible for care and maintenance of the site where his injuries/damages were sustained. For further information, refer to "Insight into Land Owners and Occupants Cases" on the preceding pages.

Issues in a Slip and Fall Case

Whether you are represented in your slip and fall case by a lawyer or you serve as your own legal counsel, your trial presentation must include the following:

Slip and Fall Plaintiff

As plaintiff, you must prove by a preponderance of the evidence:

- The defendant did not exercise reasonable care in the use and maintenance of the premises.

- While at defendant's premises, you slipped and fell and sustained injuries and other damages.

- Defendant's negligence proximately or legally caused your injury and other damages.

- You were unaware of the dangerous or otherwise unsafe condition(s) at the time you ventured into or onto the accident location, but defendant knew or should have reasonably known the dangerous condition.

- The nature, degree, and extent of your injury and other damages.

Slip and Fall Defendant

As the defendant, you must prove one or more of the following issues:

- The plaintiff did not sustain injury or damage from falling.

- The plaintiff's injuries and/or damages were not sustained at the site of the accident.

- Plaintiff knew of the condition and assumed the risk in using the premises.

- The plaintiff was contributorily negligent.

- The accident site was not dangerous or unsafe at the time the plaintiff slipped and fell.

- You (or the public agency or firm you represent) had exercised ordinary care in the use, management, or maintenance of the accident site.

- The plaintiff's harm was less than he claims it to be.

- Defendant did not know or could not have reasonably known the condition.

Insight into Accident Cases
In this type of general case category, an accident occurs which injures one's person and/or damages his property. All kinds of accidents basically fall into this category, although specific classes of actions which frequently result in lawsuits are broken down into such self-explanatory subcategories as the aforementioned "slip and fall," "personal injury," and "landowners and occupants." The basic guidelines given here may be adapted to fit every type of accident case involving negligence as the proximate or legal cause.

Issues in an Accident Case
Whether you are represented in your accident case by a lawyer or you serve as your own attorney, your trial presentation should be built around the following issues:

Accident Case Plaintiff
As plaintiff in an accident case, you must prove by a preponderance of the evidence:

- Defendant was negligent.

- Defendant's negligence was the proximate or legal cause of plaintiff's injuries and other damages.

- The nature, extent, and degree of your injuries and other damages.

Accident Case Defendant
As the defendant in an accident case, you must prove one or more of the following issues:

- The plaintiff did not have an accident; or

- The plaintiff was contributorily negligent, causing his own accident or contributing to its occurrence.

- You were not negligent but, instead, exercised due care.

- The plaintiff did not sustain his damage or injury as a result of his accident.

- The plaintiff's damages are less than he claims them to be.

Insight into Product Liability Case
This type of case differs from other accident categories because products, usually those which have been commercially manufactured and sold, are the cause of the plaintiff's injuries and/or damages. Insurance settlements are frequently involved in this type of lawsuit. If your product liability case involves serious injuries and, therefore,

possibly a large settlement, you will be best represented by an attorney who specializes in product liability matters. The same advice which applies to personal injury (P.I.) cases pertains to product liability.

If, however, yours is a fairly uncomplicated small claims case in which you are seeking a refund from the manufacturer of a defective product and compensation for minor injuries sustained from an accident caused by the product, you should have no difficulty serving as a *Pro Per*, provided you can substantiate your position with convincing evidence.

Issues in a Product Liability Case

Whether you are represented by a lawyer or serve as a *Pro Per*, your product liability presentation must be based on these issues:

Product Liability Plaintiff

As plaintiff, you must prove by a preponderance of the evidence:*

- You were injured by a defective, dangerous, or harmful product.

- Defendant's negligence proximately or legally caused your injury or damages.

- Defendant's negligence consisted of:
  a. Supplier did not reasonably warn of the dangerous conditions of the product when he had reason to believe that the consumer would not notice the danger.
  b. Manufacturer did not exercise reasonable care in the manufacture, testing, and inspection of the product.
  c. Seller did not reasonably inspect and test the product before selling it when he had reason to know that the product was likely to be dangerously defective.

- The nature, degree and extent of your injury or other damages.

In addition to your cause of action for negligence, as plaintiff in a products liability case, you may also proceed on two theories: "Strict Liability in Tort" and "Warranty Liability."

Strict Liability in Tort

As plaintiff, you must prove:

- The defendant's status as manufacturer of the article, retailer or otherwise.

---

*BAJI 9.20, 9.21, 9.24, California Jury Instructions. If you are not a California resident, similar provisions are contained in your area's jury instructions.

- That the article was defective.

- That the defect existed when the article left the possession of the defendant.

- That the article was used in a manner reasonably foreseeable by the defendant.

- That the defect was a proximate or legal cause of injury to the plaintiff.

- The nature and extent of plaintiff's injuries.*

Warranty Liability
As plaintiff, you must prove that:

- The defendant expressly warranted the goods and the plaintiff relied on the warranty (express warranty); or

  a. The defendant knew why the plaintiff needed the goods and the plaintiff relied on the defendant's skill or knowledge in the selection of the needed goods; or

  b. The defendant sold goods which are reasonably expected to be reasonably fit for its purpose (implied warranty of merchantability). Example: the defendant sells items he labeled as shoes and, therefore, he impliedly warrants that the buyer can use the goods just like any other pair of shoes.

- The defendant breached the warranty.

- The plaintiff gave notice of the breach to the defendant and asked for damages; the defendant did not pay the plaintiff's damages.

- The nature, degree, and extent of the plaintiff's damages.

Product Liability Defendant
As the defendant in a product liability case, you must prove one or more of these issues in your affirmative defense:

- The plaintiff was not injured; or

- The plaintiff's injury was not proximately or legally caused by your product.

- You were not negligent because you exercised reasonable care in the manufacture, inspection, testing, and distribution of the product.

---

*BAJI 9.00, California Jury Instructions. If you are not a California resident, similar provisions are contained in your area's jury instructions.

• The plaintiff's injuries and damages were not what he claims them to be.

• You honored your warranty.

Insight into Professional Malpractice Cases

Negligence is the key issue in a professional malpractice case. Although professional malpractice cases may be difficult for *Pro Pers* to win if they are not well prepared, you may be able to successfully handle your own matter by working with one or more expert witnesses (whom you will have to pay to testify as your witnesses).

Because the plaintiff's expert witnesses are pitted against the defendant's expert witnesses, the professional malpractice trial is unofficially called "the battle of the experts."

The reason a professional malpractice case is difficult for an inexperienced *Pro Per* to win is that you are suing an expert in his own field. If your injuries or damages are serious, you would be best represented by a lawyer; however, if your matter is a small claims case or relatively uncomplicated, you may handle it yourself.

In a professional malpractice trial the plaintiff testifies about his problem(s) which require(d) the services of the professional person (defendant). He testifies that he hired the professional, but that instead of solving the plaintiff's problems, the professional made them worse.

The plaintiff testifies that he suffered damages; he describes their nature, degree, and extent, and he introduces proof of his claim. The plaintiff then calls an expert witness who is in the same profession as the defendant. The expert witness testifies about the standard of learning and skill of reputable professionals in the locality, and that the defendant does not have that same degree of learning and skill; and/or, he testifies that reputable professionals in the locality, using their care, skill, diligence, and best judgment, would have handled the plaintiff's problems differently and/or would have applied other procedures or methods.

The expert witness would then give his opinion: the defendant was negligent because he failed to fulfill his duty of care as a professional in this particular field.

The defendant in the professional malpractice trial testifies about his degree of learning and skill. He testifies that he used the care, skill, diligence, and best judgment exercised by any reputable practitioner in the locality.

The defendant calls an expert witness who testifies that the defendant had the degree of learning and skill, and that he used the care, skill, diligence, and best judgment exercised by any reputable professional in the locality.

The expert witness testifies that it is his opinion that the defendant fulfilled his duty of care and is, therefore, not negligent.

Issues in Professional Negligence Cases
Whether you are represented in your professional malpractice matter by an attorney or yourself, your trial presentation must include these issues:

Professional Malpractice Plaintiff
As plaintiff, you must prove by a preponderance of the evidence:

- The defendant who treated you did not have the degree of learning and skill of reputable professionals in the locality; or

- The defendant did not use the care, skill, and best judgment exercised by reputable professionals in the locality.

- The failure to fulfill the foregoing duty of care proximately or legally caused the damages.

- The kind, nature, extent, and degree of your injuries.

Professional Malpractice Defendant
As defendant, you must prove in your affirmative defense:

- You do have the degree of learning and skill of reputable professionals in the locality; or

- You did use the care, skill, and best judgment exercised by reputable professionals in the locality.

- The plaintiff's own negligence caused his injuries and damages.

Overview of Negligence Cases

Regardless of the category of negligence case in which you are involved, the key to winning is evidence. Your power to persuade the judge to find for you is summed up in three words: strong, convincing evidence.

If you are the plaintiff claiming damages, include proof of all expenses you contend were proximately or legally caused by your accident. For instance, if yours is a personal injury case in which the defendant, who was driving too fast, rear-ended your car, causing you to lose a month's income during your recovery period, you must present proof of lost income.

If you had to rent an automobile while your own vehicle was being repaired, present your rental car bill as well as your out-of-pocket expenses for your own car's repairs. If insurance paid a portion of the bill, you may sue the defendant only for the amount of damages you paid personally and for recovery of the deductible. The sum total of all expenses associated with the accident constitutes the basis of the judgment you may seek for damages.

Never ask for more than you honestly deserve to receive. The judge who hears your case is a dispenser of justice. He is not a banker, so do not expect him to act like one.

How to Try Your Own Negligence Case in Court

You are now ready to receive instructions about how to try your own negligence case in court. Before proceeding, there are a few facts about which you should know:

- If yours is a small claims case, the judge will ask the questions. However, if your matter will not be heard in small claims court, your trial will be conducted according to the basic civil trial outline contained in Chapter 22, "The Courtroom Drama and How it Works."

On your day in court, have your exhibits in order before the trial, so you will not waste time hunting for them each time you introduce a piece of evidence. Organize the exhibits in the order you will introduce them through your witnesses. Be prepared to call all your witnesses.

In a negligence trial, the plaintiff is the first party to introduce himself after the case has been called and the litigants have approached the counsel table. Your trial will proceed according to the following general outline.

Outline of a Negligence Trial

(The plaintiff should be standing behind the counsel table, closer to the jury box than the defendant. Use your own words to fill in the appropriate blanks which apply to your case.)

PLAINTIFF: Your Honor, my name is *(your name)* _____, the plaintiff. I am ready to proceed.

DEFENDANT: Your Honor, my name is *(your name)* _____, the defendant. I am ready to proceed.

JUDGE: The plaintiff may proceed.

DEFENDANT: *(sits down at counsel table)*

PLAINTIFF: Your Honor, may I call myself as my own first witness?

JUDGE: Yes.

(Follow the judge's instructions about taking the witness stand; you will be sworn or affirmed by the court clerk.)

PLAINTIFF: (*Tell the judge about your accident, injuries, and damages by including these facts.*) Your Honor, on (*date*) _____, I was involved in an accident caused by (*name the cause*) _____. The details are as follows (*explain what happened*): At (*time*) _____ (*A.M./P.M.*), I was (*describe what you were doing*) _____ _____ (*tell where you were*) _____ when (*explain what happened next, such as a crash, fall, etc.*) _____ _____.

(*in as much detail as possible, describe what you saw, felt, heard, etc. after the accident*) _____.
As a result, my injuries and damages were (*name them*): _____ _____ _____. Your Honor, the amount of my injuries and damages totaled: \$_____.

(*Introduce evidence by holding it up so the judge and adverse counsel can see it; repeat this process with each piece of evidence you introduce. Practice this step even if opposing counsel has examined the exhibits before trial. State the exhibit numbers you have assigned when making your requests.*)

Your Honor, I have this (*describe the piece of evidence*) _____ which I request be marked Plaintiff's (*number*) _____ for identification. Your Honor, (*Explain why this evidence is important, how it proves your claim against the defendant.*) _____ _____ _____.

(*When you have finished giving your testimony say:*) Nothing further, Your Honor.

(*Remain in the witness box.*)

DEFENDANT (*rises to cross-examine plaintiff*): (*Cross examine plaintiff by asking questions about important facts related in his testimony*): _____ _____ _____. (*When finished, tell the judge:*) No further questions, Your Honor.

(*Return to the counsel table and be seated.*)

JUDGE: The witness may step down.

PLAINTIFF (*return to counsel table and continue. If more witnesses are to be called for your side, you are now ready to conduct their direct examination*): Your Honor, may I call plaintiff's witness (*number*)_____, (*name of witness*) _____

_____?

(When the next witness for your side takes the stand, ask questions which elicit the answers you seek.) _____

_____.

(When finished, tell the court:) Nothing further.

(Plaintiff takes his seat at the counsel table.)

DEFENDANT *(rises and cross-examines witness from counsel table):* *(Cross-examine plaintiff's witness by asking questions related to facts elicited during the direct examination):* _____

_____.

(When finished, tell the judge:) No further questions, Your Honor.

(Be seated.)

This process continues until all the plaintiff's witnesses have been examined. When the plaintiff finishes the direct examination of all his witnesses, and the defendant is through cross-examining them, the plaintiff advises the court his side's examination is finished:

PLAINTIFF: Your Honor, this concludes the plaintiff's presentation of testimony and evidence. May I now offer my exhibits in evidence?

JUDGE: *(If the judge has any instructions to give about how the plaintiff should offer his exhibits, he will now outline them. Otherwise, he will say:)* Yes.

PLAINTIFF *(offers exhibits in the order introduced in trial):* Plaintiff's 1, *(describe the item or document)* _____. Plaintiff's 2, *(describe the item or document)* _____. Plaintiff's 3, *(describe the item or document)* _____.

(When all your exhibits have been admitted, you have finished your presentation.)

Plaintiff rests, Your Honor.

(Take your seat at the counsel table.)

The defendant now presents his case in the same manner the plaintiff was heard, starting with the defendant's testimony. If your attorney will be conducting your direct examination, he will ask a series of questions which elicit answers that establish your affirmative defense. However, if you are appearing as a *Pro Per,* do the following:

DEFENDANT (*stand at the counsel table and address the judge*): Your Honor, the defendant is ready to proceed. May I call myself as my own first witness?

The judge will grant permission. After you have taken the stand and been sworn or affirmed, proceed as suggested here:

DEFENDANT: (*Present your affirmative defense by telling in narrative form your side of the issue in dispute. This is your response to the plaintiff's claim, allegation, or other statements; build your defense from the applicable points suggested here or on other issues explained elsewhere in this chapter.*)

Your Honor, (*explain your side of the matter in issue, including where you were, what happened, how it occurred, when it took place, and who was involved—keeping in mind that you wish to show the court: [1] you exercised proper care and, therefore, were not negligent; or [2] the plaintiff did not use care and was, therefore, negligent*)

_____.

_____

_____

_____

_____.

When you have finished testifying, the plaintiff may cross-examine you. After he advises the judge he has no further questions, you may step down and conduct the examination of your witnesses. Each time you conclude the direct examination of a witness, the plaintiff may cross-examine him. The procedure is the same as outlined for the plaintiff's examination of his side's witnesses.

At the conclusion of the examination, you are ready to offer your exhibits in evidence.

DEFENDANT (*continuing*): Your Honor, this concludes the defendant's case. May I now offer my exhibits in evidence?

JUDGE: Yes.

DEFENDANT (*offer exhibits in the order introduced in the trial*): Defendant's A (*describe the item or document*) _____. Defendant's B (*describe the item or document*) _____. Defendant's C (*describe the item or document*) _____.

(*When you are finished, you are through presenting your case.*)

Defendant rests, Your Honor.

(Take your seat at the counsel table.)

At the time one party offers his exhibits, the adverse party may have one or more objections. In the event this happens in your case, the objectionable exhibits must be "argued."

Here is a summary of this process:

- First, the opponent raises his objections and states his ground for objecting to the exhibit.

- Second, the proponent (party offering the evidence) rebuts the objection by arguing for admission of the exhibit.

- Third, the judge considers both parties' statements and rules in one of two ways: the exhibit is admitted as evidence (allowed) or excluded (disallowed).

When he decides the case, the judge will only consider the evidence which has been admitted.

Introducing the Trial Argument

If your negligence case will be heard in small claims court, or is a short, uncomplicated matter which can be tried in less than one day, there is no need for you to prepare a "trial argument." However, if yours is a fairly complex negligence suit or countersuit, the trial argument concludes the proceedings. Briefly, in this final phase of the proceedings, both parties present the summation of their cases and pray that the court find in their favor. The plaintiff has two opportunities.

- *Plaintiff*—Gives opening argument.

- *Defendant*—Gives summation.

- *Plaintiff*—Gives closing argument.

In the event you will deliver an argument to conclude your presentation, the following information will help you with your preparations.

How to Argue Your Negligence Case

In your argument, remind the court of the highlights of the trial. Recite those portions of the evidence which are favorable to your case (witnesses' testimonies and exhibits).

If your presentation is based upon a law, court ruling, statute, or rule, you may recite it in your argument. Although citation of applicable law is not necessary, it may help you win. Note how space is provided in the following outline for recitation of testimony, exhibits, and applicable law. Use this outline for the preparation of your own argument.

Outline of a Negligence Argument

(The plaintiff's argument should show the defendant was negligent and is, therefore, liable. The defendant's argument should show: [1] he was not negligent; [2] the plaintiff was contributorily negligent; [3] he is not liable, or plaintiff's liability is not what plaintiff claimed.)

PLAINTIFF *(rises for Opening Argument)*: Your Honor, by the evidence presented in this court today, the plaintiff has proved that *(summarize what your side has proven or the defendant has failed to prove)* _____

_____.

_____.

_____.

I recite *(name of applicable law)* _____

which states *(quote or paraphrase the applicable law)* _____

_____.

(Remain standing)

DEFENDANT *(rises for Argument)*: Your Honor, the evidence presented in this court today (proves/disproves) _____ (defendant's/plaintiff's) contention that *(summarize contention)* _____

_____.

(Summarize evidence) _____

_____.

_____.

_____.

I recite *(name of applicable law)*_____

which states *(quote or paraphrase the applicable law)* _____

_____.

For these reasons, Your Honor, I pray the court finds for the defendant and renders judgment in his favor. Thank you, Your Honor.

(Remain standing.)

When the defendant has finished his argument, the plaintiff may now give his closing argument. The closing argument offers the plaintiff the opportunity to rebut the defendant's argument. Since the plaintiff has the "burden of proof," he is allowed to have the last word.

> PLAINTIFF (*delivers Closing Argument*): Your Honor, in his argument the defendant contended that (*summarize the defendant's argument of why he should win*)
>
> _____
>
> _____.
>
> The plaintiff contends (*state why you believe the defendant was wrong and you are right*) _____
>
> I base my argument on (*name of applicable law or rule*) _____
>
> _____, which states (*quote or paraphrase the law*) _____
>
> _____.
>
> Therefore, Your Honor, I pray the court finds for the plaintiff and awards judgment in his favor. Thank you, Your Honor.
>
> (*Remain standing.*)

When arguments have been delivered, the trial is ended. All that remains is for the judge to hand down his decision and render judgment. The court's ruling is final unless the matter is taken on appeal. For more information about appealing your case, read Chapter 28, "Reaching the Decision—Win, Lose, or Appeal."

More About Negligence Trials

A few more points which may be helpful with your negligence case are summarized here. Although the same information appears elsewhere in this book, it is condensed here to assist you in your preparation for trial.

- *Taking the Oath*—You and your witnesses must each take the oath administered by the court clerk before you can testify. Each witness should decide before the trial whether he prefers to be sworn or affirmed, and the court clerk should be so notified so he may administer the proper form of oath. Select one of the following versions of the oath:

> COURT CLERK (*sworn oath*): Raise your right hand. Do you solemnly swear that the testimony you are about to give in the matter pending before this court is the truth, the whole truth, and nothing but the truth, so help you God?

> COURT CLERK (*affirmation*): Raise your right hand. Do you solemnly swear, under pain and penalty of perjury, that the testimony you are about to give in the

matter pending before this court is the truth, the whole truth and nothing but the truth?

WITNESS (*with right hand raised*): I do.

• *Opening Statement*—At the start of the trial, the plaintiff may deliver an "opening statement," in which he tells the court exactly what he intends to prove. For example:

JUDGE: The plaintiff may proceed.

PLAINTIFF: Your Honor, I expect the evidence to show that (*state your cause of action*) _____.
Witness number 1 will testify to facts (*state all facts about which he will testify*)

_____.

Witness number 2 will testify to facts (*state all facts about which he will testify*)

_____.

Witness number 3 will testify to facts (*state all facts about which he will testify*)

_____.

Your Honor, with the admission of the evidence, I am confident the court will render judgment in my favor.

The defendant may also make an opening statement; the time when he delivers his opening statement is optional: he may make it after the plaintiff's opening statement or reserve it until he is ready to begin the direct examination of his own side's witnesses.

Opening statements are optional; they are not required by law. In small claims court matters or other short, simple civil cases, opening statements are not necessary because the judge has already read the complaint and does not need to be reminded of the issue(s) to be tried. In trials by jury, however, a plaintiff's trial attorney will always make an opening statement.

The advantage of making an opening statement is that the plaintiff gets to tell his case twice. However, if the plaintiff fails to state all the elements of his cause of action, the defendant can move for non-suit; this means the defendant can ask the court to render judgment in his favor because the plaintiff showed by his opening statement that he cannot satisfy the necessary elements for his action.

When a defendant makes an opening statement, he also gets to tell his case twice. The defendant's opening statement consists of his denial of the plaintiff's cause of action and his affirmative defenses which he expects to be proven.

He states what each of his witnesses will say. The defendant is not required to make an opening statement because the plaintiff does so. If you do not wish to make an opening statement, say:

DEFENDANT (*to waive opening statement*): The defendant waives opening statement, Your Honor.

If you wish to make an opening statement at the time you begin trying your case, rather than at the opening of the trial, say:

DEFENDANT (*to make opening statement later*): The defendant reserves his opening statement, Your Honor.

Generally, the defendant should give an opening statement if the plaintiff makes one; this allows him to counteract the "sting" of the plaintiff's statement. Should you make an opening statement? In an opening statement, you could lock yourself into narrow specifics that you promise to deliver in trial. Consider these questions: what could happen if one of your side's witnesses gives unexpected testimony, or says something other than what you told the court he would talk about? What if your exhibits fail to prove the point you stated they would? You could lose your credibility.

Is an Opening Statement Necessary?
By not making an opening statement, you allow yourself greater flexibility during your presentation. Furthermore, since your case will probably not be lengthy or complicated, you need not make an opening statement.

• *Arguments and Objections*
During trial proceedings, it may be necessary for you and the other party to "argue" one or more issues before the judge by stating your respective viewpoints. After hearing both side's arguments, the judge will make a ruling which the litigants must follow.

Both parties may raise objections to each other's testimony and exhibits during the trial. The longer and more complex your trial may be, the more objections are likely to be made by both sides. To make an objection, the objector must stand and state both his objection and the grounds upon which he bases it. Four common objections are:

Objection! The plaintiff is leading the witness.

Objection! Beyond the scope of direct examination.

Objection! Hearsay.

Objection! Irrelevant.

The proponent of the objectionable evidence responds to his opponent's objection by telling the court his reason for asking a specific question or seeking a certain answer. The judge will rule to "sustain" or "overrule" the objection. If sustained, the objection stands and the question cannot be answered by the witness; if overruled, the question shall be answered.

If you do not agree with the court's ruling on an objection which has already been examined by the judge, you may move that it be reconsidered by saying:

Motion for reconsideration. (*state your reason*) _____
_____.

The judge will re-examine the objection and will either reverse his ruling on it or allow it to stand.

If a witness responds to a question before you are able to raise your objection, you may seek to have it stricken from the record by making a "motion to strike." If sustained by the court, the objectionable material will be deleted from the record and will not be considered by the judge in reaching his decision in the matter. A "moving party" says:

Move to strike, Your Honor. (*state your reason*) _____
_____.

Shortcuts to Judgment
Can a negligence case pending on the court calendar be decided without having to go to trial? Yes. Three shortcuts to judgment are briefly discussed here. In the event you decide to use one of these legal tools, the clerk at the courthouse where the lawsuit was filed can provide you with the proper forms and detailed instructions.

Introducing the Demurrer
A demurrer is an objection by the defendant to the sufficiency of the plaintiff's pleadings. It is a written motion which affords the defendant the opportunity to have the matter dismissed. Your demurrer will be heard by the judge in a hearing at which both you and your opponent appear to present your respective sides on the matter.

If your motion is granted, the opposition's complaint or cross-complaint will be dismissed and you, the defendant or cross-defendant, win without trial; or the judge may require the plaintiff or cross-complainant to file an amended complaint or cross-complaint in which he states correctly and sufficiently the points with which you take issue in your demurrer. In such an event, the matter remains pending for trial.

Grounds for the Demurrer

Every jurisdiction determines the grounds for demurrers applicable to the area. The sample *Motion [to Dismiss] with Memorandum of Points and Authorities* and following grounds for demurrers in California, are given as examples. You may research the grounds for demurrers in your area by checking with your local law library; they will probably include these grounds:

1. The court named in the plaintiff's complaint lacks jurisdiction.

2. The plaintiff has no legal capacity to sue defendant (for example, the plaintiff is a minor).

3. The complaint does not state sufficient facts to constitute a cause of action.

4. The plaintiff's pleading is unintelligible.

Introducing the Motion for Judgment on the Pleading

This is a motion which either party may make to the court to request that the matter be considered, and judgment rendered, without being tried.

Here, by making the motion, the moving party simply asks the Court to look at the pleadings and then render judgment in his favor. He reasons that the action has no merit, or there is no defense thereto.

The parties cannot introduce extrinsic evidence to support or defend the motion for judgment on pleading.

For example, the plaintiff in a slip and fall case makes the following motion. First he makes the motion, then gives his reasons for doing so:

> PLAINTIFF: Motion for Judgment on the Pleadings, Your Honor. In his Answer, the defendant [restaurant owner] does not deny the allegations of plaintiff's Complaint. He raises as his affirmative defense that he was at home asleep when the accident happened. That is not a valid defense to my action. I ask the Court to find judgment in my favor.

As a matter of practice, the trial judge will allow the opposing party to amend his pleading to add the missing element. Here, defendant may be trying to raise the defense that he did not have notice of the dangerous condition. Otherwise, the Court will grant the defendant's motion.

Introducing Judgment of Non-suit

This is a legal tool the defendant may use to ask the court to render judgment without completing trial. If you are the defendant, you may use this motion in two ways:

Sample Demurrer

(Can be prepared on pleading paper, as shown here,
or 8½ x 11 inch white bond paper.)

William Reed
1000 Main Street
Anytown, California 90000
(213) 100-0000

Defendant, in Pro Per

MUNICIPAL COURT OF THE STATE OF CALIFORNIA
FOR THE COUNTY OF LOS ANGELES

JAMES GARCIA,	)	Case No. 91 H 18066
	)	
Plaintiff	)	NOTICE OF DEMURRER
	)	MEMORANDUM OF POINTS
versus	)	AND AUTHORITIES
	)	
WILLIAM REED,	)	Date: October 19, 1997
	)	Time: 9:00 A.M.
Defendant.	)	Div.: 7/8
—————————	)	

TO: PLAINTIFF AND HIS COUNSEL

PLEASE TAKE NOTICE that on October 19, 1997, at 9:00 A.M. in Division 7 of this Court, the undersigned will present and argue his Demurrer to the Complaint and seek other relief as the Court may deem proper.

The Motion will consist of this Notice and the attached Memorandum of Points and Authorities.

Dated: October 1, 1997

_____
(Defendant)
Defendant, in Pro Per

—1—

MEMORANDUM OF POINTS AND AUTHORITIES

I

PLAINTIFF HAS NO LEGAL CAPACITY TO SUE.

Plaintiff alleged in paragraph three of his Complaint, by way of introduction, that on September 9, 1995, his sixteenth birthday, he was driving his car when the collision took place, etc.

Therefore, on September 11, 1996, when he filed his Complaint against this defendant, plaintiff was only seventeen years old. He was and still is a minor. Ergo, he does NOT have any legal capacity to sue.

II

THE COMPLAINT IS BARRED BY THE STATUTE OF LIMITATIONS

The Complaint alleges that the accident occurred on September 9, 1995. The Complaint was filed on September 11, 1996, *one year and two days after the accident.*

California Code of Civil Procedure Section 340(3) provides that an action for injury of one caused by the wrongful act or neglect of another must be filed within one year.

WHEREFORE, defendant respectfully asks the Court for the dismissal of the Complaint and other relief it may deem proper.

Dated: October 1, 1997

_____ (Defendant)

Defendant, in Pro Per

-2-

at the start of the proceedings, or after the plaintiff has rested his case. Both methods are briefly described here.

Following the plaintiff's presentation of his opening statement, do not deliver an opening statement for the defense. Instead, move for non-suit by saying:

DEFENDANT: Motion for non-suit, Your Honor.

This motion says, in effect, "Your Honor, even if all the facts stated by the plaintiff are true, still he does not have a case and, therefore, I ask for judgment in favor of the defendant."

The judge will give the plaintiff an opportunity to supplement his opening statement and you should do the following:

- If you know that the plaintiff stated everything that is alleged in his complaint, you should vigorously argue your motion for judgment of non-suit. You must show the court that even if all the allegations in the complaint are considered proven, it does not state a cause of action and should, therefore, be dismissed.

If the plaintiff does not make an opening statement, wait until he has put on his case. When the plaintiff has rested his case, rise as if to begin trying your case; however, instead of calling your first witness for direct examination, make your motion for judgment of non-suit.

In the ensuing arguments by both parties, the defendant can argue vigorously about the insufficiencies of the plaintiff's case, which has just been presented. The plaintiff will then have the opportunity to rebut the defendant's argument, following which the court will rule to grant the motion or deny it.

A word of advice: the court will consider the evidence at this stage in the light most favorable to the plaintiff.

Summarizing Negligence Cases

In summary, there are now more cases involving negligence tried in civil courts than five years ago. Because so many types of negligence cases exist, they are subcategorized into six main groups:

- Personal Injury

- Land Owners and Occupants

- Slip and Fall

- Other Accidents

- Product Liability

- Professional Malpractice

To reach his decision, the judge considers the following issues in negligence matters:

- *Duty of Care*—Did the defendant have a duty of care? If yes, did the defendant exercise due care as a reasonably prudent person would do under the same or similar conditions?

- *Proximate or Legal Cause*—Did the defendant proximately or legally (in California) cause the plaintiff's injuries, damages, or harm?

- *Damages*—What was the nature, extent, and degree of plaintiff's injuries and damages?

- *Contributory Negligence*—To what extent and degree, if any, was the plaintiff's negligence a contributory element in the proximate or legal cause of the injury, damage, harm or other wrong which he sustained?

NOTES

Chapter 25

How to Try Your Own Unlawful Detainer (Eviction) and/or Collection Case

Do you own or manage a building in which a tenant has failed to comply with your *Notice to Pay Rent or Quit?* Is the tenant still occupying the premises although he has not paid his rent? Or are you a tenant who has withheld rent to compel your landlord to make needed repairs in your apartment?

In either instance, your matter may wind up as an "Unlawful Detainer" trial in civil court if you cannot resolve it yourselves. As the name implies, unlawful detainer means "illegal detention of property" by a party or parties not entitled to hold, possess, or occupy it. Unlawful detainer is known in legal and judicial circles as "U.D.," a term used also in this book.

Some U.D. cases are tried—and won—by parties serving as their own attorneys. This chapter will help you decide whether to retain a lawyer or appear as a *Pro Per*.

Should You Retain a Lawyer?
In U.D. matters that are heard in Small Claims Court, you may have to handle the matter as a *Pro Per*. In California, for example, litigants are not allowed to be represented by lawyers, with one exception: if a party in a small claims matter is a lawyer, he may serve as his own legal counsel by appearing *in Propria Persona*.

California's maximum judgment that can be awarded in Small Claims Court is $5,000. U.D. matters in which a combined total of back rent and other damages does not exceed $5,000 may be heard in Small Claims Court in California. Outside of

California, the maximum monetary judgment allowed for small claims may be more or less than that allowed in California. Check with your local court clerk regarding this amount; the clerk can also tell you whether you must represent yourself in your area's Small Claims Court, or whether you may retain legal counsel.

All U.D. cases not filed in Small Claims Court will be heard in Municipal Court; both the plaintiff and litigant may be represented by lawyers, although in a fairly large percentage of such cases the tenants (defendants) represent themselves for economic reasons.

Introduction to Eviction Proceedings

There are two basic types of situations involving the vacation of property, as broadly defined by law, and you should have a clear understanding of the difference between them before proceeding:

- *Ejectment*—In this situation, a party occupies a premises or land without the permission of the owner or landlord. He is, in effect, a trespasser. Because no contract or agreement with the owner or landlord grants him permission to be in or on the property, he may be ejected without notice.

- *U.D.*—In this situation, the party unlawfully detaining the premises or property has violated his lease/rental contract/agreement by nonpayment of rent due. (See the next page for a sample rental agreement.) The landlord may start eviction proceedings against the tenant by serving him notice to pay or quit.

Can a landlord in a U.D. case literally toss a tenant out onto the street, by entering the premises occupied by the individual and ejecting him "bag and baggage"? No! In a U.D. matter, the law allows the defendant the right to defend his position; if he wins with his "affirmative defense," he may not be evicted.

Introducing the "Habitability Defense"

"Habitability" is one of the most common grounds upon which the affirmative defense of defendants in U.D. cases is based. This approach involves proving the premises is not habitable (capable of being lived in). For example, the plaintiff-manager was attempting to evict a seven-year tenant because of nonpayment of rent on his apartment. The tenant defended himself on the ground his apartment was not habitable because of broken doors and windows, and an infestation of roaches. In his presentation, the defendant-tenant testified that despite complaining several times to the manager, and giving him written notices, the plaintiff-manager did nothing to correct the condition.

RENTAL AGREEMENT

(MONTH - TO - MONTH TENANCY)

THIS AGREEMENT, entered into this_____day of_____, 19_____, by and between

_____ and _____, hereinafter called respectively lessor and lessee.

WITNESSETH: That for and in consideration of the payment of the rents and the performance of the covenants contained on the part of lessee, said lessor does hereby demise and let unto the lessee, and lessee hires from lessor for use as a

residence those premises described as_____

located at_____ Street,_____, California, for a

tenancy from month-to-month commencing on the_____day of_____, 19_____, and

at a monthly rental of _____ ($_____) Dollars per month,

payable monthly in advance on the_____day of each and every month.

It is further mutually agreed between the parties as follows:

(1) Said premises shall be occupied by no more than_____adults and _____ children.

(2) Lessee shall not keep or permit to be kept in said premises any dog, cat, parrot, or other bird or animal.

(3) Lessee shall not violate any city ordinance or state law in or about said premises.

(4) That all alterations, additions, or improvements made in and to said premises shall, unless otherwise provided by written agreement between the parties hereto, be the property of Lessor and shall remain upon and be surrendered with the premises.

(5) Lessee shall not sub-let the demised premises, or any part thereof, or assign this agreement without the lessor's written consent.

(6) Any failure by lessee to pay rent or other charges promptly when due, or to comply with any other term or condition hereof, shall at the option of the lessor, and after lawful notice given, forthwith terminate this tenancy.

(7) Lessee shall keep and maintain the premises in a clean and sanitary condition at all times, and upon the termination of the tenancy shall surrender the premises to the lessor in as good condition as when received, ordinary wear and damage by the elements excepted.

(8) Except as to any condition which makes the premises untenantable, lessee hereby waives all right to make repairs at the expense of lessor as provided in Section 1942 of the Civil Code of the State of California, and all rights provided in Section 1941 of said Civil Code.

(9) The _____ agrees to properly cultivate, care for, and adequately water the lawn, shrubbery, trees and grounds.

(10) The _____ shall pay for all water supplied to the said premises. The lessee shall pay for all gas, heat, light, power, telephone service, and all other services, except as herein provided, supplied to the said premises.

(11) Nothing contained in this agreement shall be construed as waiving any of lessor's rights under the laws of the State of California.

(12) This agreement and the tenancy hereby granted may be terminated at any time by either party hereto by giving to the other party not less than

_____ (_____) days prior notice in writing.

(13) The prevailing party in an action brought for the recovery of rent or other moneys due or to become due under this lease or by reason of a breach of any covenant herein contained or for the recovery of the possession of said premises, or to compel the performance of anything agreed to be done herein, or to recover for damages to said property, or to enjoin any act contrary to the provisions hereof, shall be awarded all of the costs in connection therewith, including, but not by way of limitation, reasonable attorney's fees.

(14) Remarks:

IN WITNESS WHEREOF the parties hereto have executed this agreement in duplicate the day and year first above written.

233

_____   _____
Lessor   Lessee

WOLCOTTS FORM 1030—REV. 10-77 (price class 6-1P)

The defendant also produced photographs of the broken windows, doors, and cockroaches, along with a copy of his memos outlining the problems and notifying the manager that he would withhold rent if the conditions were not cleared up. He deposited the rents due in a trust account, proof of which he offered in evidence, and he testified that the plaintiff still did nothing to make the apartment habitable.

Based on the testimony and exhibits, the court found for the defendant. The plaintiff was ordered to accept the defendant's back rent minus twenty per cent (20%) thereof for the roach infestation and broken windows and doors. The tenant paid his rent and continued living in his apartment.

In this type of habitability case, the landlord should remedy the problem, or the tenant can again withhold rent.

In a similar U.D. case, the plaintiff prevailed. In this matter, the defendant, who was habitually late with his rent, eventually quit paying altogether after he lost his job. During the trial, the plaintiff-manager presented proof that the defendant owed $1,200 in rent; he also presented his records, including all the legal notices to the defendant as required by law in eviction cases.

The defendant raised the habitability defense, claiming he had withheld rent because the building was unsanitary and, therefore, a hazard to his health. He cited an illness he incurred from allegedly eating food tainted by rats which had gotten into his cupboards, but offered no tangible evidence to support his position.

The plaintiff-manager called the building's assistant manager, who testified that he had served the tenant with the proper *Three Day Notice to Pay Rent or Quit* (vacate the premises). The tenant had ignored the notice.

The assistant manager also testified that the interior of the defendant's apartment, which he had visited many times, was often dirty, smelling of bags of unemptied garbage which collected in the kitchen.

The judge ruled for the plaintiff. The defendant was ordered to vacate the premises.

Introducing Grounds for Eviction

The single most common cause for U.D. lawsuits is failure by a tenant to pay rent. However, two other grounds for U.D. lawsuits are summarized here:

- *Failure to Move*—If a tenant has received from the landlord a thirty-day notice terminating the lease on the premises he is renting, and requiring him to move on or by the date specified on the notice, the tenant may be subject to eviction if he does not vacate the premises.

  A landlord may not arbitrarily serve a tenant with a thirty-day notice simply on a whim; he must abide by the terms of agreement set forth in the lease or rental contract with the tenant. A thirty-day notice serves as notification that the landlord is terminating a lease with the tenant; if the tenant paid his last month's rent at the time the lease agreement was signed, no further rent will be due for his final month of occupancy of the premises.

Note carefully that in a thirty-day notice, the plaintiff seeks only possession, not rent; therefore, if on January 1st, the plaintiff serves the defendant a thirty-day notice and the defendant has not paid the rent for December and January, the court will award rent only after the thirtieth day, or February 1st.

If a tenant who has been served with a thirty-day notice has not vacated the premises or quit the property at the expiration of the rental/lease period, the landlord may initiate U.D. proceedings to evict him.

Thirty Day Notice to Quit forms, similar to the example shown here, are available from stationery and legal supply stores. You may also prepare your own form by typing the same basic information on a sheet of white paper; include a *Proof of Service* similar to the example shown here.

In a case involving *the expiration of a lease period contracted by the parties,* there is no need for the plaintiff to give the defendant a thirty-day notice before filing suit; if the tenant continues occupying the premises after the lease expires, the plaintiff can start eviction proceedings immediately.

When, however, a landlord has consented to a tenant's continued occupation of premises after the lease has expired, the matter becomes a month-to-month contract; if the landlord wants the tenant to vacate the premises, he should give the tenant a thirty-day notice.

• *Nuisance*—If a tenant has received from the landlord one or more notices to cease and desist from misconduct, and the tenant has not complied with such requests, the landlord may initiate action to evict the tenant.

"Nuisance" is anything injurious to health, indecent or offensive to the senses, obstructing the free use of property, or interfering with the comfortable enjoyment of life or property. A few of the most common grounds for nuisance are: disturbing the peace through noisy or other disruptive activity; threatening the welfare of other tenants through dangerous or illegal activity; destroying property through willful acts; holding noisy pool parties on the common grounds every weekend.

Another common ground for eviction of tenants is "breach of contract." In breach of contract, the tenant fails to fulfill one or more terms to which he agreed by signing the lease or rental agreement with the landlord. Some common grounds for this type of breach include: keeping pets in premises in which no pets are allowed; harboring guests beyond the time limit for visitors as specified in the agreement; allowing individuals to occupy the premises without knowledge of, or permission from, the landlord and, thereby, causing the premises to be occupied by persons in excess of the number of authorized occupants.

THIRTY DAY NOTICE TO QUIT

_____

To

Tenant in Possession.

TAKE NOTICE, that you are hereby required to quit, and deliver up to the undersigned the possession of the premises now held and occupied by you, being the premises known as

at the expiration of the rental period ending on _____, 19____.

This Notice to Quit specifically terminates any oral/written agreement you may have with respect to the said premises at the date specified above.

THIS IS INTENDED as a thirty (30) day notice to quit, for the purpose of terminating your tenancy aforesaid.

DATED this _____ day of _____, 19____.

_____

Landlord.

_____

_____

PROOF OF SERVICE

I, _____, served

(print name)

_____

_____

(person(s) served)

with a copy of the Notice to Quit described on the reverse hereof by serving _____

(person(s) papers given to)

_____

at _____ _____ on

(address where served)

_____, 19____, at _____m. o'clock.

(date)   (time)

At the time of service I was at least 18 years of age.

Executed this _____ day of _____, 19____, at _____, California.

I declare, under penalty of perjury, under the laws of the State of California, that the foregoing is true

and correct.

_____

(Signature)

_____

(Address)

_____

If a tenant continues engaging in nuisance after the landlord has asked him to stop, the landlord may issue a written request; it need not be threatening in nature, but should clearly state the reason the note or memo is being issued. For example:

Date: May 30, 1996
To: Bob and Janice Smith, Apt. 334
From: Bruce West, Manager
Re: Complaint about Noise

Bob and Janice, I have received three complaints from other tenants in the past 10 days about loud TV and music coming from your apartment after midnight. I have also received four complaints about noisy guests coming and going from your apartment after midnight on week nights.

The other tenants and I would appreciate it if you please observe Section 3.a of your Rental Agreement which states: Noise will be kept to a minimum after 10:00 P.M. Sunday through Thursday and and after 11:30 P.M. Friday and Saturday.

Thank you for your cooperation in this matter.

The landlord should keep a copy of every letter, memo, or notice issued to tenants; in the event he brings a U.D. case against a tenant, he may offer the documents as evidence he gave several notices to the defendant(s) to stop being a nuisance.

If a tenant does not stop committing the nuisance, the landlord may serve him with a *Three Day Notice to Cease and Desist or Vacate the Premises.* A sample form is shown on the next page. If the tenant continues his conduct, the landlord may initiate a U.D. action to evict him.

How to Initiate an Eviction Proceeding

Most rental agreements or lease contracts allow a grace period; this is a period beyond the date the rent is actually due in which the tenant may pay his rent. The average grace period is three days, including the date the rent is due.

If, for example, the rent is due on the first of the month, the tenant may pay it on the second or third day of the month without being late; however, if he does not pay the rent until the fourth day of the month, he is late.

The landlord may now take action, by serving the tenant with a three-day notice ordering him to (1) pay the overdue rent or (2) vacate the premises he now occupies within three days from date of receipt of the notice.

In effect, the tenant has three days to pay up or get out.

(Sample)
THREE-DAY NOTICE TO CEASE AND DESIST OR QUIT

TO: _____

      Please take notice that you have violated Paragraph _____ of our Lease Agreement executed on (date)_____.

      Paragraph _____ provides that: (example) "No animal shall be kept or maintained in or upon the premises without the Landlord's written consent."

      (Continuation of example) For the last one-week period you have been keeping a boa constrictor in the premises without my written consent. Even if you had asked, I would have never given you my consent because most people, including myself, are scared of that animal.

      Therefore, you have three days after receipt of this Notice to remove the boa constrictor OR to vacate the premises located at (address)_____, (city) _____ (state) _____ and deliver possession of the premises to me.

      Should you fail to cease and desist, i.e. to remove the boa constrictor or to vacate the premises within the above-stated three-day period, then I shall file legal action against you for forfeiture of the lease agreement, possession of the premises, and damages consisting of rents, attorney's fees, court costs, etc.

Dated:_____

                                _____

                                  _____

                                  _____

A sample three-day notice entitled *Notice to Pay Rent or Quit* is included on the next page. You may purchase a similar form at a legal supply or stationery store, or type your own three-day notice on white paper; a *Proof of Service* form should appear on the back page.

The three-day notice can be rendered null and void by the tenant if he pays his rent within the three-day period specified on the notice; if he does not pay his rent and continues occupying the premises, further action may be taken by the landlord.

How to File an Unlawful Detainer Complaint

If a tenant does not pay his rent or vacate the premises in compliance with the three-day notice he has been served by the landlord, the landlord may now file an *Unlawful Detainer Complaint*. When an official U.D. complaint has been filed with the court, the matter becomes a lawsuit.

Two U.D. complaint forms are shown here, one for a small claim U.D. and the other for a non-small claim U.D. matter. All jurisdictions have similar forms, which are available from the clerk of the court where the matter is filed. They are easy to fill in, since the plaintiff merely has to check the spaces which fit the case. The complaint establishes the grounds for the plaintiff's lawsuit (his written pleading) and spells out the judgment he seeks (his prayer to the court).

How to File a Summons

In a non-Small Claims Court U.D. case, the plaintiff also files a *Summons,* a sample of which is provided in this chapter. The two documents are served together. A summons is a court order for the defendant to respond within the time limit shown on the document.

In most jurisdictions, a defendant must respond within five calendar days from the date he received the Summons and Complaint. Failure to respond may result in the tenant losing the case. He may be evicted, his wages garnished, and his personal property sold to satisfy the judgment.

In a small claims U.D. matter, the complaint and summons are both contained on the same form. See the sample form entitled *Plaintiff's Claim and Order to Defendant.*

How to File a U.D. Answer

A defendant-tenant, upon learning he has been sued, may consult an attorney or legal aid foundation. Or he may handle the matter himself by filing his own response, legally called an "Answer," to the Summons and Complaint within the time period allowed. The defendant may purchase his Answer form from the clerk of the court where he files his response; he must file his Answer at the same court which issued the plaintiff's Summons and Complaint.

NOTICE TO PAY RENT OR QUIT

(C. C. P., Sec. 1161)

_____

TO _____

_____

_____

Tenant—in Possession

Within THREE DAYS, after the service on you of this notice, you are hereby required to PAY THE RENT of the premises hereinafter

described, of which you now hold possession, amounting to the sum of _____

_____ Dollars ($_____)

at the rental rate of _____ Dollars ($_____)

per month (or week), being the _____ rent due from the _____ day of

_____, 19____, to the _____ day of _____, 19____,

or you are hereby required to DELIVER UP POSSESSION of the hereinafter described premises, within THREE DAYS after service on you

of this notice, to the undersigned, or _____ agent, who is

authorized to receive the same or the undersigned will institute legal proceedings against you to recover possession of said premises

with ALL RENTS DUE and DAMAGES. The undersigned, as a landlord, declares and gives notice that, if the said rent is not paid within

three days after service on you of this notice, I do hereby elect to declare a forfeiture of the lease and agreement under which you occupy

the hereinbelow-described property:

The premises herein referred to are situated in the _____ of

_____ County of _____

STATE OF CALIFORNIA, designated by the number and street as _____

_____ and more particularly

described as follows: _____

_____

_____

_____

Dated this _____ day of _____, 19____.

_____

_____

Penal Code Section No. 594 reads: "Any person or persons who wilfully or maliciously destroys or damages any Real or Personal Property not their own will be punished by Fine or Imprisonment or both."

241

WOLCOTTS FORM 1006—NOTICE TO PAY RENT OR QUIT —Rev. 12-87 (price class 3A)

ATTORNEY OR PARTY WITHOUT ATTORNEY (NAME AND ADDRESS):	TELEPHONE:	FOR COURT USE ONLY

ATTORNEY FOR (NAME):

Insert name of court, judicial district or branch court, if any, and post office and street address:

PLAINTIFF:

DEFENDANT:

DOES 1 TO _____

COMPLAINT—Unlawful Detainer	CASE NUMBER:

1. This pleading including attachments and exhibits consists of the following number of pages: _____

2. a. Plaintiff is ☐ an individual over the age of 18 years. ☐ a partnership.
   ☐ a public agency. ☐ a corporation.
   ☐ other (specify):

   b. ☐ Plaintiff has complied with the fictitious business name laws and is doing business under the fictitious name of (specify):

3. Defendants named above are in possession of the premises located at (street address, city and county):

4. Plaintiff's interest in the premises is ☐ as owner ☐ other (specify):

5. The true names and capacities of defendants sued as Does are unknown to plaintiff.

6. a. On or about (date):   defendants (names):

   agreed to rent the premises for a ☐ month-to-month tenancy ☐ other tenancy (specify):
   at a rent of $_____ payable ☐ monthly ☐ other (specify frequency):
   due on the ☐ first of the month ☐ other day (specify):

   b. This ☐ written ☐ oral agreement was made with
      ☐ plaintiff   ☐ plaintiff's predecessor in interest
      ☐ plaintiff's agent   ☐ other (specify):

   c. ☐ The defendants not named in item 6.a. are
      ☐ subtenants   ☐ assignees   ☐ other (specify):

   d. ☐ The agreement was later changed as follows (specify):

   e. ☐ A copy of the written agreement is attached and labeled Exhibit A.

7. Plaintiff has performed all conditions of the rental agreement.

8. ☐ a. The following notice was served on defendant (name):
      ☐ 3-day notice to pay rent or quit   ☐ 3-day notice to quit
      ☐ 3-day notice to perform covenant or quit ☐ 30-day notice to quit
      ☐ other (specify):

   b. The period stated in the notice expired on (date):   and defendants failed
      to comply with the requirements of the notice by that date.

   c. All facts stated in the notice are true.

   d. ☐ The notice included an election of forfeiture.

   e. ☐ A copy of the notice is attached and labeled Exhibit B.

(Continued)

Form Approved by the
Judicial Council of California
Effective January 1, 1982
Rule 982.1 (90)

76C568 CI193JC- (11) PS 1-86

COMPLAINT—Unlawful Detainer

CCP 425.12

COMPLAINT—Unlawful Detainer Page two

9. ☐ a. The notice referred to in item 8 was served
    ☐ by personally handing a copy to defendant on *(date):*
    ☐ by leaving a copy with *(name or description):*   , a person
    of suitable age or discretion, on *(date):*   at defendant's ☐ residence
        ☐ business AND mailing a copy to defendant at his place of residence on *(date):*
        because defendant cannot be found at his residence or usual place of business.
    ☐ by posting a copy on the premises on *(date):*   (☐ and giving a copy
    to a person residing at the premises) AND mailing a copy to defendant at the premises on
    (date):
        ☐ because defendant's residence and usual place of business cannot be ascertained OR
        ☐ because no person of suitable age or discretion can there be found.
    ☐ *(not for 3-day notice. See Civil Code section 1946 before using)* by sending a copy by certified or
    registered mail addressed to defendant on *(date):*
    b. ☐ Information about service of the notice on the other defendants is contained in attachment 9.

10. ☐ Plaintiff demands possession from each defendant because of expiration of a fixed term lease.
11. ☐ At the time the 3-day notice to pay rent or quit was served, the amount of rent due was $ _____
12. ☐ The fair rental value of the premises is $_____ per day.
13. Plaintiff is entitled to immediate possession of the premises.
14. ☐ Defendants' continued possession is malicious, and plaintiff is entitled to treble damages. *(State specific facts supporting this claim in attachment 14.)*
15. ☐ A written agreement between the parties provides for attorney fees.
16. ☐ Defendants' tenancy is subject to the local rent control or eviction control ordinance of *(city or county, title of ordinance, and date of passage):*

    Plaintiff has met all applicable requirements of the ordinances.
17. ☐ Other allegations are stated in attachment 17.
18. Plaintiff remits to the jurisdictional limit, if ány, of the court.

19. PLAINTIFF REQUESTS
    a. possession of the premises.
    b. ☐ costs incurred in this proceeding.
    c. ☐ past due rent of $_____
    d. ☐ damages at the rate of $_____ per day.
    e. ☐ treble the amount of rent and damages found due.
    f. ☐ reasonable attorney fees.
    g. ☐ forfeiture of the agreement.
    h. ☐ other *(specify):*

. . . . _____   _____
(Type or print name)   (Signature of plaintiff or attorney)

VERIFICATION
(Use a different verification form if the verification is by an attorney or for a corporation or partnership.)
I am the plaintiff in this proceeding and have read this complaint. I declare under penalty of perjury under the laws of the State of California that this complaint is true and correct.

Date:

. . . . _____   _____
(Type or print name)   (Signature of plaintiff)

SUMMONS
(CITACION JUDICIAL)

NOTICE TO DEFENDANT: *(Aviso a Acusado)*

FOR COURT USE ONLY
(SOLO PARA USO DE LA CORTE)

YOU ARE BEING SUED BY PLAINTIFF:
(A Ud. le está demandando)

You have *5 CALENDAR DAYS* after this summons is served on you to file a typewritten response at this court.	*Después de que le entreguen esta citación judicial usted tiene un plazo de 5 DIAS CALENDARIOS para presentar una respuesta escrita a máquina en esta corte.*
A letter or phone call will not protect you; your typewritten response must be in proper legal form if you want the court to hear your case.	*Una carta o una llamada telefónica no le ofrecerá protección; su respuesta escrita a máquina tiene que cumplir con las formalidades legales apropiadas si usted quiere que la corte escuche su caso.*
If you do not file your response on time, you may lose the case, you may be evicted, and your wages, money and property may be taken without further warning from the court.	*Si usted no presenta su respuesta a tiempo, puede perder el caso, le pueden obligar a desalojar su casa, y le pueden quitar su salario, su dinero y otras cosas de su propiedad sin aviso adicional por parte de la corte.*
There are other legal requirements. You may want to call an attorney right away. If you do not know an attorney, you may call an attorney referral service or a legal aid office (listed in the phone book).	*Existen otros requisitos legales. Puede que usted quiera llamar a un abogado inmediatamente. Si no conoce a un abogado, puede llamar a un servicio de referencia de abogados o a una oficina de ayuda legal (vea el directorio telefónico).*

CASE NUMBER: *(Número del Caso)*

The name and address of the court is: *(El nombre y dirección de la corte es)*

The name, address, and telephone number of plaintiff's attorney, or plaintiff without an attorney, is:
(El nombre, la dirección y el número de teléfono del abogado del demandante, o del demandante que no tiene abogado, es)

DATE:
(Fecha)

Clerk, by _____, Deputy
(Actuario)   *(Delegado)*

[SEAL]

NOTICE TO THE PERSON SERVED: You are served
1. ☐ as an individual defendant.
2. ☐ as the person sued under the fictitious name of *(specify)*:

3. ☐ on behalf of *(specify)*:

     under: ☐ CCP 416.10 (corporation)   ☐ CCP 416.60 (minor)
                  ☐ CCP 416.20 (defunct corporation)   ☐ CCP 416.70 (conservatee)
                  ☐ CCP 416.40 (association or partnership)   ☐ CCP 416.90 (individual)
                  ☐ other:
4. ☐ by personal delivery on *(date)*:

(See reverse for Proof of Service)
SUMMONS — UNLAWFUL DETAINER

PROOF OF SERVICE — SUMMONS – Unlawful Detainer
(Use separate proof of service for each person served)

1. I served the
   a. ☐ summons ☐ complaint ☐ amended summons ☐ amended complaint
      ☐ completed and blank Case Questionnaires ☐ Other *(specify)*:
   b. on defendant *(name)*:

   c. by serving ☐ defendant ☐ other *(name and title or relationship to person served)*:

   d. ☐ by delivery ☐ at home ☐ at business
      (1) date:
      (2) time:
      (3) address:

   e. ☐ by mailing
      (1) date:
      (2) place:

2. Manner of service *(check proper box)*:
   a. ☐ **Personal service.** By personally delivering copies. (CCP 415.10)
   b. ☐ **Substituted service on corporation, unincorporated association (including partnership), or public entity.** By leaving, during usual office hours, copies in the office of the person served with the person who apparently was in charge and thereafter mailing (by first-class mail, postage prepaid) copies to the person served at the place where the copies were left. (CCP 415.20(a))
   c. ☐ **Substituted service on natural person, minor, conservatee, or candidate.** By leaving copies at the dwelling house, usual place of abode, or usual place of business of the person served in the presence of a competent member of the household or a person apparently in charge of the office or place of business, at least 18 years of age, who was informed of the general nature of the papers, and thereafter mailing (by first-class mail, postage prepaid) copies to the person served at the place where the copies were left. (CCP 415.20(b)) *(Attach separate declaration or affidavit stating acts relied on to establish reasonable diligence in first attempting personal service.)*
   d. ☐ **Mail and acknowledgment service.** By mailing (by first-class mail or airmail, postage prepaid) copies to the person served, together with two copies of the form of notice and acknowledgment and a return envelope, postage prepaid, addressed to the sender. (CCP 415.30) *(Attach completed acknowledgment of receipt.)*
   e. ☐ **Certified or registered mail service.** By mailing to an address outside California (by first-class mail, postage prepaid, requiring a return receipt) copies to the person served. (CCP 415.40) *(Attach signed return receipt or other evidence of actual delivery to the person served.)*
   f. ☐ Other *(specify code section)*:
      ☐ additional page is attached.

3. The "Notice to the Person Served" (on the summons) was completed as follows (CCP 412.30, 415.10, and 474):
   a. ☐ as an individual defendant.
   b. ☐ as the person sued under the fictitious name of *(specify)*:
   c. ☐ on behalf of *(specify)*:
      under: ☐ CCP 416.10 (corporation) ☐ CCP 416.60 (minor) ☐ other:
              ☐ CCP 416.20 (defunct corporation) ☐ CCP 416.70 (conservatee)
              ☐ CCP 416.40 (association or partnership) ☐ CCP 416.90 (individual)
   d. ☐ by personal delivery on *(date)*:

4. At the time of service I was at least 18 years of age and not a party to this action.

5. Fee for service: $

6. Person serving:
   a. ☐ California sheriff, marshal, or constable.
   b. ☐ Registered California process server.
   c. ☐ Employee or independent contractor of a registered California process server.
   d. ☐ Not a registered California process server.
   e. ☐ Exempt from registration under Bus. & Prof. Code 22350(b).

   f. Name, address and telephone number and, if applicable, county of registration and number:

I declare under penalty of perjury under the laws of the State of California that the foregoing is true and correct.

(For California sheriff, marshal, or constable use only)
I certify that the foregoing is true and correct.

Date:

Date:

▶ _____ 245 ▶ _____
        (SIGNATURE)   *(SIGNATURE)*

982(a)(11) [Rev. January 1, 1984]

The *Answer—Unlawful Detainer* form shown here is typical of similar forms used by courts throughout the country. The defendant checks the appropriate spaces, and fills in blanks where explanations are required to state his general denial or affirmative defense(s) in the matter.

Failure of a defendant to file an answer results in default; the plaintiff may win the case without taking the matter to trial.

If the defendant denies all allegations made in the plaintiff's complaint, the matter may now be set for trial by the plaintiff.

How a U.D. Trial is Set

The plaintiff must send the clerk of the court a *Memorandum to Set the Case for Trial* to get the U.D. matter on the court calendar. The clerk will set the trial date and notify both parties of the time and place of the hearing.

How Much Money Can the Plaintiff Seek?

The plaintiff may seek all unpaid rent due from the defendant, including rent computed on a per diem (daily) basis for every day he has continued to occupy the property beyond the date he was asked to vacate the premises up to the date of judgment.

The plaintiff may also seek costs associated with the U.D. case; if he wins, the defendant will be ordered to compensate him for all expenses he incurred to bring the matter to trial, but if he loses he must absorb the expenses and pay the defendant's court costs.

What You Need as Evidence

In trial you must be able to prove that the adverse party received any and all legal documents you claim he got from you. Therefore, never drop a legal document in the mail or slip it under the other party's door. Deliver it through personal service and keep the original *Proof of Service* form for each document he has received from you. Without such proof, the other party may claim he never got the information from you and, therefore, had no knowledge about it.

Instructions about service of documents are thoroughly covered in Chapter 6, "How to File Your Case in Court." You may wish to review them now. Copies of *Proof of Service* forms specifically designed for U.D. cases are included as examples in this chapter.

You also need copies of such things as ledger sheets, rent receipts, cancelled checks, and any correspondence or notes involving the other party. The more documentary evidence you can present in court, the more you are likely to win. Of particular importance is evidence proving that a contract of tenancy exists between the two parties.

ATTORNEY OR PARTY WITHOUT ATTORNEY (NAME AND ADDRESS):

TELEPHONE:

FOR COURT USE ONLY

ATTORNEY FOR (NAME):

Insert name of court, judicial district or branch court, if any, and post office and street address:

PLAINTIFF:

DEFENDANT:

ANSWER— Unlawful Detainer

CASE NUMBER:

1. This pleading including attachments and exhibits consists of the following number of pages: _____

2. Defendants *(name):*

   answer the complaint as follows:

3. ***Check ONLY ONE of the next two boxes:***

   a. ☐ Defendant generally denies each statement of the complaint. *(Do not check this box if the complaint demands more than $1,000.)*

   b. ☐ Defendant admits that all of the statements of the complaint are true EXCEPT:

       (1) Defendant claims the following statements of the complaint are false *(use paragraph numbers from the complaint or explain):*

       ☐ Continued on Attachment 3.b.(1).

       (2) Defendant has no information or belief that the following statements of the complaint are true, so defendant denies them *(use paragraph numbers from the complaint or explain):*

       ☐ Continued on Attachment 3.b.(2).

4. AFFIRMATIVE DEFENSES

   a. ☐ *(nonpayment of rent only)* Plaintiff has breached the warranty to provide habitable premises. *(Briefly state the facts below in item 4.k.)*

   b. ☐ Plaintiff waived, changed, or canceled the notice to quit. *(Briefly state the facts below in item 4.k.)*

   c. ☐ Plaintiff served defendant with the notice to quit or filed the complaint to retaliate against defendant. *(Briefly state the facts below in item 4.k.)*

   d. ☐ Plaintiff has failed to perform his obligations under the rental agreement. *(Briefly state the facts below in item 4.k.)*

   e. ☐ By serving defendant with the notice to quit or filing the complaint, plaintiff is arbitrarily discriminating against the defendant in violation of the constitution or laws of the United States or California. *(Briefly state the facts below in item 4.k.)*

   f. ☐ Plaintiff's demand for possession violates the local rent control or eviction control ordinance of *(city or county, title of ordinance, and date of passage):*

       (Briefly state the facts showing violation of the ordinance in item 4.k.)

(Continued)

Form Approved by the
Judicial Council of California
Effective January 1, 1982
Rule 982.1 (95)

247

ANSWER—Unlawful Detainer

CCP 425.12

76A506 **CI194JC**(11) PS 1-86

ANSWER—Unlawful Detainer

g. ☐ Plaintiff accepted rent from defendant to cover a period of time after the date stated in paragraph 8.b. of the complaint.

h. ☐ *(nonpayment of rent only)* On *(date):*   defendant offered the rent due but plaintiff would not accept it.

i. ☐ Defendant made needed repairs and properly deducted the cost from the rent, and plaintiff did not give proper credit.

j. ☐ Other affirmative defenses. *(Briefly state below in item 4.k.)*

k. FACTS SUPPORTING AFFIRMATIVE DEFENSES CHECKED ABOVE *(Identify each item separately.)*

☐ Continued on Attachment 4.k.

5. OTHER STATEMENTS
   a. ☐ Defendant vacated the premises on *(date):*
   b. ☐ Defendant claims a credit for deposits of $_____
   c. ☐ The fair rental value of the premises in item 12 of the complaint is excessive *(explain):*

   d. ☐ Other *(specify):*

6. DEFENDANT REQUESTS
   a. that plaintiff take nothing requested in the complaint.
   b. costs incurred in this proceeding.
   c. ☐ reasonable attorney fees.
   d. ☐ other *(specify):*

. . . .
_____   _____
(Type or print name)   (Signature of defendant or attorney)

. . . .
_____   _____
(Type or print name)   (Signature of defendant or attorney)

*(Each defendant for whom this answer is filed must be named in item 2 **and** must sign this answer unless represented by an attorney.)*

VERIFICATION

(Use a different verification form if the verification is by an attorney or for a corporation or partnership.)

I am the defendant in this proceeding and have read this answer. I declare under penalty of perjury under the laws of the State of California that this answer is true and correct.

Date:

248

. . . .
_____   _____
(Type or print name)   (Signature of defendant)

Understanding the Contract of Tenancy

A written agreement signed by both parties thereto constitutes a contract. A contract of tenancy may be any lease agreement or rental agreement between the landlord and tenant.

Such a written contract contains specific terms and conditions to which the parties agree to perform in accordance with the duties and obligations specified therein.

Standard rental agreement and lease contract forms are available at most stationery and legal supply stores; however, a typewritten or handwritten agreement signed by both parties is also considered legal and binding.

In court, a written contract of tenancy is much easier to prove than an oral contract because it is tangible; however, an oral agreement may also be admitted in evidence *if it can be proven to exist through the testimony given during the trial.*

Example of Contract of Tenancy

In a U.D. case based on an oral contract the plaintiff testified: "Your Honor, Mr. Smith and I sat down and agreed that this was going to be our contract: He would rent the house from me for $350 a month for only three months while I was waiting for my sister and her family to arrive from England sometime shortly after November 1. They would move into the house and pay $900 per month rent.

"In exchange for the reduced rent, Mr. Smith agreed to paint the living room, landscape the yard, and lay new linoleum tile in the kitchen. When he moved in on August 1, Mr. Smith offered to pay two months' rent. I accepted his $700. He never paid another dime, nor did he move out at the end of October, Your Honor, so my sister's family had to move into my crowded house."

The defendant testified: "Your Honor, when Mr. Greene and I made our oral agreement, he said he would reduce my rent if I would manage the property for him. I painted, cleaned up the yard, and put down a new kitchen floor. Then, on September 30, he told me I had to be out at the end of October. It was the first I heard about his sister coming to live in the house. I did not pay any further rent because I had performed approximately $1,000 worth of free service for Mr. Greene. He deliberately used me, Your Honor."

If you were the judge hearing this case, would you have found for the plaintiff or defendant? Would you have favored evicting the tenant or ordering him to pay his past-due rent and allowing him to continue living in the house?

Such decisions are difficult to make in matters in which one party's word is pitted against the other's. Protect yourself by bringing as much documentary evidence as possible to prove your side of the U.D. case in court.

Strategies for Landlords

Eviction proceedings against a tenant begin with the landlord's service to the tenant of a three-day notice or thirty-day notice. He may perform this service personally; he should always keep a copy of the notice so it may be offered as evidence in trial.

During the trial, the plaintiff introduces his evidence and says, "Your Honor, I personally served the three-day notice to the tenant by placing it in his hands."

If a tenant refuses to answer the door or accept the notice offered by the landlord, he may serve the document through a strategy known as "nail and mail." Here is how this technique is performed:

"Nail & Mail" Service of Notice
(A landlord may use this technique to serve a tenant with a three-day or thirty-day notice.)

1. The landlord tacks or tapes the original notice to the tenant's front door.

2. He takes a photograph of the doorway to which the notice is affixed; this may be offered as evidence of the landlord's service of the document.

3. The landlord mails a copy of the notice through the U.S. Postal Service; he sends it Certified Mail, Return Receipt Requested.

4. The signed receipt will be returned to the sender, who may use it in trial as proof of mailing.

Taking a photograph of a notice affixed to a doorway, and sending a copy by certified mail, is not required by law; however, it is our suggestion as a technique you may use, as a landlord, to have a stronger case.

To Whom May Service Be Made?

If the party for whom the landlord's notice is intended is not at home or in his usual place of business, the landlord may serve the notice to another person at either place by requesting it be delivered to the tenant by the recipient. For example, he might say: "Would you please give this to John Smith?" or "Will you make certain Alice Williams gets this?" He *should not* explain what is in the envelope; he *should* get the name of the person to whom he gives the document and *should* keep a note in his file telling him:

- The name of the individual to whom the notice was given.

- The date and time on which it was delivered.

- The place the notice was delivered (apartment, office, etc.).

He should also send a copy by mail, addressed to the tenant at his place of residence.

The people to whom a landlord might deliver a document in the absence of a tenant include any person of "reasonable age and discretion," usually sixteen years of age or older; such a recipient could be a tenant's roommate, house guest, child, or spouse.

If the place of residence or business cannot be ascertained, or a person of suitable age and discretion cannot be found, you may affix a copy in a conspicuous place on the property (e.g., front door) and send a copy by mail to the tenant at the place where the property is situated.

Introducing Co-defendants

When two or more individuals are named on the landlord's three-day or thirty-day notice, they will be joined in the lawsuit as "co-defendants." A co-defendant can be a spouse, adult child, roommate, or other co-tenant. A notice states, in effect, that everyone named therein is duly notified to pay the overdue rent within three days or vacate the premises, or to vacate the premises within thirty days. However, a notice in which only one tenant is named is legally binding only on that individual.

Therefore, if you plan to start eviction proceedings against more than one tenant occupying the same premises, be certain they are all named in your three-day or thirty-day notice.

The Landlord's Role After Notice Is Served

The landlord's "service of process" should end when the lawsuit begins. Therefore, after you have filed your U.D. lawsuit with the court, you should engage a neutral third party to serve the Summons and Complaint on the tenant(s).

To be assured that any proof of service which you offer in trial is admitted as evidence, hire a professional process server to serve the defendant(s) your Summons and Complaint. He may be a sheriff, marshal, or registered process server. Refer to Chapter 6, "How to File Your Case in Court," for more information.

Why Pay If You Can Get Service of Process Free?

Why should you pay a professional process server if a friend or acquaintance could serve your documents free of charge and vouch for their delivery? To protect your evidence. Proof of service by a noncertified or unregistered process server will be inadmissible hearsay unless the person who served the documents appears in court and testifies about the service he performed. On the other hand, the written declaration of service by a registered process server is admissible, even if he is not in court, by express statutory provision.

Issues the Litigant Must Prove

If you are the plaintiff in your unlawful detainer trial, you must prove one or more of these issues to the court:

- That there was a contract of tenancy (oral or written) with the defendant.

- That the defendant breached the contract.

- That you served a proper notice on the defendant demanding that he perform.

- That the defendant failed to comply with the terms of the notice and is still in possession of the premises.

- The amount of damages which you claim the defendant owes.

If you are the defendant in your U.D. case, you must raise and prove one or more of the following defenses during the trial:

- Notice was improper because it demanded more rent than was owed; it was not in the alternative;* it was not served; or it asked rent for a period more than one year.

- Retaliation.

- That the premises is uninhabitable.

- That you spent money to correct a condition or you made repairs to the premises, expenses for which were deducted from the rent; the landlord knew those repairs were needed but did not make such repairs within a reasonable time.

- That the landlord accepted the rent beyond the expiration date of the notice period.

- That the tenant had tendered payment within the notice period but the landlord rejected it.

Besides the amount of money due the landlord by the tenant for the delinquent rental period, the plaintiff-landlord may also seek judgment for any damage done by the tenant to the premises if, indeed, any such damage existed.

---

*The term "pay rent or quit," which is standard legal language required in a three-day notice, gives the tenant the alternative of paying rent or quitting (vacating) the premises. If no alternative appears in the notice, the defendant may show the court the notice was "not in the alternative."

The plaintiff must itemize all damages and be able to present proof such alleged damage happened; i.e., by the testimony of witnesses, photographs, and statements, bills, or receipts for each repair job.

Insight Into Witnesses

People who live near each other (in the same neighborhood, apartment house, or condominium complex) may be reluctant about testifying against a neighbor. Even a person harboring deep dislike for an individual outside of court may be reluctant to take the stand against him inside the courtroom.

If the testimony of one or more eyewitnesses is crucial to your U.D. case, do not run the risk of winding up in court without any witnesses. Serve each witness with a *Subpoena,* a court order that demands a person to appear for the purpose of giving testimony and/or providing evidence.

The law does not demand that a litigant subpoena his witnesses; however, you should demand it of yourself.

Instructions on how to subpoena your witnesses, along with other helpful tips and techniques about working with witnesses, are contained in Chapter 17, "How to Organize Your Witnesses."

The Difference Between Small Claims and Other U.D. Cases

Small claims trials are noted for being short and quick. If your U.D. matter will be heard in Small Claims Court, the trial will be much less formal than if it were being tried in another court.

In Small Claims Court, the judge participates actively in the proceedings by asking most of the questions, conducting the examination of witnesses, and calling a halt when he feels he has heard enough.

The litigants neither make opening nor closing statements, nor do they argue exhibits at the close of each side's examination of witnesses. Instead, if the opposition objects to an exhibit, both parties argue the exhibit at the time it is introduced in evidence, and the judge makes his ruling about whether or not it is admissible.

Although Small Claims Court proceedings are neither stiff nor formal, they are patterned around the rules of court which govern every type of trial.

In a non-small claims U.D. matter, the parties conduct their own direct and cross-examinations; the judge, as neutral third party, listens and observes as opposing counsel elicit testimony and introduce exhibits as evidence.

(Note: Most U.D. cases are filed in Municipal Court, not in Small Claims Court, because landlords prefer to be represented by lawyers.)

How to Try Your Own Small Claim U.D. Case

A Small Claims Court matter begins when the case is called and the parties take their places at the counsel table or podium provided by the court. Their witnesses, usually numbering no more than two for each side, may accompany them. The parties and their witnesses remain standing throughout the trial. Only the judge is seated. In the following order, the judge will:

- Ask the plaintiff why he believes he is entitled to judgment.

- Ask the plaintiff's witnesses if they can corroborate plaintiff's testimony.

- Ask the defendant and his witnesses what they have to say about why the plaintiff should not get anything.

Understanding the Judge

If a person hesitates, hedges, or fishes around for words while testifying, rather than giving a direct answer to his question, the judge may take such factors into account when determining the individual's credibility.

When a litigant or witness fidgets, shifts about nervously, or refuses to look at the judge while speaking, by his own action that individual indicates he is trying to hide something, or is evading a point he does not want brought out. The judge may then dig for information to uncover the truth.

The judge will ask you if you have brought any exhibits to offer as evidence. The more physical proof you can offer, the better your chance becomes of winning.

To help yourself win your Small Claims Court U.D. case, look at the judge, not above, below, or around him. Answer his questions honestly and without hesitation. Last, never try to raise an issue in court which is not included in your lawsuit.

After hearing both sides' cases, the judge will reach his decision and render judgment. Unlawful detainer matters tried in Small Claims Court usually take only a few minutes to resolve.

For complete details about proceedings in Small Claims Court, refer to Chapter 27, "How to Try Your Own Small Claims Court Case."

How to Try Your Own Unlawful Detainer Case

In a non-small claims U.D. case, the plaintiff is the first party to introduce himself after the case has been called and the litigants have approached the counsel table.

Have your exhibits in order so you will not have to search through your file to find them each time you introduce a document; organize them so the first exhibit is on top, the second is beneath it, and the last piece of evidence is at the bottom.

You may use the following outline as a guide in the preparation of your U.D. trial presentation.

Outline of an Unlawful Detainer (U.D.) Trial
(Non-Small Claim)
(To prepare your presentation for court, read through this trial
outline and fill in the blanks with your own words.)

PLAINTIFF: Your Honor, my name is (your name) _____
_____, the plaintiff. I am ready to proceed.

DEFENDANT: Your Honor, my name is (your name) _____
_____. I am the defendant.

JUDGE: The plaintiff may proceed.

DEFENDANT: (sits down at counsel table)

PLAINTIFF (if testifying as own key witness): Your Honor, I wish to call myself as
   plaintiff's first witness. May I please proceed in narrative form?

JUDGE: Yes.

PLAINTIFF: I am the (owner/manager/landlord) _____ of the
   (property/premises) _____ known as (*name of building, if*
   any)_____ located at (*street*
   address) _____
   (*city*) _____ (*state*) _____.
   I have entered into a contract, which is (written/oral)_____, with
   the defendant (*name the defendant*)_____.
   (*If the contract is written, plaintiff introduces it.*)
      Your Honor, I have this document which is our (lease/rent agreement)
   _____. May it be marked Plaintiff's (*number*) ____ for identification.
      (*Point to defendant's signature.*) This is the defendant's signature. I know it
   is his signature because (*state your reason: he signed it in front of you, you have*
   seen his signature many times before, etc.) _____
   _____.

      (*Explain reason for taking U.D. Action.*) Your Honor, the issues(s) in this mat-
   ter (is/are) that (*tell how the defendant breached the contract, did not pay rent, and*
   did not vacate the premises) _____.
   I show the court this (three-day notice/thirty-day notice) _____, which I personally served (*the defendant*) _____ (*or identify other per-*
   son served) _____ because the defendant was not there, on
   (*date*) _____. May it be marked plaintiff's (*number*)____ for identification. I also show the court the return receipt. May it be marked plaintiff's
   (*number*) ____ for identification.

Plaintiff's Direct Examination of Witnesses

The purpose of direct examination is to enable the plaintiff to build his case; therefore, a series of questions which you may ask your witness is included, along with responses the witness may give. When planning your side's direct examination, you may use any of these questions which apply to your case, and ignore the others.

PLAINTIFF (*to direct examine key witness other than himself*): Plaintiff calls his first witness, (*name of witness*) _____.

WITNESS NUMBER 1: (*takes stand: states name and is sworn or affirmed by clerk*)

PLAINTIFF (*remain at counsel table to conduct direct examination by asking questions applicable to your case from this suggested list*): (Mr./Mrs./Ms.) _____, what is your relationship to plaintiff?

WITNESS NUMBER 1: (*Witness should respond that he manages plaintiff's property.*)

PLAINTIFF: What is the name of the building which you manage?

WITNESS NUMBER 1: (*Witness tells name of the apartment or other building, if any.*)

PLAINTIFF: What is the address of the property which you manage?

WITNESS NUMBER 1: (*Witness tells street address, city, and state.*)

PLAINTIFF: How long have you been manager of this property?

WITNESS NUMBER 1: (*Witness tells date he took the position and length of time in months or years he has served in this capacity.*)

PLAINTIFF: Do you know the defendant, (Mr./Mrs./Ms. last name _____?

WITNESS NUMBER 1: Yes.

PLAINTIFF: How long have you known (him/her/them)_____?

WITNESS NUMBER 1: (*Witness responds in months or years.*)

PLAINTIFF: Explain how you know the defendant?

WITNESS NUMBER 1: The defendant is a tenant in the building I manage.

PLAINTIFF: Does the defendant have a relationship with the plaintiff?

WITNESS NUMBER 1: A landlord-tenant relationship through the lease/rental contract which exists between them.

PLAINTIFF: On what date did the plaintiff and defendant enter into this contract?

WITNESS NUMBER 1: (*Witness names the date the lease/rental agreement was signed.*)

Three Essential Elements of a Civil Trial

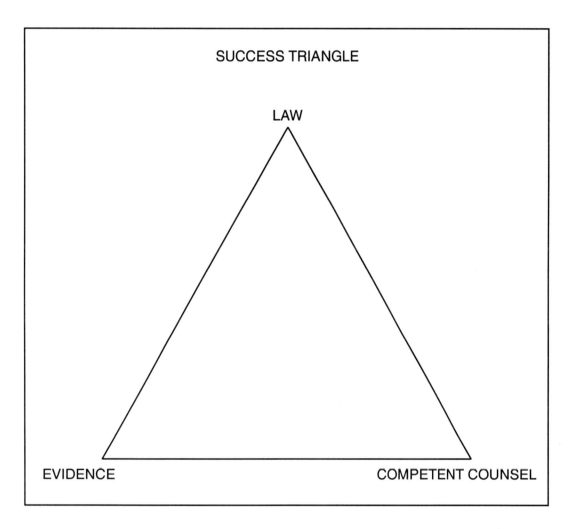

To win in trial, you must be adequately prepared on all three points shown in this illustration. If your case is weak in one or more of the elements, concentrate on strengthening such weaknesses before attempting to try your own unlawful detainer (eviction) matter in court.

Through the foregoing series of questions, the direct examiner has laid a proper foundation that establishes the landlord-tenant relationship in the disputed U.D. matter. When you have accomplished this portion of your direct examination, proceed with the introduction of specific evidence and facts which prove your case.

If you wish to approach the witness to show him a piece of evidence, you must ask the court's permission to do so. Name each piece of evidence by its identifying mark, such as Plaintiff's 1, Plaintiff's 2, etc. You will offer these exhibits in evidence later. Now you only ask the witness to identify the exhibits.

The questions you will ask depend upon your grounds for eviction; therefore, select only questions which are applicable to your matter from those given in the following guidelines.

PLAINTIFF (*to prove breach of contract has occurred*): Your Honor, with the court's permission, may I approach this witness?

JUDGE: Yes.

PLAINTIFF (*approach witness; take exhibit[s] with you*): I show you this document marked Plaintiff's 1 for identification. (*Show witness the contract.*) Do you recognize it?

WITNESS: (*identifies it as the contract between plaintiff and defendant*)

PLAINTIFF (*points out signature*): Do you recognize this signature?

WITNESS: (*identifies it as the defendant's signature*)

PLAINTIFF: Please tell the court how you know this is the defendant's signature.

WITNESS: (*explains that he was present when the defendant signed the lease, he has seen the signature before, etc.*)

PLAINTIFF: Did the defendant not do anything which is required in this contract?

(*If answer of witness is yes, ask:*)

PLAINTIFF: What?

WITNESS (*responds in narrative form in one of two ways*): The defendant committed nuisance by (*explain the nuisance*) _____

_____.

or

The defendant did not pay his rent according to terms of the (lease/rental contract/agreement). (*Explain what happened*)_____.

At this point, you have established how the defendant breached the contract. If, however, instead of proving that the defendant breached the contract, it is your intention to show that he failed to vacate the premises after plaintiff served him with a thirty-day notice, proceed as follows:

PLAINTIFF (*to prove defendant did not comply with thirty-day notice*): Your Honor, with the court's permission, may I approach this witness?

JUDGE: Yes.

PLAINTIFF (*approach witness; take exhibit(s) with you*): I show you this document marked Plaintiff's 1 for identification. (*Show witness the contract.*) Do you recognize it?

WITNESS: (*Identifies it as the contract between plaintiff and defendant.*)

PLAINTIFF: (*Has witness identify signatures, as explained in the foregoing portion of this trial outline.*)
(*Points to portion of contract in which terms state a thirty-day notice to vacate may be served by either or both parties upon each other.*) Will you please read Section (*name the section*) _____. (*Hand contract to witness.*)

WITNESS: (*Reads the section requested by direct examiner and returns contract to the examiner.*)

PLAINTIFF (*shows witness the thirty-day notice*): I now show you a document marked Plaintiff's 2. Can you identify it?

WITNESS: (Responds that it is a copy of the thirty-day notice served on the defendant, notifying him to vacate the premises.)

PLAINTIFF: How was it served?

WITNESS: (*Explains how he served defendant the thirty-day notice.*)

PLAINTIFF: After the expiration of the thirty-day period, (*date*)_____, did the defendant vacate the premises?

WITNESS: No.

At this point, you have established that a proper thirty-day notice to vacate the premises was served by the plaintiff on the defendant and that the defendant did not comply but, instead, continued occupying the premises. If no thirty-day notice was involved, because the lease expired and the defendant should have moved—but did not—proceed as follows.

The plaintiff will now give the witness the opportunity to testify in narrative form to further prove the plaintiff's U.D. case against the defendant.

PLAINTIFF: After the defendant breached the contract, what happened next?

WITNESS (*testifies in narrative form*):
(*For nuisance:*) He was served with a three-day notice to cease and desist or vacate the premises.
> *or*

(*For nonpayment of rent:*) He was served with a three-day notice to pay rent or vacate the premises.

PLAINTIFF: How was the defendant served with the three-day notice (*to cease and desist or pay or quit*)?

WITNESS (*tells in narrative form how defendant was served*):
(*If witness served defendant:*) I served the defendant myself with a (*name the kind of notice*) _____.
> *or*

(*If served to person other than defendant:*) I served (*name of recipient*) myself and asked (him/her) to give the document to the defendant.
(*Describe method used to serve the notice; i.e., hand delivery, posted notice on door, and took photo*) _____
_____.

I then mailed a copy of the notice through the U.S. Postal Service by Certified Mail, Return Receipt Requested.
> *or*

(*If witness did not personally serve the defendant, identify and offer in evidence the proof of service of the registered process server.*) _____
_____
_____
_____.

At this point, the direct examiner will seek corroboration of the witness' statements. He will ask the witness to identify the documents just mentioned; he may then finalize his presentation by introducing documents to prove his damages.

PLAINTIFF: (*Show witness the three-day notice and then the proof of service. Each time an exhibit is shown to the witness, repeat:*)
(*Show witness document*) I show you this document marked Plaintiff's (*number*) _____ for identification. What is that?

WITNESS (*identifies each exhibit as it is presented by saying:*) That is the (*name the document*) _____ that (I served/was served) _____
_____ the defendant.

PLAINTIFF (*you are now ready to prove damages*): Because of the defendant's action, did the plaintiff suffer damages?

WITNESS: Yes.

PLAINTIFF: Will you please explain the damages or losses sustained by the plaintiff?

WITNESS (*explains one-by-one the damage or loss: costs for repairs to the premises, rent due from defendant, etc.*): _____
_____
_____

The total amount of (damages/loss) sustained by the plaintiff was (*give the amount in dollars*) $_____.

PLAINTIFF (*asks witness to identify corroborating exhibits: bills, receipts for repairs, cancelled checks, etc. He repeats this step with every exhibit*):
I show you this (*describe exhibit*) _____ in the amount of $_____, which is marked Plaintiff's (*number*) _____ for identification. What is that?

WITNESS (*identifies each exhibit*): It is the (bill/receipt/check, etc.) _____ for (*explain what the charge covered*) _____
_____.

PLAINTIFF (*when he has finished with this witness*): No further questions, Your Honor. (*Take your exhibits and be seated at the counsel table.*)

This concludes the direct examination of the plaintiff's key witness. By selecting the appropriate questions, and ignoring those which do not apply to your matter, you will be able to direct examine your witness swiftly, accurately, and professionally.

Following the direct examination of each of your side's witnesses, the opposition will have the opportunity to conduct cross-examination. The trial will proceed in this manner:

JUDGE (*to defendant's lawyer or Pro Per*): Does the defendant wish to cross-examine this witness?

If the defendant does not wish to cross-examine the witness by asking further questions related to the witness's testimony given on direct examination, he advises the court:

DEFENDANT (*rise to address judge*): No cross-examination, Your Honor. (*Sits down.*)

The plaintiff may now rise, call his next witness and proceed with the direct examination of that person. The defendant may cross-examine each witness following the direct examination.

Cross-Examination in the U.D. Trial

As a legal tool, cross-examination allows a litigant the opportunity to "punch holes" in the opponent's case.

The cross-examiner will try to elicit answers from the witness that will be favorable to his own side of the case. Cross-examination is an art.

Briefly, cross-examination should be confined to facts brought out during direct examination, but questions which are "beyond the scope of direct examination" may be allowed if their purpose is to impeach (undermine) the witness or otherwise challenge his (and, consequently, the adverse party's) credibility. Objections may be raised and argued during cross-examination.

When the cross-examiner has received answers helpful to his case, he should end the cross-examination or go on to another topic. Several hypothetical sample questions are given here to show how the defendant in a U.D. case might cross-examine the plaintiff's witness. Using these examples as your guide, formulate your own cross-examination questions on your day in court.

When the plaintiff has finished with the direct examination of his witness, the defendant may rise and, standing behind the counsel table, conduct his cross-examination of the plaintiff's witness.

DEFENDANT: (Mr./Mrs./Ms. *last name*) _____, on direct examination, you said the defendant did not pay his rent within the three-day grace period allowed following its due date of March 1st, correct?

WITNESS: Yes.

DEFENDANT: Is it also true that you said you personally reminded the defendant that he had a three-day grace period in which to pay the rent?

WITNESS: Yes.

DEFENDANT: Is it also true that the defendant offered you his check dated March 3, 1996, but your refused to accept it?

PLAINTIFF (*rising to make objection*): Objection! Beyond the scope of direct examination.

DEFENDANT (*in answer to objection*): Your Honor, my reason for the question is to impeach the plaintiff, who claims that the defendant did not offer to pay rent.

JUDGE: Overruled.

DEFENDANT: Did the defendant offer you his rent check dated March 3, 1996?

WITNESS: Yes.

DEFENDANT: No further questions, Your Honor.

If the defendant had not ended his cross-examination at this point, the plaintiff's witness could have testified, "The reason I did not accept the defendant's check dated March 3, 1996, was because it was back-dated. He did not offer it to me until March 5, 1996." This testimony would have been harmful, not helpful, to the defendant. Note that an alert plaintiff can being up this harmful evidence in re-direct examination.

When the plaintiff has completed the direct examination of his witnesses, and the defendant has cross-examined the last of plaintiff's witnesses, the plaintiff is now ready to offer his exhibits in evidence. At this point, you do the following:

PLAINTIFF (*stand behind counsel table*): Your Honor, this concludes the plaintiff's presentation of evidence. May I now offer my exhibits in evidence?

JUDGE: Yes.

PLAINTIFF (*name each exhibit and hand exhibits collectively to the clerk*): Plaintiff's 1, (*describe it*) _____
    Plaintiff's 2, (*describe it*) _____
    Plaintiff's 3, (*describe it*) _____

If the defendant objects to any of plaintiff's exhibits, he will make an objection. Both plaintiff and defendant then argue their respective reasons for wishing the exhibit to be admitted or excluded. The judge will rule to admit or exclude the objectionable exhibit.

When the plaintiff's exhibits have been admitted in evidence, he is through trying his case. If you are the plaintiff, you now say:

PLAINTIFF (*to conclude your presentation*): Plaintiff rests. Thank you, Your Honor. (*Be seated at counsel table.*)

The defendant now rises and seeks the court's permission to call his first witness. If you are the defendant, and you are representing yourself, proceed as follows:

DEFENDANT: The defendant is ready to proceed, Your Honor. May I call myself as my own witness?

JUDGE: Yes.

DEFENDANT (*Take the witness stand; if you have any exhibits to introduce, take them with you. After being sworn or affirmed, say:*) May I testify in narrative form, Your Honor?

JUDGE: Yes.

DEFENDANT: Your Honor, I have been a tenant at (*the property/address*) _____
_____ (owned/managed) _____by the plaintiff
for (*length of time of tenancy*) _____. On (*date*)_____, I received
a summons and complaint notifying me that I was being sued by the plaintiff
for (*name the ground of the complaint*)_____.
(*In your own words, you now present your affirmative defense by telling the judge
what happened and by corroborating your testimony with exhibits which prove your
statements. Several suggestions about how to proceed are given here; build your defense
around the one which most closely depicts your case.*)

(*Complaint partially true*)
Your Honor, the defendant admits all the statement's of the plaintiff's complaint are true, except (*explain one-by-one any statements which are untrue*)
_____
_____.

(*Introduce evidence to prove each point you are making.*) I show the court this
(*describe the exhibit*) _____, which is marked Defendant's (*letter*) _____
for identification, _____, which (shows/states)
_____ (*explain what it proves*) _____
_____.

(*Affirmative defenses—Select the one applicable to your case.*)
    (*Non-payment of rent:*)
Your Honor, the plaintiff has breached the warranty with the defendant to
provide habitable premises. (*Explain the conditions which make the premises non-habitable:*) _____
_____.

(*Introduce proof, such as photographs, etc.*) I show the court this (*describe the exhibit*)
_____, which I request to be marked Defendant's (*letter*) _____ for
identification, to show the court that (*describe the condition of premises*)
_____
_____.

    (*Nuisance "order to quit" cancelled:*)
Your Honor, the plaintiff waived, changed, or canceled the notice to quit which
had been served on me for nuisance and I complied with the notice. (*Briefly
explain what happened, as, for example, you stopped playing loud music, etc.*)

_____. (*If you have any proof of your statement, offer it now.*) I show the court this (*affidavit or note from manager, etc.*) _____, which I request to be marked Defendant's (*letter*) _____ for identification. It (shows/indicates/proves) _____. (*If the order to quit was issued for a reason other than nuisance, substitute that reason in your presentation, and offer corroborative evidence.*)

(*Plaintiff's retaliation against defendant:*)
Your Honor, the plaintiff served the notice to quit, or filed the complaint, to retaliate against the defendant. (*Briefly explain your reason for claiming the plaintiff wishes to get even with you, punish you, etc.*) _____ _____.

(*If you have any documentary proof of your statement, offer it now.*) I show the court this (*describe the exhibit*) _____, which is marked Defendant's (*letter*) _____ for identification, which (shows/tells/explains) _____ _____ _____.

(*Plaintiff's failure to perform:*)
Your Honor, the plaintiff failed to perform his (duties/obligations) _____ under the terms of our (rental/lease) _____ (agreement/lease/contract)_____. I show the court this (agreement/lease/contract) _____, which I request to be marked Defendant's (*letter*) _____ for identification. With the court's permission, I will read from page (*number*) _____, (section/paragraph/item) _____: (*Read applicable section*) "_____ _____." (*Tell how plaintiff failed to perform*) _____ _____. (*If you have any other exhibits to corroborate your statement, present them now.*)

(*Discrimination by plaintiff:*)
Your Honor, the plaintiff arbitrarily discriminated against the defendant in violation of the Constitution of the United States. (He/she) did this by (*serving defendant with the notice to quit/filing the complaint*) _____. (*Briefly state the facts about your discrimination claim*) _____. (*If you have any exhibits to corroborate your claim, introduce them now.*)

(*Violation of local rent/eviction-control ordinance:*)
Your Honor, the plaintiff's demand for possession of the premises violates local (rent control/eviction control) ordinance for the (city/county) of _____, which is entitled (*name or other identification of ordinance*) _____, which was enacted into law on (*date of passage*) _____. According to this ordinance, plaintiff's action of (*explain*

plaintiff's action) _____ was a violation of this law which states (*tell what the ordinance says about the issue in dispute)* _____ _____. (*If you have a copy of the ordinance with you, you may now introduce it as evidence.)*

    (Rent accepted after period stated in plaintiff's three-day notice to pay or vacate the premises had expired:)
Your Honor, the defendant accepted rent in the amount of $_____ from the defendant after (*date stated in plaintiff's complaint for rent to be paid or premises to be vacated)*_____. This was the date the defendant was notified to pay or quit the premises and, therefore, renders the plaintiff's complaint null and void. (*If you have proof, such as cancelled checks or rent receipts, introduce them now.)*

    (Refusal by plaintiff to accept defendant's rent in eviction action based on ground of "non-payment:")
Your Honor, on the date of (*date you tried to pay rent)* _____, the defendant offered to pay the rent due, but the plaintiff would not accept it. (*If you have any proof, such as non-cancelled check, statement of cash deposit in a rent trust account, etc., introduce it now.)*

    (Defendant deducted costs of repairs from the amount of rent due:)
Your Honor, the defendant made needed repairs to the premises in the amount of $_____, and properly deducted the cost from the rent. The plaintiff did not give the defendant proper credit. (*If you have exhibits to prove your statement, you may now present them one at a time.)* I show the court this (receipt/cancelled check/bill)_____, which is marked Defendant's (*letter)*_____, in the amount of $_____ for (*name the repair)* _____.
(*When all exhibits have been introduced, say:)* The total cost of repairs was $_____, which I deducted from the rent due in the amount of (*amount of rent)* $_____. (In California, Civil Code 1942 requires the tenant to give notice to the landlord of the dilapidations. Then tenant must wait for landlord for a reasonable time to repair. Thirty days is presumed reasonable. If landlord neglects to act, tenant can then repair and deduct for an amount not exceeding one month's rent.)

    The foregoing examples illustrate the most common affirmative defenses offered by defendants in U.D. trials; if your matter differs from those given here, you may structure your defense around these guidelines. You may also wish to include in your testimony one or more of the following statements of fact:

- Your Honor, on the date of (*date*)_____, defendant vacated the premises at (*address*)_____.

- Your Honor, the defendant claims from plaintiff a credit for deposits in the amount of (*amount of refund due you*) $_____.

- Your Honor, the fair rental value of the premises as shown in the plaintiff's complaint, (*amount*) $_____is excessive. (*Explain the grounds upon which you base your statement.*) _____
_____.

Advise the judge when you are finished with your presentation, and remain on the witness stand, by saying:

DEFENDANT: Nothing further, Your Honor.

The plaintiff now has the opportunity to cross-examine the witness, according to cross-examination techniques already explained in this trial outline. If the plaintiff has no cross-examination questions, you may now step down and continue trying your case, as follows:

DEFENDANT: The defendant calls his next witness, (*name of witness*) _____
_____.

When the witness has taken the stand and been sworn or affirmed, you may now ask direct examination questions designed to build your defense. When you have finished with the witness, the plaintiff may cross-examine him.

When all witnesses for the defense have testified, you are ready to offer your exhibits in evidence and conclude your presentation, as follows:

DEFENDANT: This concludes the presentation of the defense. May I now offer my exhibits in evidence?

JUDGE: Yes.

DEFENDANT (*name each exhibit and give exhibits collectively to the clerk*): Defendant's A (*describe the exhibit*) _____. Defendant's B (*describe the exhibit*) _____. Defendant's C (*describe the exhibit*) _____.

If the plaintiff objects to any of the defendant's exhibits, both parties will argue their respective reasons for wishing each exhibit to be excluded or admitted. When all exhibits have been admitted, the defendant is through trying his case.

DEFENDANT (*to conclude presentation*): The defendant rests. Thank you, Your Honor. (*Be seated at counsel table.*)

When the defendant has rested his case, the litigants' portion of the proceedings is finished. In many types of civil matters, particularly those involving jury trials or negligence, arguments may be given by both sides to offer summations of their cases and pray for judgment. Final arguments are not necessary in the average U.D. trial because the judge already knows the facts, as well as judgment being sought by both parties. Therefore, when the defense has rested, only one step remains to conclude the proceeding:

The Court's Judgment

After considering the evidence and the law, the judge will hand down his decision and render judgment. The court will probably issue one of three decisions:

- *Judgment for plaintiff.* The defendant is ordered to vacate the premises and to pay rent due until the date of judgment.

- *Judgment for defendant.* The plaintiff is ordered to accept the defendant's reduced rent to be paid within a specific date to compensate for any out-of-pocket expenses incurred by the defendant for repairs, etc., and the defendant may continue occupying the premises, or for reduction due to habitability problems. If the defendant fails to pay, then judgment for the plaintiff will be entered awarding him possession of the premises, the reduced rent, and costs.

- *Judgment for defendant upon plaintiff's failure to prove an element in his case.* For example, notice was not properly served; therefore, the defendant is ordered to have possession of the premises.

Even if the court renders judgment which differs from these examples, the judge's decision stands—unless the matter is taken on appeal.

Assuming your U.D. matter will not be appealed, the steps which should be taken next are explained below.

What Happens After Trial

If the plaintiff loses his U.D. case, he does not get possession of the presmises and cannot collect rent, damages, or other money he sought in his complaint. However, if he loses on a technicality (i.e., improper three-day notice because the amount stated is wrong, or the notice was only mailed, not hand delivered), he can file another complaint based on the same unpaid rent.

If the defendant wins, he remains in possession of the premises and recovers costs of the suit.

Winning Plaintiff's Procedure

If you, the plaintiff, win your U.D. case against the defendant and the court orders him to vacate the premises, proceed immediately as follows:

1. *File a Writ of Execution*—The plaintiff files in the court a completed form known as a *Writ of Execution/Possession.* This is a written order directing the sheriff, marshal, constable, or other authorized law enforcement agency or registered process server to enforce the court's order.

   (The sample shown here is for Los Angeles; however, every jurisdiction has similar writs of execution/possession.) When filed, you now become the "judgment creditor."

2. *Arrange for Delivery*—Take your *Writ of Execution/Possession* to the sheriff, marshal, or constable and arrange for him to handle the matter for you. The writ authorizes him to go to the defendant's premises and post a *Notice to Vacate.* (A sample of this form is also provided for your reference.) This notice orders the defendant, who now becomes known as the "judgment debtor," to vacate the premises by or before the date decreed by the court.

3. *Taking Possession of Property*—After the expiration period, if the tenant has not vacated the premises, the sheriff, marshal, or constable returns to the property and evicts him. If the judgment debtor leaves peaceably, no force is required; however, if not, the law enforcement agency so empowered may force the tenant and/or his personal property from the premises. This same method may be used to collect money or other debts due the judgment creditor by the judgment debtor.

4. *Satisfaction of Judgment*—When the judgment has been satisfied (paid in full, or other terms or conditions fulfilled), the plaintiff must file a form known as *Satisfaction of Judgment* with the court. The case will then be closed.

Landlord-Tenant Rights

Landlords and tenants both have rights; therefore, it is important that you know the law applicable to your case. For example, every tenant served with a *Notice to Vacate* may claim his right to possession of the premises by showing the court he has the right to remain there, as follows:

- *Right of Possession*—When a notice to vacate the premises is posted by an authorized sheriff, marshal, or constable, it is accompanied by a copy of the *Writ of Execution/Possession* filed by the judgment creditor. Along with the writ will be a form known in California as *Claim of Right to Possession.* If any person occupying

ATTORNEY OR PARTY WITHOUT ATTORNEY *(Name and Address)* :

☐ Recording requested by and return to:

TELEPHONE NO.:

FOR RECORDER'S USE ONLY

☐ ATTORNEY FOR ☐ JUDGMENT CREDITOR ☐ ASSIGNEE OF RECORD

NAME OF COURT:
STREET ADDRESS:
MAILING ADDRESS:
CITY AND ZIP CODE:
BRANCH NAME:

PLAINTIFF:

DEFENDANT:

WRIT OF	☐	EXECUTION (Money Judgment)
	☐	POSSESSION OF ☐ Personal Property
		☐ Real Property
	☐	SALE

CASE NUMBER:

FOR COURT USE ONLY

1. **To the Sheriff or any Marshal or Constable of the County of:**

   You are directed to enforce the judgment described below with daily interest and your costs as provided by law.

2. **To any registered process server:** You are authorized to serve this writ only in accord with CCP 699.080 or CCP 715.040.

3. *(Name)* :
   is the ☐ judgment creditor ☐ assignee of record
   whose address is shown on this form above the court's name.

4. **Judgment debtor** *(name and last known address)* :

   ☐ additional judgment debtors on reverse

5. **Judgment entered** on *(date)* :

6. ☐ **Judgment renewed** on *(dates)* :

7. **Notice of sale** under this writ
   a. ☐ has not been requested.
   b. ☐ has been requested *(see reverse)*.

8. ☐ Joint debtor information on reverse.

[SEAL]

9. ☐ See reverse for information on real or personal property to be delivered under a writ of possession or sold under a writ of sale.

10. ☐ This writ is issued on a sister-state judgment.

11. Total judgment . . . . $

12. Costs after judgment (per filed order or memo CCP 685.090) . $

13. Subtotal *(add 11 and 12)* . . . . . $

14. Credits . . . . $

15. Subtotal *(subtract 14 from 13)* . $

16. Interest after judgment (per filed affidavit CCP 685.050) . . . . . . $

17. Fee for issuance of writ . . . . . . $

18. **Total** *(add 15, 16, and 17)* . . . . $

19. Levying officer: Add daily interest from date of writ *(at the legal rate on 15)* of . . . . $

20. ☐ The amounts called for in items 11–19 are different for each debtor. These amounts are stated for each debtor on Attachment 20.

Issued on
(date) :

Clerk, by _____ , Deputy

— NOTICE TO PERSON SERVED: SEE REVERSE FOR IMPORTANT INFORMATION —

(Continued on reverse)

Form Adopted by the
Judicial Council of California
EJ-130 (Rev. January 1, 1989)
76W791 CI-75JC(11) (Rev. 1/89) PS 2/90

WRIT OF EXECUTION

270

CCP 699.520, 712.010, 715.010

SHORT TITLE:

CASE NUMBER:

Items continued from the first page:

4. ☐ Additional judgment debtor *(name and last known address)*:

7. ☐ **Notice of sale** has been requested by *(name and address)*:

8. ☐ **Joint debtor** was declared bound by the judgment (CCP 989–994)

a. on *(date)*:

a. on *(date)*:

b. name and address of joint debtor:

b. name and address of joint debtor:

c. ☐ additional costs against certain joint debtors *(itemize)*:

9. ☐ *(Writ of Possession or Writ of Sale)* **Judgment** was entered for the following:

a. ☐ Possession of real property. The complaint was filed on *(date)*:

(1) The court will hear objections to enforcement of the judgment under CCP 1174.3 on the following dates *(specify)*:

(2) The daily rental value on the date the complaint was filed is *(specify)*: $

b. ☐ Possession of personal property

☐ If delivery cannot be had, then for the value *(itemize in 9e)* specified in the judgment or supplemental order.

c. ☐ Sale of personal property

d. ☐ Sale of real property

e. Description of property:

— NOTICE TO PERSON SERVED —

Writ of execution or sale. Your rights and duties are indicated on the accompanying Notice of Levy.

Writ of possession of personal property. If the levying officer is not able to take custody of the property, the levying officer will make a demand upon you for the property. If custody is not obtained following demand, the judgment may be enforced as a money judgment for the value of the property specified in the judgment or in a supplemental order.

Writ of possession of real property. If the premises are not vacated within five days after the date of service on the occupant or, if service is by posting, within five days after service on you, the levying officer will remove the occupants from the real property and place the judgment creditor in possession of the property. Personal property remaining on the premises will be sold or otherwise disposed of in accordance with CCP 1174 unless you or the owner of the property pays the judgment creditor the reasonable cost of storage and takes possession of the personal property not later than 15 days after the time the judgment creditor takes possession of the premises.

A Claim of Right to Possession form accompanies this writ.

EJ-130 [Rev. January 1, 1989]   **WRIT OF EXECUTION**

NOTICE TO VACATE

CASE NUMBER: _____

TO: Judgment debtor, members of the judgment debtor's household, and any occupants holding under the judgment debtor

By virtue of a **Writ of Possession of Real Property**, a copy of which is attached,

YOU ARE HEREBY ORDERED TO VACATE THE PREMISES DESCRIBED IN THE WRIT

NOT LATER THAN: _____ , 19____

MARSHAL'S DIVISION (Name, Address, and Telephone Number)

ROBERT F. MANN, MARSHAL

By: _____
                    Deputy

Date: _____

NOTICE TO OCCUPANTS

IF YOU ARE NOT NAMED in the attached writ and if you claim a right to possession of the premises described in the writ based upon the fact that you were in possession on or before the date of filing of the unlawful detainer (eviction) proceeding, YOU MUST ACT AT ONCE.

You must claim a legal right to possession with the Marshal's Office, or you will be removed by the Marshal's deputies at the time of the eviction.

TO CLAIM YOUR RIGHTS, if any, you must complete the attached **Claim of Right to Possession** form in which you state under penalty of perjury that you were in possession of the premises on or before the date of filing of the unlawful detainer proceeding. You can complete and SUBMIT THE CLAIM FORM

(1) at the Marshal's Office located at the address above before the date of eviction, **OR**

(2) at the premises at the time of the eviction.

If you do not complete and submit the form (and pay a filing fee or file the appropriate form for proceeding in forma pauperis if you cannot pay the fee), YOU WILL BE EVICTED along with the parties named in the writ.

- GIVE THE CLAIM FORM to the Marshal at the address above. *(Do not take or send the claim form to the court.)*

- **TO OBTAIN A COURT HEARING**
  1. You must PAY A FILING FEE of $ directly to the court *(see attached writ for the address)* within 48 hours after you give the claim form to the Marshal. *(INCLUDE THE CASE NUMBER ON ALL DOCUMENTS)*
  2. IF YOU CANNOT PAY THE FEE, you must file with the court the appropriate form for proceeding in forma pauperis. *(Ask the court clerk for the form "Application for Waiver of Court Fees and Costs.")* You must file that application form within 48 hours after you give the claim form to the Marshal.
  3. IF YOU MAIL to the court the fee or the application for waiver, you must make sure the envelope is postmarked within 48 hours after you give the claim form to the Marshal. *(Write the case number on your check, money order, or application form.)*
  4. *IF YOU DO NOT pay the fee or file an application for waiver of the fee, you will not have a court hearing and YOUR CLAIM OF RIGHT TO POSSESSION WILL BE DENIED.*

[New January 1, 1987]
76 P 475

**NOTICE TO VACATE
and
NOTICE TO OCCUPANTS**

CCP 715.010, 715.020, 1174.3

the premises has a legal right to possession of the premises, he must act at once by filling in this form and filing it with the court. A court hearing will then be scheduled to give him the opportunity to explain to the judge why he has the right to remain in the premises. In the event no person occupying the illegally detained premises files such a claim, everyone present may be evicted by the sheriff, marshal, or constable. However, if such a claim has been filed, and a copy is presented to the law enforcement agency handling the eviction, the party(ies) claiming right of possession to the premises may not be evicted.

In California, landlords represented by counsel serve *Prejudgment Claim of Right to Possession* forms to all occupants (under CCP 415.46) to preclude occupants, whether named or not named in the judgment for possession, from objecting to the enforcement of the judgment. Every jurisdiction has its own forms. If you have any questions about claims to right of possession, ask the law enforcement agency which you engage to serve your *Notice to Vacate* on the defendant-judgment debtor.

Other aspects of the law which you should also take into consideration regarding your U.D. matter are briefly discussed here.

Observing U.D. Time Limits

Time limits in your area may differ from those for evictions in California. However, the law regulates time limits in all U.D. matters, the primary one being the date on which rent must be paid or the date by which a tenant must vacate the premises.

Another time factor to consider involves when a judgment creditor may dispose of any or all of the judgment creditor's personal property which may now be in his possession.

When a Landlord May Dispose of a Former Tenant's Personal Property

According to the California Civil Code (CC 1983), for example, notice of disposition of personal property remaining on the premises at termination of tenancy must be given by the landlord to the former tenant, or to any person the landlord reasonably believes to be the owner of the personal property. Such notice must contain:

- A description of the property

- A statement of reasonable storage charges for the property

- The date before which the property must be claimed (not less than fifteen days if notice is personally delivered, or not less than eighteen days if the notice is deposited in the mail)

Suppose, for instance, a tenant was evicted from his apartment on the first day of November. He left a small portable television set and box of old books in the storage shed above the parking space for his vacated apartment; he also left some clothes in the closet. The judgment creditor immediately re-rented the vacated apartment; however, by law, he was not allowed to dispose of the former tenant's personal property without first complying with the law.

In this case, the tenant, who had moved out of the area, agreed to pay the landlord a reasonable storage fee for his personal property, which he claimed on November 23. California CC 1965 provides that a landlord should release property to a former tenant who pays a reasonable storage charge.

Know the Applicable Law in Your Area

The same basic laws applicable in California also exist in other areas, although they may be slightly different in your state. For example, under CC 1988, if a former tenant does not claim his personal property, such unreleased property shall be sold by competitive bidding. The landlord or former tenant can bid. However, if the landlord reasonably believes that the total resale value of the property is less than $300, the landlord may retain such property for his own use.

After deduction of the costs of storage, advertising, and sale, the balance not claimed by the former tenant shall be deposited within thirty days after the date of sale with the county treasury. Claimants must file claim within one year from the date of deposit with the county treasury. Before the above-mentioned sale is held, it shall first be published once a week, for two consecutive weeks, in a newspaper with at least five days intervening between the respective publication dates.

In the hypothetical case cited above, if the former tenant had not reclaimed his personal property, the landlord might have kept the portable television set, sold the books at a garage sale, and donated the clothing to a nonprofit organization which distributed them to homeless families.

If you become the possessor of personal property belonging to a tenant whom you evict, be certain you know the applicable law pertaining to the time in which you must hold these items before disposing of them. If you do not know the law, check your state's civil code and code of civil procedures. In the event you get rid of such personal property before the time limit has run out, the former tenant may sue you.

Miscellaneous Facts About Unlawful Detainer

The balance of this chapter contains miscellaneous facts about various aspects of U.D. matters which were not touched upon in the previous pages. Some of them may be helpful to you; others may have no relevance to your case.

As with all other material in this book, you may use the information which is beneficial to you and ignore the rest.

Landlord-Tenant Laws

Thousands of landlord-tenant laws are in effect throughout the United States. They are too numerous to include in this chapter about how to try your own unlawful detainer case. Some of these laws are local while others are specific to your state. Still others are federal rules or regulations.

Before attempting to try your own U.D. matter, you should know the applicable law(s) governing your kind of case. If you do not know the law, and need help finding the information you need, a local legal aid office or community service agency operated by volunteers may be of assistance. These organizations frequently offer free or low-cost counseling about landlord-tenant relations. You may research such laws in your local law library; also, city hall or the public library may have local ordinances and codes which include landlord-tenant rights and rent control regulations. Also, many county courthouses have this information available to the public. What do you need to know? This list will help you decide:

- *Rent control*—Is there a rent-control law in effect in your area? If yes, what are the landlords' rights? What are the tenants' rights?

- *Federal regulations*—Are your property or premises governed by federal regulations? If the building is a low-income project, does it fall under federal, state, city, or county law—or a combination of them all? If the building is a high-rent property, what are the laws governing landlord's and tenants' rights?

- *Lease rules*—What are the provisions of your lease or rental agreement? What, if any, local laws govern whether or not a landlord can terminate a lease before it expires? Can a landlord evict a tenant who has already paid both first and last months' rent? If a tenant who has paid first and last months' rent defaults on his monthly rental payments, can the landlord force him to continue paying rent until the year expires? Can the tenant break his lease and forfeit his first and last months' rent?

Whether you are the plaintiff or defendant in your U.D. matter, you must know the applicable law before you can fight for your rights. Instructions about finding the laws that apply to your type of case are given in Chapter 16, "How to Research the Law."

Residential vs. Business and Commercial Tenancy

For simplicity, this chapter has been slanted toward the residential landlord-tenant relationship. Also, to keep the instructions clear, only one tenant has been included in the examples. Therefore, the guidelines in the trial blueprint are specifically designed to show how one landlord conducts his own U.D. trial against one tenant whom he is attempting to evict. Such a residential tenant may rent an apartment, condominium, trailer, room, house, or other living quarters.

Simple residential U.D. matters are the types most frequently tried, and won, by *Pro Pers*; however, the basic guidelines given here are also applicable to situations in which a tenant rents business or commercial property from the landlord. If yours is a case involving a business or commercial enterprise, and you know the applicable laws pertaining to your matter, you may adapt the suggestions given in this chapter to fit your trial.

Understanding the law, as it applies to your case, is the key to winning your U.D. case in court. For example, the "habitability defense" used by vast numbers of tenant-defendants to win their residential unlawful detainer cases across the country cannot be raised in California U.D. matters involving business or commercial leases.

Another ground for the defendant-tenant's affirmative defense in residential U.D. matters, "retaliation," may not be available in commercial or business leases in California; however, the law might allow both defenses in your area.

How well versed are you about the law governing your U.D. matter? If in doubt, check it out!

Understanding Habitability

The term "cohabit" means "live together." Married couples and their offspring, as well as entire families, frequently cohabit in the same residential premises; that is, they share the same living quarters. Unrelated roommates, as well as unmarried partners sharing "significant other" (unmarried) relationships, often make their homes together.

Although by popular inference the word cohabit refers to unmarried partners (both heterosexual and homosexual) who live together in an intimate relationship, by the broadest legal definition "cohabitants" are any persons who are domiciled (live) together.

The term "habitable" means "able to be lived in." In a rental agreement, the landlord is usually responsible for the habitability of the rented premises. He must provide a safe place for his tenants, one which is neither a health hazard nor poses risks to his tenants' personal safety or the safety of their personal property.

While a tenant is not responsible for repair of a broken water pipe or leaking roof, for example, he is responsible for the upkeep of the premises he has rented. That is, he must do his own cleaning and exercise reasonable care in keeping the house, apartment, condominium, or other living quarters habitable.

Reasonable Care and Habitability

Suppose a tenant allowed garbage to collect in his kitchen for six weeks, creating a health hazard. His negligence, not the landlord's, is the cause of the infestation of roaches which occurred in his premises, making the living quarters uninhabitable.

"Habitability" means "livability." Since tenants renting premises for business or commercial purposes do not generally live where they work, the habitability defense may not be allowed in your area for U.D. matters which do not involve living quarters.

If you are the defendant in a business or commercial U.D. matter, and your affirmative defense is that the plaintiff-landlord failed to provide safe, healthful, risk-free living quarters, as agreed upon, you should argue that you actually have a residential lease contract on at least a major portion of the premises. Therefore, you can raise the habitability or retaliation defense.

Breach of Contract and Other Defenses

Technically, breach of contract is not a valid affirmative defense because unlawful detainers are summary proceedings; breach of contract is an ordinary civil action that does not have precedence in the trial calendar. However, you may raise the breach-of-contract defense in your Answer to the plaintiff's Complaint.

It is better practice to raise every conceivable defense that you have (breach of contract, habitability, retaliation). If the judge rejects your defense, accept his decision graciously.

Aggrieved Commercial Tenant's Remedy

An aggrieved commercial tenant's remedy is to give written notice of the breach to the landlord, demanding that the landlord:

• Cure the breach, or

• Tenant will vacate premises and sue for damages.

Advice for Co-defendants

The subject of co-defendants was mentioned previously in this chapter; however, if two or more persons are defendants in your U.D. suit, the following information may be helpful.

If more than one tenant is named in an unlawful detainer complaint, the parties are known as "co-defendants."

For example, three unrelated roommates who shared one apartment were named in their lawsuit as *George Smith, Thomas Brown, and Albert Wilson, defendants.*

An unmarried couple sharing a house was named as *Janice L. Green and Alexander C. Hall, defendants.*

The spouses who rented a condominium in another U.D. lawsuit were named as *John Smith, husband, and Mary Smith, wife, defendants.*

Co-defendants are defendants who are sued jointly.

However, here is how two business partners, who operated a furniture upholstery business from the commercial property they rented, were named in the U.D. complaint filed by the plaintiff-landlord: *Gregory B. Jackson, partner, and Harold R. Anderson, partner, dba Furniture Facelift, defendants.* Note that their names and the name of their business were both included on the complaint.

Legally, two abbreviations denoting aliases (other names) are frequently used in legal documents. They are:

- *dba*—"Doing business as" is a term denoting the name of a business. If, for example, Missouri writer Samuel Clemens had operated a newspaper called the *Midwest Gazette,* he would have been named in a lawsuit as: *Samuel Clemens, dba Midwest Gazette, defendant.*

- *aka*—"Also known as" is a term most often used to denote an alias. For example, Samuel Clemens wrote *The Adventures of Huckleberry Finn* under his alias "Mark Twain." If he were sued, he would have been named in a lawsuit as: *Samuel Clemens, aka Mark Twain, defendant.*

An alias is a phony name, as a pen name (*nom de plume*) or stage name. Television and film stars are noted for changing their names. For instance, actor Bernard Schwartz took the professional name "Tony Curtis."

Some people change their names legally; others do not. In a lawsuit an individual should be named by his legal name and, if pertinent to the case, also by his business or professional name.

Regardless of the names by which defendants are sued, if more than one defendant is named in the plaintiff's complaint, they are co-defendants. This means they are both (or all, if more than two persons are named) being sued.

Insight into Partnerships and Corporations

In business and commercial U.D. matters, the plaintiff-landlord sues the leaseholder(s) of the premises where business is conducted. The basic differences between partnerships and corporations are briefly summarized here.

- *Partnership*—A partnership may be formed when two or more parties, capable of entering into a contract, make an agreement between or among themselves to associate themselves together for the performance of certain functions which an individual, acting for and by himself, could do for and by himself. In a business partnership, the method by which the true extent of the relationship is measured is through the manner in which the parties contribute capital and divide their profits.

If the parties associated together are mutual agents—one for the other, in transacting business—these parties are legally considered regular partners within the scope of their joint business venture, which may have been entered into by written or oral agreement. Every partnership is unincorporated.

The partners in a partnership are not immune from prosecution; that is, the individual partners, rather than the business entity which they operate, may be sued; however, the liability of a limited partner is limited to his investment.

If a U.D. lawsuit is filed against a partnership, the plaintiff's petition (complaint) may read: *William Smith of Los Angeles, California, and John Brown of Pasadena, California, doing business under the style and the firm name of Smith & Brown, and having a place of business in Beverly Hills, California.*

In a partnership, the partnership itself is not different from its members. A partner's liability includes all of the debts of the partnership itself. A regular partner authorized by the Articles of Partnership may bind the partnership by issuing a negotiable instrument in the name of the partnership. In other words, one partner may incur debts for the partnership; all the other partners are, therefore, liable for the partnership's debt.

However, if one partner has been grossly negligent, the other partners may sue him for the purpose of recovering damages to the extent the partnership has been injured.

Therefore, if a partnership is sued for unlawful detention of premises, the partners, not the business name under which they operate, are co-defendants. Each partner may appear in *Pro Per*; or, the partners may elect to engage a lawyer to represent them.

If one former partner sued the other for unlawful detention of property, the two former partners might both appear as *Pro Pers*, trying their U.D. cases against one another in court.

However, if the leased premises is jointly owned by the partners, ownership is in issue; the Municipal Court (in California) does not have jurisdiction to hear this type of matter and, therefore, will dismiss the case or transfer it to Superior Court.

• *Corporation*—A corporation is an "incorporated" legal entity. As such, a corporation is an "artificial person." By virtue of its charter, it is a separate and distinct "entity" from its stockholders. Generally, a corporation may have no less than three officer-stockholders; however, every jurisdiction has its own corporation codes and the rules of one venue may differ from those in another area. There is no federal corporations code; each state, therefore, establishes its own codes governing both "for-profit" and "not-for-profit" corporations. The following points apply to most corporations:

Once a year, an annual meeting of shareholders is held in which an annual report is given about the past year's business operations and financial standing, and a forecast of the coming year is also made. Shareholders vote for various proposals put before them, and the board of directors and other officers of the company may be elected. A stockholder is usually entitled to one vote for each share of stock which he owns. Meetings, chaired by the chief executive officer, are conducted by Parliamentary Procedure. Minutes of all meetings are made by the corporate secretary and constitute, along with quarterly and annual financial reports, the records of the corporation.

In not-for-profit corporations, in which there is no stock and, therefore, no shareholders, the officers and/or board of directors meet annually. Volunteers, contributors and other supporters may participate..

A corporation may enter into contracts and purchase, sell, or lease property in the name of the corporation; duly appointed representatives of said corporation have power to execute such contracts in the name of the corporation (i.e., corporate lawyers, officers, etc.). A corporation may sue and be sued; also, a corporation is subject to federal and state taxation. The parties representing the corporation may not be held personally liable for the corporation's legal liabilities or its tax liabilities. This basically means that the officers of a corporation cannot be made to pay the corporation's debts with their personal assets or properties. Corporate stock is the personal property of shareholders who own it.

How is a corporation—an "artificial entity"—formed? The basics are: a corporation must file articles of incorporation with the state in which it intends to be incorporated, following which the state will issue a charter of incorporation which allows the corporation to operate in that state. When the charter is secured, the stockholders meet to elect a board of directors and approve the corporation's bylaws, which outline the methods of achieving the corporation's business and conducting business. Corporate officers are also named. Ordinarily they are: president, vice president, secretary, and treasurer; however, the secretary-treasurer position may be combined.

The board of directors determines the policy, practices, and business goals of the corporation.

Nonofficers who are employees of a corporation may not be held to answer for, nor represent, the corporation in legal matters pertaining to the corporation unless so duly empowered by corporate authority.

Big corporations have large business operations which often have hundreds, or even thousands, of employees; these big corporations frequently have branch offices in many cities and states.

On the other hand, small corporations are functioning under a sole owner whose staff comprises the corporate officers and/or the board of directors. Some of these small firms are a variety of professional persons, including but not limited to doctors, dentists, attorneys, accountants, and tax-accounting firms.

Others include freelance writers, artists, and a wide variety of service-oriented operations owned and operated by sole practitioners/proprietors or one or two other individuals as, for example, a group of doctors operating a clinic, several lawyers operating their own independent law firm, or an organization of professional business persons operating a secretarial service.

Instead of owning their own buildings, as many large corporations do, these small corporations frequently lease the premises from which they do business or perform their services.

In the event a small corporation is the defendant in an unlawful detainer lawsuit, is it necessary to retain a lawyer (if none is already on the corporation's staff) to handle the U.D. matter? Or can the corporation represent itself in court?

If you are the sole owner of your own corporation, you will still have to hire an attorney to represent the corporation. The reason is: a corporation is a distinct, separate entity; therefore, you cannot represent it unless you are a lawyer.

If you are not a sole owner of a small corporation, and your firm neither has its own attorney nor retains outside counsel, you and the other officers should hold a meeting; in this meeting, the question of which attorney would best represent your firm's needs should be resolved.

Only an attorney can represent a corporation in court.

How Unnamed Defendants Are Indicated

An unnamed defendant is designated in the Summons and Complaint as "Doe." You may be familiar with the term "John Doe," which designates an unnamed (or unidentified) person or dead body.

If ten unnamed defendants are involved in a case, they will be designated as "Does 1 to 10." However, it is always better practice that you have five times the number of unidentified defendants. This way, if another fifteen persons should turn out to be involved in the case as defendants after the statute of limitations had run, you could still include them in your complaint. Therefore, in our example you should have "Does 1 to 50."

If only five unnamed defendants are designated, they will be shown as "Does 1 to 5." The number of "Does" designate the number of unnamed defendants.

Understanding "Doe(s)"

"Doe" is a standard name meaning "unknown person."

For example, while an unidentified male is referred to as John Doe, an unidentified female is called Jane Doe for identification. In legal actions involving more than a few persons, the collective term "Does 1 to 15" or "Does 1 to 30" must appear on the plaintiff's petition (complaint). This is a technique lawyers use for the timely filing of petitions if they do not know the names of the other individuals being sued, so they may later add their names to their lawsuits.

The term "Doe" allows lawyers latitude.

The plaintiff in a U.D. matter may also use this technique. For example, in a U.D. case in which several unauthorized (and unknown) persons had moved in with a tenant who was being sued by his landlord, the plaintiff's petition was filed as: *Greenwood Apartments, plaintiff vs. Robert Ames and Does 1 to 15, defendants.*

Introducing *et al.*

This is another legal term used to indicate unnamed persons in a lawsuit. *Et al.* is a Latin term meaning "and all" or "all others."

Et al. is used when there are several parties on either side.

Subsequent pleadings may use the term *et al.* after one named party in lieu of all the remaining named parties.

For example, Western Properties filed an unlawful detainer suit against tenant Rose Ann Smith, Johnny Smith, Maggie Smith, Caroline Smith, and Marjorie Smith, all adult family members occupying the premises.

Following filing of the initial complaint, the plaintiff's subsequent pleadings designated the defendants as: *Western Properties, plaintiff, vs. Rose Ann Smith, et al., defendants.*

Space-Saving Terms

Not only do both terms, "Doe" and *et al.*, lend legal latitude to the lawyers or *Pro Pers* using them, they also serve as time and energy conservers, as well as space savers.

There is seldom room on legal forms, of the types used in U.D. and many other matters involving civil torts, for long lists of individual names.

Advice for Plaintiffs

If the plaintiff who brought the U.D. action against the defendant(s) fails to show up in court, the judge will dismiss the entire case; therefore, if you are the plaintiff and you really want to win your case in court, be there!

Advice for Defendants

If you are the only defendant named in the plaintiff's summons and complaint, and you are, therefore, the sole signatory on your answer, your presence in court is mandatory—if you hope to win your U.D. case.

If you fail to appear, the plaintiff will be allowed to prove his claim in your absence.

When a Married Couple is Sued

Under California law (CCP 371), provisions of which are similar to laws in other states:

If a husband and wife are sued together, each may defend for his or her own right; but if one spouse neglects to defend, the other spouse may defend for that spouse's right also.

Suppose your wife (who did not sign the answer) appears, but you do not. The plaintiff may "prove up" his claim against you. In such a case, your wife will not be allowed to participate in the hearing because she does not have any personality in court unless she is able to successfully argue to the court (in California by virtue of CCP 371) that:

- She can defend her husband,

- She should be allowed to join her husband's answer, and

- The court should grant her waiver of the Answer filing fee.

The court may or may not grant the motion that she be allowed to try the case.

As a general rule, therefore, every defendant should appear for the trial. To do otherwise is a concession of defeat.

Introducing "Prove-up"

Generally, if both defendants file their answers to your complaint, they should both appear during the hearing.

If only one shows up in court, however, the trial will proceed against the defendant who is present and prove-up hearing on the absent defendant.

If no one shows up for the defense, then it will just be a prove-up hearing.

As plaintiff, you will "prove up" your case against the absent defendant, which means you will still have to prove all the elements of your case in order to get judgment. These suggestions simplify the prove-up process:

How to Prove-Up Your Case

In your file will be your copy of the clerk's Notice of Hearing; this is the notice mailed to litigants by the court which notifies the parties when and where the U.D. trial will be held. In your file will also be the other exhibits, if any, which you plan to introduce as evidence. These exhibits may already be marked; for example, Plaintiff's 1, Plaintiff's 2, etc.

If you have not included the clerk's notice of hearing as one of your exhibits, do so now.

To prove up your case against the absent defendant, you may now rearrange the numbering of your exhibits, as follows:

- At the start of the trial, the plaintiff says:

  Your Honor, with the court's permission, the plaintiff requests that the clerk's "Notice of Hearing" be marked as Plaintiff's 1.

- The judge will grant permission. The clerk's notice now becomes your key piece of evidence to be offered against the absent defendant. If another exhibit was originally marked Plaintiff's 1, it now becomes Plaintiff's 2, etc.

- The plaintiff now calls his first witness. If you are testifying on your own behalf, you testify in narrative form. Use whichever of the following examples fits your situation:

Plaintiff proceeds against absent defendant.

PLAINTIFF (*present the elements of the case: the contract, notices, etc.*): Your Honor, by the clerk's notice of hearing the defendant was notified of this hearing (*introduce the Notice of Hearing as evidence*). The elements in this case are: the defendant did not pay rent in compliance with this (*introduce the contract/rental agreement/lease*) for premises he rented from me at (*address of premises*) _____ _____. The terms of the (contract/rental agreement/lease) _____ are (*read the terms pertaining to payment of rent*) _____ _____. I served the defendant with this Three-Day Notice (*introduce the three-day notice*) on (*date*) _____. Defendant did not pay his rent and is still in possession of the premises.

If the judge's decision is for the plaintiff, he may now render judgment against the defendant.

Review of Unlawful Detainer

All unlawful detainer (U.D.) petitions allege the illegal possession of property or premises by one or more parties. The party seeking to regain possession of the property or premises is the plaintiff; the party unlawfully detaining the property or premises is the defendant.

Are all U.D. matters covered under a blanket set of laws? No, as you have seen from the facts presented in this chapter. Not only do different laws exist in numerous jurisdictions, various aspects of applicable laws also govern specific U.D. situations.

Before proceeding with your U.D. matter, know the law as it applies in your jurisdiction! If you do not yet know the law, research it by visiting your local law library and studying your state's code of civil procedures.

The ways partnerships and corporations may handle their U.D. matters have already been introduced; not covered, however, was the matter of unlawful detainer cases involving unincorporated companies. In the event such a company is involved in your unlawful detainer matter, the following facts may be helpful.

Introducing the Company

America is truly the land of opportunity. Each year thousands of small businesses are opened by enterprising individuals. Many of these new businesses use the word "company" in their names. For instance: *The Olde Bookbinding Company, Adams Antique Company, or Parsons & Company Jewelers.*

The word company is derived from "community" or "communal," both terms which mean "more than one person" or "a group of persons." The word company used in connection with business implies that a group of individuals all offer the same special services. However, this name is often misleading, because many independent businesses are operated by only one person.

For instance, William Walton is a freelance plumber whose business operates under the name "Walton Plumbing Company." He usually answers all his own calls and gives personal service to his clients. Occasionally, however, he needs another plumber to help him on jobs that require four hands. He pays his helper for only the hours he actually works. His helper is not his employee but an independent subcontractor.

Other companies may actually have a company payroll, several employees, and a benefit plan for the people who are paid wages; however, by the time a company grows large enough to be a profit-making business enterprise, the owner or partners usually incorporate for legal and tax purposes. For example, Parsons & Company Jewelers becomes Parson & Company Jewelers, Inc.

The word "Incorporated" or, in its shortened version, "Inc." in a business name indicates that the business is an "artificial person" which is sole and separate from its owner(s). Conversely, a "company" and its owner(s) are one and the same entity(ies).

Many small businesses are "partnerships." Others are not. A company may be less structured than a partnership; for instance, a man and wife may run their own company without establishing operating agreements, internal standards of conduct or control, or policies related to distribution of income or payment of salaries or wages. However, small companies usually have one thing in common with partnerships and corporations: the majority operate under fictitious names.

How New Businesses Get Their Names

The term "dba" means a person or group of persons is doing business under a fictitious name. In America, an individual may call himself any name he desires; to do business under a fictitious name, however, most areas require that proper legal steps are taken before a bank will even open a business account in the fictitious name. This means the person(s) wishing to go into a new business must apply for a *Fictitious Name Certificate.*

Although laws may vary from area to area, basic rules applicable to obtaining fictitious names are:

1. *A Fictitious Business Name Statement* is filed with the clerk of the county or township in which the business will be located.

2. Notice of the Fictitious Business Name Statement shall be published in a newspaper of general circulation once a week for four consecutive weeks, with at least five days intervening between the respective publication dates. (California law; this requirement may vary slightly in your area.)

3. After the publication requirement has been met, the proprietor(s) of the new business come into possession of the certified (signed, sealed, and dated) document from the county, which authorizes the use of the fictitious name for a specified period of time (five years in California, four in others, etc.)

4. The bank account of the new business is established in the fictitious business name; many banks will not open accounts under fictitious names unless the aforementioned documents are given as proof that the proprietor(s) went through the legal channels described here.

Many new businesses are kicked off with little more than business cards, letterhead stationery, business checks, and a post office box or street address. A bedroom, garage, or kitchen table often serves as company headquarters in the owner's own home.

Legal Status of an Unincorporated Company
While a corporation must file separate state and federal tax returns from those filed by its owners, the reverse is true of an unincorporated company.

Income (or loss), along with operating expenses of a company, whether operated full-time or part-time by the owner, may be reported on the same state and federal tax returns in which the business owner reports all other sources of income: wages, or salary, dividends, earnings on investments, etc. Why only one tax return? Because the real person and the business operating under a fictitious name are legally the same person.

This means that the owner of an unincorporated company can be sued for his firm's liabilities, and in U.D. matters the litigant is always the individual, never the fictitious name under which he operates. Therefore, if John Smith, who operates "The Smith Mail Order Company" from an apartment leased from Williams Properties, is being sued for non-payment of rent, the complaint is worded this way:

Williams Properties, plaintiff, vs. John Smith, dba "The Smith Mail Order Company," defendant.

Not all companies are small businesses, and not all small businesses are companies. If your legal matter involves your own small business, make wise decisions about the company you keep.

Summarizing Unlawful Detainer

Unlike other types of civil matters, which may not come to trial for months or even years, U.D. matters are entitled to precedence (priority) and are scheduled for early trials on court calendars.

A U.D. matter involving one tenant and one landlord, in which both sides are well-prepared, may be tried and disposed in fifteen minutes or less.

If you are the plaintiff in a U.D. matter, you may ask for the rent money due from the time the defendant quit paying the monthly amount owed; you may also ask for the amount owed on a daily basis between the time his last month's rent was due and the date judgment is ordered.

If money is being sought for damages caused by the defendant, include this in your complaint.

You may also ask the court to award you court costs and all other legal fees associated with your lawsuit. Attorney's fees will be awarded if you are represented by counsel and it is provided for in the lease contract.

Introducing the "Collection" Case

If the defendant who owes you rent has vacated the premises before the trial, possession is no longer in issue. Therefore, it is no longer a U.D. case deserving precedence in the court calendar; it has become a simple "collection" case.

The court will then reset the matter for another trial date in the non-precedence calendar unless you can convince the court (and you should try):

- That this is going to be a short trial.

- That defendant does not have any new affirmative defenses in the collection case.

- *That defendant must agree to these representations.*

- That it will be in the interest of fairness and judicial economy that the court hears the case now.

If the court hears the collection case, then you proceed as previously discussed, with one exception: when you ask for judgment, do not ask for possession of the premises or forfeiture of the lease agreement; ask only the amount you are collecting, plus interest and court costs.

Understanding "Collection"

Because U.D. and collection cases have two common elements, and because the majority of cases heard in Small Claims Court are collection cases, the next few paragraphs cover the basics about collection which every *Pro Per* should know.

The two elements common to U.D. matters and collections cases are:

- There is a contract (oral or written), and

- The defendant breached that contract.

The most common types of contracts or agreements, oral or written, are briefly summarized below as they pertain to collections cases.

The Promissory Note (I.O.U.)

A collection case involving a *Promissory Note* (note of promise to pay) is one in which a contract of loan existed between the parties; the plaintiff loaned money to the defendant who, in turn, obligated himself to pay the plaintiff on a certain date.

The defendant did not pay on the date of maturity; or, the payment (check) was dishonored for insufficiency of funds, as, for instance, in the case of a "bounced" check.

Despite demands by the plaintiff, the defendant failed to pay; therefore, the defendant breached (broke) the contract.

When trying this type of matter, proceed as outlined in the U.D. cases discussed in this chapter by incorporating these points in your presentation:

Plaintiff
- Plaintiff testifies to the execution of the Promissory Note and offers it as evidence.

- Plaintiff testifies to the giving of the money and offers his cancelled check as evidence.

- Plaintiff points out the date of maturity of the Promissory Note.

- Plaintiff points out the demand-for-payment which he made and offers his letter of demand as evidence.

- Plaintiff testifies to the defendant's continued non-payment.

- Plaintiff states the amount of his damages.

Defendant
(May raise any or all of these defenses as applicable.)

- Defendant may claim that the Promissory Note is a forgery.

- Defendant may defend that the true interest rate, which is usurious, is not shown in the Promissory Note and that he got only fifty percent of the amount.

- Defendant may defend that the proceeds of the Note were actually spent by the parties on a joint business venture that failed.

- Defendant may testify that the Note had not yet matured.

- Defendant may testify that the plaintiff had already been paid.

- Defendant may testify that the plaintiff had forgiven the loan.

- Defendant may testify about any other valid reasons for his non-payment of the Note.

The defendant should present evidence, if any is available, to prove each point in his defense.

Contract of Sale or Service

In this type of collection case, there was a contract between the parties whereby the plaintiff delivered goods or services to the defendant; the defendant, in turn, obligated himself to pay for the goods or services.

The defendant's check bounced, or he failed to pay despite repeated demands by the plaintiff; hence, the defendant breached the contract.

When trying a matter involving goods furnished or services performed, proceed as outlined in the U.D. cases discussed in this chapter by incorporating these points in your presentation:

Plaintiff
- Plaintiff testifies as to the goods furnished the defendant and offers receipt for goods signed by the defendant; or

- Plaintiff testifies about services performed for the defendant and offers the contract of services.

- Plaintiff testifies about demands made to the defendant for payment and offers letters of demand, bills sent, etc. as evidence.

- Plaintiff testifies about the defendant's continued nonpayment.

Defendant
(Include the applicable points in your defense.)
- Defendant defends he did not ask for the goods delivered.

- Defendant defends that the goods were never delivered.

- Defendant defends that the goods were not delivered on time (when time was of the essence).

- Defendant defends that the goods supplied were of very inferior quality and offer to return was seasonably made (within the time frame allowed for returns), but such offer was rejected by the plaintiff.

- Defendant defends that service furnished was inadequate or unsatisfactory, or was the cause that damaged his property or injured his body.

- Defendant here files cross-complaint for damages.

Non-sufficient Funds (NSF) or Stop-Payment Checks
In this type of collection case, a check given the plaintiff by the defendant bounced because funds to cover it were not sufficient, or the defendant stopped payment on the check given plaintiff as payment by the defendant.

When trying a matter involving NSF or stop-payment checks, proceed as outlined in the U.D. cases discussed in this chapter by incorporating these points in your presentation:

Plaintiff
- Plaintiff testifies how goods were furnished, or service was performed.

- Plaintiff testifies how check payment was made, how the check was deposited in plaintiff's account and returned for insufficient funds or payment was stopped, and offers dishonored check as evidence.

- Plaintiff testifies about notice and demand made by the plaintiff to the defendant to make the check good, and offers the notice as evidence.

- Plaintiff testifies to the defendant's continued nonpayment.

Defendant
The defendant uses similar defenses asserted in "Goods Furnished or Services Performed" (above).

Introducing Treble Damages
In California (and other areas), a plaintiff may be entitled to "treble" (add to the actual amount of) damages in his collection case.

To get treble damages in California, the payee (plaintiff) shall give written demand by certified mail to the maker (defendant), informing him of the applicable law (CC 1719) stating that maker is liable, in addition to the amount owing upon that check, for not less than $100 and not more than $1,500, plus the cost of mailing the demand, if the maker fails to pay within thirty days from the demand date.

But in the case of the maker stopping payment in order to resolve a good-faith dispute with the payee, the payee can only recover the treble damages upon clear and convincing evidence that there was no good-faith dispute.

If you are not familiar with the law in your area as it applies to treble damages, we suggest you become so before proceeding with your matter in court.

Do You Need a Lawyer?

The majority of collection and U.D. matters are uncomplicated and may be tried by *Pro Pers* as outlined in this chapter. However, there are exceptions to the general laws which give plaintiffs the right to sue—and evict—tenants. For example, suppose you are a litigant in this hypothetical case involving spousal rights:

Back in 1987, John Brown, who was then single, bought a "fixer-upper" home as a real estate investment. He planned to renovate the house and sell it. Instead, he married Alice Jones in 1988. They moved into the John Brown's house and lived there until 1990, at which time they separated. The Browns did not file for divorce.

John Brown moved out and Alice Brown continued living in the house as a tenant. She paid monthly rent to Mr. Brown; he, in turn, used this rent money to make the monthly mortgage payments on the house which was in his name only. In September 1990, Alice Brown's rent was two months overdue. In October 1990, John Brown filed an unlawful detainer action against her.

What Would You Do?

Supposing this was your U.D. matter. How well do you know the applicable law in your area? Is the house "community property" or the separate property of John Brown? One jurisdiction might allow John Brown to evict his wife, while another would not. If you were John Brown, what would you do?

If you do not know the applicable law pertinent to your U.D. case, learn it. If you cannot or do not wish to invest the time and effort required to research the law, consider these alternatives: try your own case in court and hope the law favors your side (which is like gong to battle hoping to win by virtue of your opponent's mercy!)—or get a lawyer!

Even the sparrow has found a home
And the swallow a nest for herself.
Where she may lay her young—
Even Your altars, O Lord of hosts,
My King and my God,
Blessed are those who dwell in Your house;
They will still be praising You.
Selah.—Psalm 84:3–4

NOTES

Chapter 26

How to Try Your Own Traffic Infraction Case

If you have received a ticket for any of these traffic infractions, you may wish to try your own case in court:

- *Parking*—You were given a citation because your parking meter was expired, or because your vehicle remained parked beyond the posted time limit on a public street.

- *Parking*—You were ticketed for illegally parking in a red, yellow, green, or other zone designated "no parking."

- *Moving Violation*—You received a ticket for exceeding the legal speed limit on a street or highway, driving in the wrong direction on a one-way street, driving too slowly, changing lanes without signalling, tailgating, cutting a U-turn in a no-U-turn zone, and running through a stop sign.

Trying your own case for such tickets means *you plead not guilty to the citation(s) issued against you.* In essence, you fight your ticket. If you take your case to court and win, your traffic record will not show the traffic citation; otherwise, traffic violations on your Department of Motor Vehicles record can cause your insurance premium to be raised and your driver's license may even be suspended.

You Are the Defendant

Traffic tickets are issued by officers of law enforcement agencies, including the police, highway patrol, or sheriff's department. The "People of the State" are the plaintiffs in such cases, and the agency issuing the ticket is the complaining witness. The person cited is the defendant; therefore, if you received a traffic ticket, you are the defendant in your matter.

The "People" have to prove your traffic infraction beyond a reasonable doubt.

What You Should Know About Traffic Cases

Every ticket issued for a traffic infraction is based on one or more applicable laws (usually a municipal code or vehicle code). The law you are charged with violating must be cited on the ticket. This "citation of applicable law" gave rise to the term "traffic citation," as now commonly used by motorists and traffic officers.

Standard forms like those used by traffic officers contain preprinted citations of applicable law. Other tickets may contain space in which the issuing officer must fill in the law which was violated.

The pertinent law must appear on your traffic ticket as legal notice of the infraction you are charged with committing. If no such law appears anywhere on your traffic ticket, you may make a motion to dismiss the traffic citation.

The chance of such a slip-up happening in your case is slim; however, since lawsuits can sometimes be won on technicalities, you should be aware of the foregoing information.

Can a traffic ticket really be considered a lawsuit? Yes, because the local prosecuting agency is charging you for violating a traffic law. Therefore, carefully read the small print on your ticket. Are you allowed to pay your fine by mail or are you required to make a personal appearance at the address shown on the ticket? Follow the instructions.

Understanding Traffic Infractions

A traffic infraction involves a breach of traffic law. You may retain a lawyer to represent you in such a case; however, in many cases involving the more common types of traffic tickets, *Pro Pers* represent themselves.

If, however, you are involved in a misdemeanor or felony matter, you need to retain legal counsel; such cases include charges of "DUI" (driving under the influence), "operating a stolen vehicle," and "vehicular manslaughter" in most areas.

Although traffic tickets are only infractions and not major offenses, failure to resolve them can result in serious consequences. For example, a young man who was afraid to tell his parents he got a speeding ticket was exposed when a bench warrant for his arrest was issued. By the time his infraction came to light, a misdemeanor complaint had also been filed against him. He ended up paying more than five times the amount of the original traffic fine.

The young man nearly lost his driver's license, and he became a "bad risk" so that his car insurance premium tripled. If his father had not paid the fines, the young man might have ended up doing jail time for his "FTA" (failure to appear).

Traffic infractions carry the penalty of a fine; if you are guilty as charged, plead guilty and pay the ticket, or go to traffic school. If you go to traffic school, upon submission of proof of your satisfactory completion of traffic school the court will dismiss the case.

If you are not guilty—and the prosecution cannot prove your guilt beyond a reasonable doubt—you may take your case to traffic court—to win!

The Burden of Proof Is on the Prosecution

The prosecution will have to prove your traffic violation beyond a reasonable doubt. Usually, the only witness against you is one law enforcement officer.

Most of the time, the judge will decide whom to believe: you or the law enforcement officer. Therefore, if you have an eyewitness, or physical evidence, to corroborate your testimony, you stand a good chance not to be found guilty.

Examples of *Pro Pers* Who Win

Pro Per Wanda Sue Parrott was a defendant in two traffic infraction matters. The first case involved a one-way street which circled through a public park. Wanda's husband, Ted, who was driving the car in which she was riding, entered the park from a public thoroughfare and continued in the wrong direction until he was stopped and given a ticket by a uniformed officer.

The Parrotts, who had not observed a one-way sign, returned to the scene and photographed the driveway leading from the city street. The pictures revealed a mass of shrubbery behind which an indistinct one-way sign was hidden almost entirely from view.

The judge, who heard the case in court, dismissed the charges and ordered the city to trim the trees.

Wanda's second traffic infraction involved three long-overdue parking tickets allegedly received by her several weeks after she had sold her car to a college student who failed to register the automobile in his name.

Several months passed before she began receiving notices that the tickets were outstanding; each time a new notice was issued, the fine per parking violation was increased.

The defendant researched the applicable law, then produced as evidence a Declaration in which she swore she was not the owner of the offending vehicle at the time the tickets were written. Other evidence included the original copy of a sales receipt signed by the car's buyer, attesting to the fact he took possession of the vehicle on the date of sale, and a transfer of ownership form the defendant had filed with the Department of Motor Vehicles after releasing the car to the new owner.

The burden of evidence required by law was that the defendant prove she was not the legal owner of the vehicle at the time the tickets were written; she was not required to prove who was the current owner of the car.

What did defendant Parrott gain by winning? She saved more than $200 in parking fines, and had her name stricken from the official records that had continued showing her as the car's registered owner because transfer of title had not been executed by the purchaser.

Is a Traffic Ticket Worth Fighting?

Is fighting a traffic ticket worth all the time and effort involved to clear your name from the record? This depends on what you stand to lose if you do not fight it.

Payment without protest of a traffic fine is an admission of your guilt in the matter for which you have been ticketed.

Fines for such infractions as overparking generate revenue for your city. This money is usually used to provide services to the city, so you are actually contributing to your own welfare when you pay a traffic fine.

Facts to Consider

Your good record will not be permanently marred because you received a few parking tickets, provided you pay them on or before the time set forth on the traffic ticket. In fact, it is much easier to mail your $5 or $10 fine as payment of a ticket than to take your matter before a judge; however, the easy way may not be the best way.

For example, if Wanda Sue Parrott had paid the three traffic tickets cited above merely to avoid getting involved in a legal matter, consider these hypothetical consequences: If the driver of the car had killed a pedestrian in a hit-and-run accident, between the time the first and last parking tickets were issued, and an eyewitness identified the car as the defendant's, Wanda would have been a suspect in a felony manslaughter case!

Proving she was no longer the owner of the car would be very difficult because, by her payment of the three tickets, she admitted her guilt in the parking matters, thus raising the question: if she was driving the vehicle when she got the parking tickets, was it not likely she was also driving it when the pedestrian was struck and killed?

If Wanda had not opted to fight city hall under the hypothetical condition cited above, she might have ended up a convicted killer serving time in prison for a crime she did not commit!

If you stand to lose something far more precious than the amount of the fine you would pay just to get your traffic ticket out of your hair, and you can prove you are not guilty as charged, ask for a trial.

How to Set Your Traffic Trial

Here is the basic procedure you must follow in order to set your traffic infraction case for trial:

- On or before the date specified on your traffic ticket, go to the address at which you are ordered to pay your fine.

- Take your traffic ticket with you.

- Take enough money to pay your fine.

- Wait in line to see the clerk of the court.

- When it is your turn, hand your ticket to the clerk and say:

  DEFENDANT: I plead "not guilty" and request a trial date.

- The clerk will require that you "post bail" (by paying your fine).

- Pay the fine. Do not argue.

- The clerk will return your ticket and set a date for your trial.

If you fail to show up for the hearing, you will forfeit your bail. Technically, this is equal to an admission of guilt. However, if you proceed with the trial and win your case, your bail will be returned and the charges dismissed.

How to Try Your Own Traffic Case

Small claims and traffic courts are two of the busiest courts in the judicial system. They are also the courts where the majority of *Pro Pers* represent themselves.

In the courtroom, you will probably find yourself surrounded by other parties also waiting for their cases to be called; take a seat and wait for your turn.

When your case is called, take your place at the counsel table. If a witness is with you, tell him to wait by being seated in the spectator section of the courtroom.

The prosecuting attorney who represents the agency which issued your ticket will probably also be present, and he may call the officer who wrote the ticket as key witness. *If the officer fails to appear, the judge shall dismiss the case.*

If the judge mistakenly asks you to testify about what happened, and to introduce your evidence, tell him politely:

Your Honor, since the prosecution did not prove any violation against me beyond a reasonable doubt, and since the defendant is presumed innocent, I will not present any evidence. I move for dismissal on the grounds of (insufficiency/lack of evidence).

If the judge tries to continue the case to another date, object politely, move to dismiss, and assert your right to a speedy trial guaranteed by the United States and your own state's constitutions. For example:

Objection, Your Honor! Defendant moves for dismissal on the grounds that under both the Constitution of the United States and the Constitution of the State of (name your state) ————————————————————, *defendant is guaranteed a speedy trial.*

Assuming that the prosecution is ready to proceed, here is how you try your own case in traffic court:

1. Both parties introduce themselves to the judge; the prosecutor goes first, followed by the defendant, as shown here:

    PROSECUTION: Your Honor, I am (*name*) ——————————————————, the prosecutor.

    DEFENSE: Your Honor, I am (*your name*) ——————————————————, the defendant.

2. The prosecution's side of the case, which is presented first, tells the court what you did, the traffic violation(s), and the action taken by the traffic officer. You then cross-examine each prosecution witness.

3. The defendant (you) moves to dismiss for insufficiency of evidence. If this is denied by the judge, then you (and your witness, if you have one) will testify, and you will introduce your physical evidence to prove your contention that you did not violate the traffic law.

4. After taking all oral testimony and physical evidence into consideration, the judge will reach his decision and render judgment.

Trials of this nature tend to run short, often lasting between five and fifteen minutes. Your best approach is to tell your side of the matter in your everyday language. Give a clear explanation of what happened and why it occurred as it did, and back it up with physical evidence.

When you have finished your presentation, show your appreciation to the court by saying:

DEFENDANT: Thank you, Your Honor.

How to Get Your Money Back
If the decision is in your favor, the judge will advise you about how your bail will be refunded to you. You may be advised that a refund check will be mailed to you.

If the judge forgets to tell you how to collect your bail, ask him before you leave the courtroom.

In the event you lose, you owe nothing since you have already paid in advance.

Tips on How to Work With the System
I was a traffic court judge many years back, so I consulted with a Trial Commissioner who is legendary for his just and expeditious handling of traffic matter in Los Angeles. I would like to share a few tips with you.

Start by being courteous to the officer who issues you the citation (ticket), but do not make any admissions to him or her.

However, there is nothing wrong with attempting to talk the officer out of issuing the ticket—provided you do so courteously; if the officer indicates through words or body language that he or she would prefer not to be listening to your argument or plea, your best approach is to be quiet and accept the citation. If you disagree with the grounds for its issuance, you may present your argument later to the judge who will hear your case in court.

Make notes of what just occurred. Why make detailed notes at the time you get the ticket? Because our human memories tend, with the passing of time, to forget specific points or to mix up facts. Instead of waiting until you are addressing the judge or commissioner in court to try recalling specific details, you make your notes as soon as possible. You can refer to them to refresh your memory during the trial.

Witnesses Can Help

Ask any witnesses to likewise make notes which, later, they may also use to refresh their memories.

If any individuals are witnesses at the scene of the incident be sure to get their names, addresses and phone numbers. They may appear voluntarily in court, if they are needed as witnesses. Or, you can have them subpoenaed to appear in court if they are reluctant to testify.

As in all legal matters, being forthright and honest are good qualities that can help you win your traffic case in court.

Photographs and Diagrams

Preparation is the key to winning your case. Take photos of the location, if possible; or, return to the scene and take pictures later, if you believe it will be of help in proving your defense in court. For example, perhaps the officer's view was obstructed. A photo can prove such a contention.

Diagrams of the scene may also help. You need not be an artist. Simple line drawings will be sufficient.

Document Your Explanations

If you were ticketed for speeding and explained, "I was rushing my mother to the hospital," be prepared to prove the truthfulness of your statement. Your mother's medical records, showing she needed emergency treatment, is suggested.

If you were under the impression you were driving the speed limit, instead of deliberately going ten miles over the legally posted speed limit for the area where the officer ticketed you, show the court a document from a mechanic or repair shop proving your speedometer was broken, just as you claimed when the officer pulled you over.

A receipt for the immediate repair of the broken speedometer would help convince the judge you are a responsible citizen, and could result in your winning.

What Not to Say in Court

Be prepared to make statements beneficial to your case. Statements of little substantive value can hinder, not help, so avoid such comments as, "I am a very careful driver" or "I saw the officer, so why would I go through the red light?" or "Yes, I was speeding. I was just going with the flow of traffic. I probably was going seventy-five miles per hour, along with everyone else."

Plausibility can go a long way in your defense, so read your citation carefully. If you find any significant errors, be prepared to give plausible reasons why you are not guilty.

How to Plead

Many people plead "not guilty" because they do not understand the meaning of "guilty."

They equate the word "guilty" with being "sinful" and, therefore, feel they cannot plead guilty—which they see as meaning they are sinful or bad people.

If you feel this way, and you have committed the infraction with which you are charged, when you appear in court you will be asked how you plead. Instead of saying "not guilty" you can simply state: "No contest."

Whether you admit to the infraction, or wish to challenge it in court:

To make a good impression on the officer of the court who hears your case, dress for business.

Being presentable cannot hurt!

Summarizing Traffic Cases

Most traffic cases take just a few minutes to try in court; your wait may be longer than the trial. Allow yourself an extra hour or two on your day in court, since you may have to wait for your case to be called.

If you live in a major metropolitan city like Los Angeles, give yourself an extra hour or two to stand in line to see the traffic court clerk. On an average day, several hundred people may appear to pay fines or post bail. The bulk of the crowd shows up between 11:00 A.M. and 2:00 P.M. daily.

If you do not like waiting in line, beat the midday crush by arriving early in the morning or after 2:00 P.M.

"Have I not commanded thee? Be strong and of a good courage; be not afraid, neither be thou dismayed: for the Lord thy God is with thee whithersoever thou goest."—Joshua 1:9

Chapter 27

How to Try Your Own Small Claims Court Case

(Bonus Chapter)

Trying your small claims case will be easy because the judge will conduct the trial. He asks the questions and you and the adverse party answer them. However, you may ask the court to allow you to question the party and his witnesses.

After considering both sides' testimony and other evidence, the judge will reach his decision and hand down judgment.

The judge's decision will be based on a combination of factors: the believability of the witnesses, the evidence and the pertinent law.

If no cross-complaint is involved (the opposing party does not sue you in return), your small claims trial may take less than fifteen minutes; most small claims matters are disposed in even less time.

When counter-suits are involved, small claims trials may run as long as thirty minutes, but they seldom last as long as one hour. For these reasons, small claims hearings are really "the original judicial fast-track trials."

Insight Into Small Claims
You are allowed to bring witnesses to court with you. Because of the streamlined nature of small claims trials, you need not prepare a lengthy presentation or plan for half a dozen witnesses to give testimony. One or two witnesses should be sufficient.

To select the right witnesses to help you win, choose the eyewitnesses who know the most and whose testimony will best corroborate your position.

Do not use witnesses whose testimony is solely based on "hearsay." It is better to have one eyewitness than two or more witnesses who repeat secondhand information about which they have no actual firsthand knowledge.

Arrive at small claims court at least one half hour before your trial is slated to start. The courtroom might be filled with other *Pro Pers* waiting for their cases to be heard, so do not be dismayed if your case is not called at the precise time it is scheduled on the court calendar.

While waiting in court, you may enjoy being an observer to the fascinating variety of cases coming before the Bench. No two small claims cases are quite alike.

Definition of Small Claims
A "small claim" is basically a "little civil lawsuit" in which the litigants are usually involved in a private dispute they cannot resolve themselves. Two criteria must be met for a matter to qualify as a small claim:

1. The matter is noncriminal in nature.

2. The dollars-and-cents relief being sought by the plaintiff does not exceed the maximum award allowed by law for a small claim.

In California, the maximum judgment which can be awarded for a small claim is $5,000; it may be slightly more or less in your jurisdiction.

The majority of small claims involve financial settlements; however, this is not true in every case.

Examples of Small Claims Cases
On a segment of *The People's Court* aired in March 1990, two litigants sought custody of a dog both had cared for and claimed to love. Since the dog could not choose who should be its master, Judge Joseph A. Wapner decided. The plaintiff won.

In another small claims case, the plaintiff alleged he had loaned an antique leather saddle to a local businessman, who used it as a wall decoration in his store. When the business moved to new quarters, the saddle went with it. The plaintiff wanted it back, but since he could not prove ownership and that an agreement had been made regarding his loan of the saddle to the shop's proprietor, the decision was for the defendant.

If the plaintiff in the above case had been able to produce strong evidence (i.e., purchase receipt and a written agreement between the parties), he would probably have prevailed.

There is no limit to the types of civil matters that qualify as small claims; however, the bulk of such cases involve such things as payment due for work performed, uncollected bills, compensation for property damage, recovery of expenses for personal injuries not covered by insurance.

How to Prepare for Small Claims Court

Bring as much physical evidence as possible to prove your position in small claims court (photocopies, documents, photographs, etc.).

If you are seeking a financial award, do not ask for the maximum award allowed by law ($5,000 in California) if your expenses only amount to a fraction of that amount.

If your expenses exceed the maximum limit allowed in small claims court, but you are willing to take a loss rather than wait many months or even years for your case to be tried in another court, you may take the matter to small claims court.

For instance, a California man whose damages in a breach-of-contract matter amounted to $5,632.54 collected $5,000.00 in small claims court. He wrote off the $632.54 which he failed to collect as a loss and explained his reason for taking the judicial shortcut by quoting the old maxim: *a bird in the hand is worth two in the bush.*

How Much Can You Seek?

Such general damages as emotional wear and tear or potential loss of income may, indeed, have resulted from your conflict with the opponent; however, unless you can prove such claims with documentary evidence, they will probably be disallowed in small claims court. Therefore, seek only what you can prove you are entitled to receive. As plaintiff, you may include court costs (filing fees, service of process expenses, etc.) in your prayer for judgment on your written pleading. If you do not ask for such compensation, it may not be awarded to you if you win.

The defendant in a small claims matter may not seek compensation for damages he also sustained in the matter unless he files a cross-complaint against the plaintiff; in his countersuit, the defendant sues the plaintiff. The judge hears the plaintiff's complaint first; then, he hears the defendant's cross-complaint.

How to Try Your Small Claims Case

When your case has been called, both parties will go to the counsel table. Your witnesses may go with you. All of you will remain standing throughout the proceedings, unless directed to do otherwise by the judge.

Instead of being sworn or affirmed individually, you will raise your right hands and swear, as a group, to tell the truth, the whole truth. and nothing but the truth about the matter now pending before the court.

The judge will then instruct you about how the proceeding will be conducted. His message will basically state:

> JUDGE: You have been sworn and I have read your written pleadings and know the issue(s) in this case. The plaintiff claims (*explains the grounds of action*)
> _____.

The judge will then ask the plaintiff what he has to say about the matter. If you are the plaintiff, you now give a narrative response to the judge.

> PLAINTIFF (*one or two short sentences*): Your Honor, (*tell what happened but do not go into elaborate detail*) _____
> _____.

The judge will then ask the defendant to make a statement about the plaintiff's claim. If you are the defendant, you now explain your denial or your affirmative defense.

> DEFENDANT (*short response stating your position*): Your Honor, I deny the plaintiff's claim because (*explain briefly your reason for the denial*) _____
> _____.
>
> *or*
>
> Your Honor, the reason I acted as I did was (*explain your reason for having acted as the plaintiff claims you did*) _____
> _____.

The judge will continue questioning the litigants and their witnesses until enough details have been elicited for him to make a decision.

Do not speak directly to the adverse party during the trial proceedings. Direct all questions and comments to the judge.

The judge will ask you to present the evidence which you have brought. If a party has brought a vital exhibit which has not come to light during the examination, he may say:

> LITIGANT (*introduce one piece of evidence at a time*): Your Honor, I have as Exhibit (*number or letter*) ____, (*name and description of exhibit*) _____
> _____. May I now introduce it in evidence?

If the opposing party objects to his opponent's evidence, he may say:

> OPPOSING LITIGANT (give brief reason for objecting): Objection, Your Honor! (*State brief reason for objecting to opponent's evidence*) _____
> _____.

After the judge has considered the evidence, he will rule on its admissibility. If your evidence is not admitted by the court, do not argue with the judge. His decision is final.

The judge may take the matter under consideration before handing down his decision and judgment, or he may immediately make a decision. In either event, he will instruct you on how the outcome of the trial is to be handled.

The trial now comes to an end. Regardless of whether or not you agree with the judge's decision, thank the judge before leaving the counsel table

LITIGANT: Thank you, Your Honor.

Summarizing Your Small Claims Trial

The burden is on the court to conduct your small claims trial, but the burden is on you to conduct yourself properly.

Small claims trials should not deteriorate into angry arguments between litigants. Anger, frustration, accusation, and other emotions should be left outside the courtroom.

If you object to any of the opposition's testimony, you may raise an objection by saying:

LITIGANT: Objection! Your Honor, (*state the ground for your objection*) _____

_____.

The judge will sustain (allow) or overrule (deny) your objection. His decision is the final word. Do not pick a fight with the judge if you disagree with his decision.

In small claims matters, the defendant may appeal the court's final decision; however, the plaintiff may not. Instructions on how to file an appeal are given in Chapter 28, "Reaching the Decision—Win, Lose, or Appeal?"

The court may not be held responsible for collecting judgments awarded in small claims court. You must do so yourself. When your award has been satisfied in full, file a *Satisfaction of Judgment* form with the court; this informs the court that your judgment has been satisfied and the case can be closed.

Examples are provided in Chapter 28, "Reaching the Decision—Win, Lose, or Appeal." These California forms are similar to those used for small claims matters in all jurisdictions. They are:

- *Notice of Entry of Judgment*—This is the notice sent to litigants by the court; it sets forth the terms of judgment to be satisfied.

- *Acknowledgment of Satisfaction of Judgment* (bottom of form)—The winning party must sign and return this form to the court immediately after the judgment owed him is satisfied in full.

If the adverse party fails to satisfy judgment according to the terms specified by the judge, the clerk of the court where the matter was tried will provide you with a form to enable you to get satisfaction of judgment.

Today you are on the verge of battle with your enemies.
Do not let your heart faint, do not be afraid and do not tremble or be terrified because of them;
For the Lord your God is He who goes with you,
to fight for you against your enemies, to save you.—Deuteronomy 20:3–4

Chapter 28

Reaching the Decision—Win, Lose, or Appeal?

By the time you reach this chapter, you may have already tried your own case in court. If so, you can now proudly call yourself a seasoned lay lawyer—a real *Pro Per*. If you have not yet tried your case, but instead are familiarizing yourself with everything you need to know before the proceedings, this chapter will tell you what occurs after you have presented your case.

When you have finished trying your case, your role in the trial is completed. Now it is the court's turn to take the next step.

This is the moment for which everyone is waiting—the announcement of the judge's decision and handing down of judgment. Here is what you may expect.

The Decision

The judge may announce his finding immediately after the plaintiff rests. Or, before he arrives at his decision, the judge may call a short recess so he can study any controverted issue(s) more closely; when court reconvenes, he will deliver his decision and hand down judgment.

If necessary to continue the matter until another date, the judge will advise you whether you must return to court or whether notice will be sent advising both parties of the court's ruling. In the majority of civil cases such as those featured in this book, disposition of a case is decided on the day of the trial.

What might that decision be: win, lose, or appeal?

You Win!

If the judge decides *for* you, you win!

Smiles are in order if you win. However, do not celebrate your victory by whistling, stamping your feet, cheering, or blowing kisses at the judge! Nor should you leer, jeer, or sneer at the losing party. Instead, shake his hand—but only if he is willing to return your handshake.

Does winning automatically assure you will collect the judgment awarded you? No! If yours was a small claims case, the court clerk will mail or deliver to you a form called the *Notice of Entry of Judgment* which outlines the court's award. *You may not collect the judgment until after the period allotted for the other party to file an appeal has elapsed.* This information will appear on the notice which you receive.

In Los Angeles it is thirty days for small claims; therefore, the losing party should satisfy judgment or file his appeal before thirty days have passed from the date the clerk has delivered or mailed notice of entry of judgment to the parties.

An example of a small claims *Notice of Entry of Judgment* appears on the following page.

If the losing party neither files an appeal nor satisfies the judgment awarded you within the time frame allowed by the court, you may file a form known as a *Writ of Execution,* which directs an officer of the law to take property of the judgment debtor to pay your claim.

Examples of the types of property the officer may be able to seize include cars, wages, bank accounts, business property, and rented property. A sample *Writ of Execution* appears on the following pages. This is the same form as in Chapter 25. We use it also for small claims.

A court is not a debt collector; you are responsible for collecting your own judgment.

When you have collected the money or other compensation due you through the judgment, you must file a form known as an *Acknowledgment of Satisfaction of Judgment,* which notifies the court that you, the "judgment creditor," have been paid (or otherwise compensated) in full by the other party. A sample of this form appears in this chapter.

When you acknowledge that judgment has been satisfied, your case will be closed.

I suggest that you work out arrangements by which the other party will satisfy the judgment awarded you before you leave the courthouse on the day of trial. Meet with him outside the courtroom to discuss details about how he plans to pay you what he owes. Such timely planning greatly reduces your risk of having to become—perhaps in vain—your own debt collector.

Name and Address of Court:

SMALL CLAIMS CASE NO.

NOTICE TO ALL PLAINTIFFS AND DEFENDANTS: Your small claims case has been decided. If you lost the case, and the court ordered you to pay money, your wages, money, and property may be taken without further warning from the court. Read the back of this sheet for important information about your rights.	*AVISO A TODOS LOS DEMANDANTES Y DEMANDADOS:* *Su caso ha sido resuelto por la corte para reclamos judiciales menores. Si la corte ha decidido en su contra y ha ordenado que usted pague dinero, le pueden quitar su salario, su dinero, y otras cosas de su propiedad, sin aviso adicional por parte de esta corte. Lea el reverso de este formulario para obtener información de importancia acerca de sus derechos.*

PLAINTIFF/DEMANDANTE *(Name and address of each)* :

DEFENDANT/DEMANDADO *(Name and address of each)* :

[ ] See attached sheet for additional plaintiffs and defendants.

NOTICE OF ENTRY OF JUDGMENT

Judgment was entered as checked below on *(date)*:

1. [ ] Defendant *(name, if more than one)*:
   shall pay plaintiff *(name, if more than one)*:
   $ principal and $ costs on plaintiff's claim.
2. [ ] Defendant does not owe plaintiff any money on plaintiff's claim.
3. [ ] Plaintiff *(name, if more than one)*:
   shall pay defendant *(name, if more than one)*:
   $ principal and $ costs on defendant's claim.
4. [ ] Plaintiff does not owe defendant any money on defendant's claim.
5. [ ] Possession of the following property is awarded to plaintiff *(address of property)*:

6. [ ] Payments are to be made at the rate of $ per month, beginning on *(date)*:   and on the   day of each month thereafter until paid in full. If any payment is missed, the entire balance becomes due immediately.
7. [ ] Other *(specify)*:

8. [ ] This judgment results from a motor vehicle accident on a California highway and was caused by the judgment debtor's operation of a motor vehicle. If the judgment is not paid, you may apply to have the judgment debtor's driver's license suspended.
9. Enforcement of the judgment is automatically postponed until the time for filing an appeal expires, and if filed, until the appeal is decided.
10. [ ] This notice was personally delivered to *(insert name and date)*:
11. CLERK'S CERTIFICATE OF MAILING — I certify that I am not a party to this action. This Notice of Entry of Judgment was mailed first class, postage prepaid, in a sealed envelope to the parties at the addresses shown above. The mailing and this certification occurred at the place and on the date shown below.
   Place of mailing: , California
   Date of mailing:

   Clerk, by _____ , Deputy

— You have a right to a small claims advisor free of charge. Read the information sheet on the reverse. —

Form Adopted by the
Judicial Council of California
SC-130 (Rev. January 1, 1987)

NOTICE OF ENTRY OF JUDGMENT
(Small Claims)

Rule 982.7

309

INFORMATION AFTER JUDGMENT	INFORMACION DESPUES DEL FALLO DE LA CORTE

Your small claims case has been decided. The **judgment** or decision of the court appears on the front of this sheet. The court may have ordered one party to pay money to the other party. The winner of the case and the person who can collect the money is called the **judgment creditor**. The loser of the case and the person who owes the money is called the judgment debtor.

Enforcement of the judgment is **postponed** until after the time for appeal ends or until after the appeal is decided. This means that the judgment creditor cannot collect any money or take any action until after this period is over. Generally, both parties may be represented by lawyers after judgment.

IF YOU LOST THE CASE . . .

1. If you lost the case on your own claim and the court did not award you any money, the court's decision on your claim is **FINAL**. You may not appeal your own claim.

2. If you lost the case and the court ordered you to pay money, your money and property may be taken to pay the claim unless you do one of the following things:

a. PAY THE JUDGMENT

The law requires you to pay the amount of the judgment. You may also ask the court to order monthly payments you can afford. Ask the clerk for information about this procedure.

b. APPEAL

If you disagree with the court's decision, you may appeal the decison *on the other party's claim*. You may not appeal the decision on your own claim. If you appeared at the trial, you *must* begin your appeal by filing a form called a **Notice of Appeal** within *20 days* after the date this Notice of Entry of Judgment was mailed or handed to you at the time of the small claims hearing. Your appeal will be in the superior court. You will have a **new trial**. You may be represented by a lawyer.

c. VACATE OR CANCEL THE JUDGMENT

If you did not go to the trial, you may ask the court to vacate or cancel the judgment. To make this request, you must file a **Motion to Vacate the Judgment** *within 30 days* after the date this Notice of Entry of Judgment was mailed. If your request is denied, you then have *10 days* from the date the motion was denied to appeal the denial.

The period to file the **Motion to Vacate the Judgment** is *180 days* if you were *not properly served* with the claim. The 180-day period begins on the date you found out or should have found out about the judgment against you.

IF YOU WON THE CASE . . .

1. If you were sued by the other party and you won the case, then the other party may not appeal the court's decision.

2. If you won the case and the court awarded you money, here are some steps you may take to collect your money or get possession of your property:

a. COLLECTING FEES

Sometimes fees are charged for filing court papers or for serving the judgment debtor. These extra costs can become part of your original judgment. To claim these fees, ask the clerk for a **Memorandum of Costs**.

b. VOLUNTARY PAYMENT

Ask the judgment debtor to pay the money. If your claim was for possession of rental property, ask the judgment debtor to move out. **THE COURT WILL NOT COLLECT THE MONEY OR ENFORCE THE JUDGMENT FOR YOU.**

c. STATEMENT OF ASSETS

If the judgment debtor does not pay the money, the law requires the debtor to fill out a form called the **Judgment Debtor's Statement of Assets**. This form will tell you what property the judgment debtor has that may be available to pay your claim. If the judgment debtor willfully fails to send you the completed form, you may ask the court to impose penalties.

d. ORDER OF EXAMINATION

You may also make the debtor come to court to answer questions about income and property. To do this, ask the clerk for an **Order of Examination**. There is no fee for this order, but there is a fee if a law officer serves the order on the judgment debtor.

e. WRIT OF EXECUTION

After you find out about the judgment debtor's property, you may ask the court for a **Writ of Execution**. A writ of execution is a court paper which tells a law officer to take property of the judgment debtor to pay your claim. Here are some examples of the kinds of property the officer may be able to take: **wages, bank account, automobile, business property, or rented property.** For some kinds of property, you may need to file other forms. See the law officer for information.

f. ABSTRACT OF JUDGMENT

The judgment debtor may own land or a house or other buildings. You may want to put a lien on the property so that you will be paid if the property is sold. You can get a lien by filing an **Abstract of Judgment** with the County Recorder in the county where the property is located. The recorder will charge a fee for the Abstract of Judgment.

NOTICE TO THE WINNING PARTY — As soon as you have been paid in full, you *must* fill out the form below and mail it to the court *immediately* or you may be fined. If an Abstract of Judgment has been recorded, you must use another form; see the clerk for the proper form.

SC-130 [Rev. January 1, 1987]

SMALL CLAIMS CASE NO.

ACKNOWLEDGMENT OF SATISFACTION OF JUDGMENT

(Do not use this form if an Abstract of Judgment has been recorded.)

To the Clerk of the Court:

I am the ☐ judgment creditor ☐ assignee of record.

I agree that the judgment in this action has been paid in full or otherwise satisfied.

Date:

▶

. . . .
(TYPE OR PRINT NAME)   *(SIGNATURE)*

ATTORNEY OR PARTY WITHOUT ATTORNEY *(Name and Address)*:	TELEPHONE NO.:	*FOR RECORDER'S USE ONLY*

☐ Recording requested by and return to:

☐ ATTORNEY FOR ☐ JUDGMENT CREDITOR ☐ ASSIGNEE OF RECORD

NAME OF COURT:
STREET ADDRESS:
MAILING ADDRESS:
CITY AND ZIP CODE:
BRANCH NAME:

PLAINTIFF:

DEFENDANT:

WRIT OF ☐ **EXECUTION (Money Judgment)**
☐ **POSSESSION OF** ☐ **Personal Property**
☐ **Real Property**
☐ **SALE**

CASE NUMBER:

FOR COURT USE ONLY

1. **To the Sheriff or any Marshal or Constable of the County of:**

   You are directed to enforce the judgment described below with daily interest and your costs as provided by law.

2. **To any registered process server:** You are authorized to serve this writ only in accord with CCP 699.080 or CCP 715.040.

3. *(Name)*:
   is the ☐ judgment creditor ☐ assignee of record
   whose address is shown on this form above the court's name.

4. **Judgment debtor** *(name and last known address)*:

   ☐ additional judgment debtors on reverse

5. **Judgment entered** on *(date)*:
6. ☐ **Judgment renewed** on *(dates)*:

7. **Notice of sale** under this writ
   a. ☐ has not been requested.
   b. ☐ has been requested *(see reverse)*.
8. ☐ Joint debtor information on reverse.

[SEAL]

9. ☐ See reverse for information on real or personal property to be delivered under a writ of possession or sold under a writ of sale.
10. ☐ This writ is issued on a sister-state judgment.
11. Total judgment . . . . $
12. Costs after judgment (per filed order or memo CCP 685.090) . $
13. Subtotal *(add 11 and 12)* . . . . . $ _____
14. Credits . . . . $
15. Subtotal *(subtract 14 from 13)* . $ _____
16. Interest after judgment (per filed affidavit CCP 685.050) . . . . . . $
17. Fee for issuance of writ . . . . . . $
18. **Total** *(add 15, 16, and 17)* . . . . $ _____
19. Levying officer: Add daily interest from date of writ *(at the legal rate on 15)* of . . . . $
20. ☐ The amounts called for in items 11–19 are different for each debtor. These amounts are stated for each debtor on Attachment 20.

Issued on
(date):

Clerk, by _____ , Deputy

— **NOTICE TO PERSON SERVED: SEE REVERSE FOR IMPORTANT INFORMATION** —

(Continued on reverse)

Form Adopted by the
Judicial Council of California
EJ-130 (Rev. January 1, 1989)
GW791 CI-75JC(11) (Rev. 1/89) PS 1-89

WRIT OF EXECUTION

CCP 699.520, 712.010, 715.010

311

EJ-130

Items continued from the first page:

4. ☐ **Additional judgment debtor** *(name and last known address)*:

7. ☐ **Notice of sale** has been requested by *(name and address)*:

8. ☐ **Joint debtor** was declared bound by the judgment (CCP 989-994)
   a. on *(date)*:
   b. name and address of joint debtor:
                                             a. on *(date)*:
                                             b. name and address of joint debtor:

   c. ☐ additional costs against certain joint debtors *(itemize)*:

9. ☐ *(Writ of Possession or Writ of Sale)* **Judgment** was entered for the following:
   a. ☐ Possession of real property. The complaint was filed on *(date)*:
       The court will hear objections to enforcement of the judgment under CCP 1174.3 on the following dates *(specify)*:
   b. ☐ Possession of personal property
       ☐ If delivery cannot be had, then for the value *(itemize in 9e)* specified in the judgment or supplemental order.
   c. ☐ Sale of personal property
   d. ☐ Sale of real property
   e. Description of property:

— NOTICE TO PERSON SERVED —

Writ of execution or sale. Your rights and duties are indicated on the accompanying Notice of Levy.

Writ of possession of personal property. If the levying officer is not able to take custody of the property, the levying officer will make a demand upon you for the property. If custody is not obtained following demand, the judgment may be enforced as a money judgment for the value of the property specified in the judgment or in a supplemental order.

Writ of possession of real property. If the premises are not vacated within five days after the date of service on the occupant or, if service is by posting, within five days after service on you, the levying officer will remove the occupants from the real property and place the judgment creditor in possession of the property. Personal property remaining on the premises will be sold or otherwise disposed of in accordance with CCP 1174 unless you or the owner of the property pays the judgment creditor the reasonable cost of storage and takes possession of the personal property not later than 15 days after the time the judgment creditor takes possession of the premises. **A Claim of Right to Possession form accompanies this writ.**

EJ-130 [Rev. January 1, 1987]

WRIT OF EXECUTION

Page two

312

ATTORNEY OR PARTY WITHOUT ATTORNEY (Name and Address):	TELEPHONE NO.:	FOR RECORDER'S OR SECRETARY OF STATE'S USE ONLY

ATTORNEY FOR (Name):

NAME OF COURT:

STREET ADDRESS:

MAILING ADDRESS:

CITY AND ZIP CODE:

BRANCH NAME:

PLAINTIFF:

DEFENDANT:

	CASE NUMBER:

ACKNOWLEDGMENT OF SATISFACTION OF JUDGMENT
[ ] FULL   [ ] PARTIAL   [ ] MATURED INSTALLMENT

FOR COURT USE ONLY

1. Satisfaction of the judgment is acknowledged as follows *(see footnote* before completing)*:

   a. [ ] Full satisfaction

       (1) [ ] Judgment is satisfied in full.

       (2) [ ] The judgment creditor has accepted payment or performance other than that specified in the judgment in full satisfaction of the judgment.

   b. [ ] Partial satisfaction

       The amount received in partial satisfaction of the judgment is
       $

   c. [ ] Matured installment

       All matured installments under the installment judgment have been satisfied as of *(date)*:

2. Full name and address of judgment creditor:

3. Full name and address of assignee of record, if any:

4. Full name and address of judgment debtor being fully or partially released:

5. a. Judgment entered on *(date)*:

       [ ] (1) in judgment book volume no.:   (2) page no.:

   b. [ ] Renewal entered on *(date)*:

       [ ] (1) in judgment book volume no.:   (2) page no.:

6. [ ] An [ ] abstract of judgment [ ] certified copy of the judgment has been recorded as follows *(complete all information for each county where recorded)*:

COUNTY	DATE OF RECORDING	BOOK NUMBER	PAGE NUMBER

7. [ ] A notice of judgment lien has been filed in the office of the Secretary of State as file number *(specify)*:

NOTICE TO JUDGMENT DEBTOR: If this is an acknowledgment of full satisfaction of judgment, it will have to be recorded in each county shown in item 6 above, if any, in order to release the judgment lien, and will have to be filed in the office of the Secretary of State to terminate any judgment lien on personal property.

Date:

                    ▶

(SIGNATURE OF JUDGMENT CREDITOR OR ASSIGNEE OF CREDITOR OR ATTORNEY)

*The names of the judgment creditor and judgment debtor must be stated as shown in any Abstract of Judgment which was recorded and is being released by this satisfaction. A separate notary acknowledgment must be attached for each signature.

Form Approved by the
Judicial Council of California
EJ-100 [Rev. July 1, 1983](Cor. 7/84)

ACKNOWLEDGMENT OF SATISFACTION OF JUDGMENT

CCP 724.060, 724.120, 724.250

You Lose!

If the judge rules for the opposing party, control your disappointment. Do not mutter curses, moan, growl, shout, or bang the counsel table with your fist. You did your best during the trial. So did your opponent.

If he offers his hand, shake it. If he does not, extend your hand to him as a goodwill gesture showing you are a true winner even if you lost the case.

Also, before you leave the courthouse, enter into a discussion with the winner about how you plan to satisfy the judgment you are obligated to fulfill. Then, follow through.

What If There Is Comparative Negligence?

Sometimes a judge finds for the plaintiff but reduces the award based on the plaintiff's contributory negligence. This is known as "comparative negligence" or negligence in which each side bears a percentage of the responsibility.

For example, in a personal injury matter, the plaintiff was the prevailing party in a lawsuit involving a neck injury caused when the defendant rear-ended his car. The court ruled that the plaintiff was forty per cent (40%) negligent and the defendant was sixty per cent (60%) negligent.

Rather than ordering the defendant to pay the full $550 of medical bills incurred by the plaintiff, the judge subtracts forty per cent ($220) and orders the defendant to pay the sixty per cent balance of $330.

The judge's reasons for reaching his comparative negligence decision were: the defendant was tailgating the plaintiff's car, but the plaintiff was driving too slow (25 miles per hour in a 35-mile zone), thus constituting a safety hazard.

If a similar type of decision is handed down in your case, look at the bright side: it could have been worse because you might have had to carry the whole burden rather than just a portion of it.

How to Appeal Your Case in Court

If you are dissatisfied with the outcome of your trial, you may wish to consider appealing your case. *Be certain you have substantial grounds for an appeal before you file because the court takes a dim view of appeals of a "frivolous" nature.*

Some states fine appellants for filing frivolous appeals. In California, for instance, sanctions are imposed for court costs against appellants whose appeals are frivolous.

In a murder case in which the verdict of capital punishment is handed down, an appeal is taken automatically. In civil cases of the types tried by *Pro Pers*, however, there are no automatic appeals. In fact, if you have a small claims case, you may not even be allowed by law to appeal the court's decision.

The following facts will help you decide whether or not to exercise the right to appeal your own case in court.

Who Can File Small Claims Appeals?

A *plaintiff* who loses his small claims case in a California municipal court *may not appeal* the judge's decision; he must abide by it. If a *defendant* loses a small claims case, however, *he may appeal* the decision by filing a *Notice of Appeal* within thirty days after the court's *Notice of Entry of Judgment* was mailed or handed to him at the time of the hearing. A sample *Notice of Appeal* appears on the next page.

A new trial, known as a *trial de novo,* will be held in superior court, and the parties may be represented by a lawyer or appear as *Pro Pers.*

The same basic rules governing small claims appeals in California also apply in other states. Your local Clerk of the Court can advise you about who may or may not appeal small claims decisions in your area.

Understanding the Appeal

An "appeal" is a request for a higher court to review your civil case for the purpose of modifying or reversing judgment.

For instance, if the defendant in the rear-end collision cited in this chapter, is not satisfied that the plaintiff was only ordered to carry forty per cent (40%) of the comparative negligence expenses, or $220 out of the total $550, he may appeal the decision.

If the defendant wins his appeal, judgment may be modified so the plaintiff is found to be one hundred per cent (100%) negligent and, therefore, the defendant is not liable to the plaintiff.

If you stand to save a substantial amount of money if you win your appeal, and you have solid grounds for filing it, this may be the right course of action for you. If you are involved in a criminal matter, however, the appeal has significantly different importance than in most civil cases:

An appeal in a criminal matter is a request for a higher court to review the case for the purpose of modifying or reversing sentence to get a new trial.

For example, a man convicted of murder in the first degree is sentenced to die by lethal injection. His automatic appeal seeks reversal of the conviction or modification of the sentence imposed to life imprisonment without the possibility of parole.

- While an appeal is pending, satisfaction of a civil judgment or carrying out a criminal sentence may be stayed (suspended).

- Never file an appeal for the sole purpose of allowing yourself more time in which to fulfill your court-ordered obligation.

How Much Time Is Involved?

In Los Angeles, appealing your case can take an average of four months (for small claims cases) to fifteen months (for other civil matters).

Name and Address of Court:

SMALL CLAIMS CASE NO.

| PLAINTIFF/DEMANDANTE *(Name and address of each)*: | DEFENDANT/DEMANDADO *(Name and address of each)*: |

☐ See attached sheet for additional plaintiffs and defendants.

NOTICE OF FILING NOTICE OF APPEAL

TO: ☐ Plaintiff *(name)*:

☐ Defendant *(name)*:

Your small claims case has been APPEALED to the superior court. Do not contact the small claims court about this appeal. The superior court will notify you of the date you should appear in court. The notice of appeal is set forth below.	*La decisión hecha por la corte para reclamos judiciales menores en su caso ha sido APELADA ante la corte superior. No se ponga en contacto con la corte para reclamos judiciales menores acerca de esta apelación.. La corte superior le notificará la fecha en que usted debe presentarse ante ella. El aviso de la apelación aparece a continuación.*

Date: Clerk, by _____, Deputy

NOTICE OF APPEAL

I appeal to the superior court from the small claims judgment or the denial of the motion to vacate the small claims judgment, as provided by law.

DATE APPEAL FILED *(clerk to insert date)*:

· · · · · · · *(TYPE OR PRINT NAME)* · · · · · · · ▶ _____
(SIGNATURE OF APPELLANT OR APPELLANT'S ATTORNEY)

CLERK'S CERTIFICATE OF MAILING

I certify that

1. I am not a party to this action.
2. This Notice of Filing Notice of Appeal and Notice of Appeal were mailed first class, postage prepaid, in a sealed envelope to
   ☐ plaintiff
   ☐ defendant
   at the address shown above.
3. The mailing and this certification occurred
   at *(place)*: California,
   on *(date)*:

Clerk, by _____, Deputy

Form Approved by the
Judicial Council of California
SC-140 [Rev. January 1, 1985]

NOTICE OF APPEAL
(Small Claims)

Rule 982.7

The length of time your appeal will require depends on the number of appeals pending on the appellate court's calendar and the amount of time required for the panel of judges or justices to review your case before the hearing.

How Much Does an Appeal Cost?

In Los Angeles, the average filing fees for civil appeals range between $61 for Municipal Court cases to $250 for Superior Court cases.

The filing fees may be slightly more, or even less, in your area.

If you cannot afford the fees associated with appealing your civil case in court, you may be eligible for a fee waiver. In criminal cases the defendants (accused) pay nothing for filing appeals.

To determine whether you are eligible for a fee waiver, discuss your financial situation with the Clerk of the Court where you plan to file your appeal.

Where to File Your Appeal

You must file your appeal in the same court where your case was tried. If your trial was held in Municipal Court, your appeal must be filed in Municipal Court; if it was conducted in Superior Court, your appeal must be filed in Superior Court.

You may purchase your *Notice of Appeal*, and any other forms associated with your appeal, from the Clerk of the Court.

Taking Your First Step

Filing your *Notice of Appeal* is the first step you must take as an "appellant" to set the appeal process in motion. File the original, with proof of service by mail, in the trial court.

Insight Into the Appeal Process

As appellant in any civil matter except a small claims case, you must file a "proposed statement on appeal" detailing what you think took place in the trial court in regard to witnesses, testimonies, objections, motions, exhibits, and court rulings; this "proposed statement" must point out the bases of your appeal.

The appellee's response includes his "proposed statement" outlining his recollection of what transpired in trial court *contrary to your proposed statement.*

If, however, you are involved in a small claims case under appeal, the procedure is considerably simplified. *A small claims appeal is a request for a Trial de Novo* (new trial) and no proposed statements are necessary. Your case will be set for retrial in a higher court than the one which rendered the earlier decision. Then you may try your own case for the second time—or be represented by a lawyer, something you were not able to do in Small Claims Court, where the law required you to serve as a *Pro Per.*

Easy-to-follow instructions are printed on all the forms which will be provided by the Clerk of the Court at the time you file your Notice of Appeal.

Your First Hearing

In civil cases on appeal—other than those involving small claims—both the appellant and appellee must appear in the court where the *Notice of Appeal* was filed. Both you and the other party must argue your proposed statements, from your respective viewpoints, before the Bench.

Following this hearing, the court "settles" and the appellant "engrosses" the statement on appeal. If the appellant engrosses the statement on appeal as ordered, then the court certifies it as the settled statement on appeal that will be sent and considered by the superior court appellate department as the official record of the proceedings taken in the trial court.

After these preliminaries have been completed, the clerk than transfers all files relevant to the case to the appellate court which will review it.

Transferring Your Appeal

Your case will be transferred to an appellate court, which is a higher court than the one where the case was filed. For instance, Municipal Court cases are transferred to Superior Court. For details on the appellate court system, refer to Chapter 5.

What Happens in the Appellate Court?

After the case has been transferred to the appellate court, the following steps are taken:

- *Filing Your Briefs*—The appellate court notifies both parties when to file "briefs." A brief is a written statement containing a party's argument why the appellate court should resolve the appeal in his favor. The sequence is:

  1. *Appellant*—He files his "Opening Brief."

  2. *Appellee*—He files his "Brief."

  3. *Appellant*—He files his "Reply Brief" (optional).

- *First Review*—One judge is assigned to write the first draft of the Opinion; he then passes it to the other members.

- *Panel Reviews*—The panel of judges or justices now reviews the matter. There may be as few as three appellate officers on the entire panel or as many as seven or more. In California the entire State Supreme Court reviews appeals. The number of panel members reviewing your case will be determined by the rules prevailing in your jurisdiction. A majority opinion must be reached.

• *Presenting Your Oral Argument*
A hearing date will be arranged by the court, at which time both the appellant and appellee will be given a specific amount of time in which to orally argue their respective sides of the appeal. You may be given as little time as ten minutes, or you may be allotted twenty minutes or more. *Throughout the course of your argument, the panel members will ask questions which you will be expected to answer.* The main points will be those contained in your brief; therefore, the fewer points your written statement contains, the more time you can devote to in-depth coverage of each topic during your oral argument before the appellate panel.

How the Opinion Is Rendered

Following the hearing at which both parties present their oral arguments, the judge or justice assigned to the appeal may or may not change the tentative opinion based on points raised during the oral argument.

If there is a majority vote for the opinion, it becomes the *Opinion* (or decision) of the court. However, if the majority of panel members disagree with the opinion written by the judge or justice, their dissenting opinion prevails as the court's judgment or opinion.

How the Parties Are Notified

The court notifies the appellant and appellee by mail of the Opinion reached by the appellate court.

If the appellant wins, the original judgment is either modified or reversed.

If the appellee wins, the original judgment handed down at the trial stands unchanged (affirmed).

The appellate court's ruling is final, unless you appeal its decision to the next higher court, which involves repeating the process highlighted here.

How Many Appeals Can Be Filed?

Filing appeals is like climbing a ladder. You start at the bottom and move up the rungs until you reach the top.

The highest state court of appeal in California is the State Supreme Court; your state may call its highest appellate court by a slightly different name.

Having even greater power than a state's courts is the federal court system, which extends across the nation. A Federal District Court is usually located near the other courthouse(s) in a city, county, or township. The highest court of the nation is the United States Supreme Court.

Small cases like those under discussion in this book do not qualify for review by a federal court because they usually deal with disputes between two private parties or agencies which are governed by state and/or local laws and which should be resolved at the local or state level.

Mountains vs. Molehills

Regardless of how important—or seemingly large—your case may appear to you, in comparison with legal matters of national or international magnitude, such small civil matters are like the proverbial "molehills" in the overall judicial system of the nation.

Cases heard and appealed in federal courts involve laws governing the welfare and conduct of the whole country, and often having a far-reaching effect on America's influence throughout the world. These cases are like the legendary "mountains" in folklore.

When deciding just how far to take your appeal remember these words: *Don't try to make a mountain out of a molehill because a molehill cannot qualify as a mountain!*

Should You File Your Own Appeal?

Now that you know the basics about how the appellate courts operate, should you appeal your own case in court? Yes, but only if what you stand to lose is of major importance to you, and you have a valid ground for appeal. Two examples are: money and freedom.

If you stand to lose a large amount of money, such as the savings you have worked a lifetime to acquire, go for the appeal. Or if you are involved in a criminal matter in which you have been sentenced to prison for many years, file your appeal, because in so doing you are filing for your freedom.

In civil cases, appellate courts may apply sanctions (require you to pay costs) for filing a frivolous appeal. The following maxim will help you decide wisely:

If you have any doubt
Leave the appeal out!

Summarizing the Appeal

Unless you have very strong grounds upon which to base your appeal, the appellate court will affirm (uphold) the lower court's judgment. In such an instance, not only will you have wasted your own precious time, as well as the court's, you might part with more money than you counted on, to lose your appeal.

The right to appeal a court decision is one of the freedoms extended to citizens through the American system of justice. The right to appeal is a freedom denied most individuals in non-democratic nations around the world. It is a great privilege.

Exercise it judiciously!

Take away from Me the noise of your songs,
For I will not hear the melody of your stringed instruments.
But let justice run down like water,
And righteousness like a mighty stream.—Amos 5:23–24

Conclusion

This concludes the basic instructions about how to try your own case in court. With this information, you should be able to try your own civil case in any Small Claims Court, Traffic Court, Municipal Court, or even Superior Court, if yours is a relatively simple, uncomplicated matter. If your matter is fairly complex, or you simply desire more knowledge and understanding about trial techniques and courtroom legal procedures, refer to this book's companion volume: *How to Try Your Own Case in Court—And Win! Book Two: A Pro Per's Guide to Law and Legalese.*

You have made significant progress since you first opened this book and started preparing your case for court. Not only have you learned how the American judiciary works, you have played an important role in making it happen in your own life.

You should now know enough about the law to share your new knowledge with others. Best, you can practice many of the principles you have learned to lead a happier, more fulfilling life—regardless of whether or not you ever appear in court again.

I hope one of the principal assets you gained from reading this book and applying the principles outlined in its pages is greater understanding of, and appreciation for, democracy in action:

• *America allows all her people to speak up to the ruling powers and to be heard.*

• *In this great nation which allows every citizen the right to a fair trial, every court is truly The People's Court.*

Congratulations, *Pro Per.* You won by trying!

He that diligently seeketh good procureth favour; but he that seeketh mischief, it shall come unto him.
He that trusteth in his riches shall fall; but the righteous shall flourish as a branch.
He that troubleth his own house shall inherit the wind; and the fool shall be servant to the wise of heart.
The fruit of the righteous is a tree of life; and he that winneth souls is wise.
Behold, the righteous shall be recompensed in the earth; much more the wicked and the sinner.—Proverbs 11:27–31

Peace be within thy walls,
and prosperity within thy palaces.
For my brethren and companions' sakes,
I will now say, PEACE BE WITHIN THEE.—Psalms 122:7–8

Index

to Volume I

To order books, please send full amount
plus $4.00 for postage and handling.

Send orders to:

GALDE PRESS, INC.
PO Box 460
Lakeville, Minnesota 55044

Credit card orders call 1–800–777–3454